Kidnap

Colin R. Armstrong

ISBN: 978-1-916732-57-5

i2i

PUBLISHING

i2i Publishing. Manchester
www.i2ipublishing.co.uk

For Leo Morris, my adoptive son and true friend
who sadly died in December 2024.
Photo of myself with Leo some years ago.

Leo and I

5

27th June 2024

There can be few moments more frightening than to wake up in the night and find your bedroom full of armed men. That is what happened to my girlfriend Kate and I at 2.00am in the morning of Saturday 16th December 2023.

So who are we? Let me introduce ourselves. My name is Colin Armstrong. I am seventy-eight years old, ex-Honorary British Consul in Guayaquil and the owner of Agripac SA, the biggest agricultural supply company in Ecuador. I have been married to Ceci (Cecilia) for almost fifty years. We have three children Nick, Diana and Alex and nine grandchildren.

I used to be six foot two inches tall, but with age, I guess I am no more than six foot one now.

Thanks to Just for Men brown hair colourant, I am told I look young for my years.

I like to think so.

Ten years ago I met Kate and we have had a relationship since then, though in December 2023 I am still living with Ceci.

Kate is Katherin Santos, aged 30, born in Ibague, Colombia but now living in Ecuador. She is a beautiful model, tall with long black hair.

She is a fitness fanatic. She practices pole dancing, telas (aerial silk), Pilates and goes regularly to the gym.

She is a member of Madrid Skydivers Club, with 74 solo jumps to her credit.

We met in August 2013 when she was nineteen, modeling for Agripac, and despite an age difference of almost fifty years, we fell in love. We have been together ever since.

But only on a part time basis.

That is to say, during the last ten years, on weekdays when Ceci is in Guayaquil, I would leave the office every day at 4.30pm, drive to Kate's place, spend two hours with her, from five to seven o'clock, and then go back to my house for dinner.

The French have an expression for it. She is my cinc a sept.

It was not a satisfactory state of affairs, from either lady's point of view.

Which they both made clear!

But Kate and I have the weekends together, including Saturdays at my ranch Rodeo Grande, when Ceci goes with friends to her beach house. For those who have read my book "Behind the Forbidden Corner", the ranch was called Mapan at that time.

We have taken a lot of holidays too. We have travelled together all over the world, to more than forty countries, for which we have wonderful memories and thousands of photos.

Dear Ceci, my wife of nearly fifty years, has had to put up with it. She is petite and attractive at seventy-three years old. We love each other and haven't separated. She knows about Kate and is obviously not happy about her. But we keep our marriage going.

Nick, our tall handsome son, is forty-eight-years old.He has inherited a family trait. His hair turned white while still in his twenties. Today he has a designer white beard too. He married Almudena (Almu) whom he met in Madrid, while working there in an employment agency. They have three children, Sophia, Willie and Victoria.

Diana is also tall with auburn hair. She is very beautiful. She worked as a model in Milan after university, and met her future husband Steve. He is from Alaska and was also a model. Today they live in Los Angeles, California. Modelling has come to an end. They both work successfully as estate agents. They have three children. Oliver Colin, like me is very tall, Rocco and Dominic.

Our beautiful younger daughter is Alexandra, once again tall with auburn hair. She met Javi (Javier) while she was working in Madrid in a marketing company. Javi's father is British and his mother Spanish. They have Sienna and the twins Christian and Olivia.

7

I came to Ecuador on 17th January 1972 to start Agripac SA. At that time it belonged to a British gentleman, Thomas Macdougal. I was seconded by ICI Ltd to act as his manager for the first three years of the company. Subsequently, I bought into Agripac and eventually became sole owner.

Ceci and I built it up together. Today it is a large company, by Ecuadorian standards. We employ fourteen hundred people.

Kate and I had come to Rodeo Grande yesterday afternoon, Friday 15th of December, to have a party with the staff to celebrate the end of the cattle inventory, which had come out 100% correct.

My 1,000 ht ranch near Baba is in the province of Los Rios on Ecuador's coastal strip.

It is low lying, only six meters above sea level at the lowest point.

I have owned it for forty seven years.

When my children were young, Ceci and I would go there regularly as a family. The kids invited their friends and we would all ride together, up to twenty horses, accompanied by one or two of the seven beagles we have had over the years.

Then came boarding school when they were away from Ecuador for long periods of time. Ceci lost interest in the ranch, and went with her group of friends to her beach house every weekend, to swim in the sea, eat wonderful seafood and play cards.

But I didn't enjoy it. The beach is not my scene, and I don't play cards.

That left me alone to go to the ranch.

Over a ten-year period I would often stay Saturday night at Rodeo Grande, and ride again on Sunday. I slept alone in the house with my beagles. It was my bachelor period. I read a lot of books, I didn't need anyone's company, just the dogs.

I was never afraid of intruders. But I kept a revolver on the bedside table, just in case. I thought that the dogs would hear anyone before I did, and I would have time to react with the gun.

That was shown to be wishful thinking, as will be seen.

Then Kate came into my life.

She loves to ride, it formed a bond between us. My lonely weekends were over. I had my fair companion.

Setting off from Guayaquil at 8am, with our beagle. Formerly it was James, but after he died she bought a puppy which we called Snoopy.

We would drive the hour and a quarter it took to get to Rodeo Grande. Once we had left the outskirts of Guayaquil we passed fields of rice and bananas. There are three possible routes to get there.

Foolishly I always took the same one, at the same time, even though I was advised to vary both the route and the time.

I was aware that there might be a kidnap attempt on the road. They are increasingly common. I even practised defensive driving, though I have never had training in this. Basically it was driving fast and overtaking dangerously. Until one day I thought I would probably kill both of us anyway, if I carried on doingit.My sight isn't that good.My family have taken to driving armoured cars. That is to say, a normal car is taken to pieces in a specialized workshop and put back together with bullet proof metal. The windows and windscreen are replaced with bullet proof glass. It makes the cars a lot heavier, so the suspension needs to be reinforced. Also the front windows will only open a fraction,the back ones not at all. There are several grades of protection available, anything from a pistol shot to a bazooka.

But I had declined to have my black BMW armoured. I like its acceleration, which would be affected by the extra weight.

Recently we had noticed suspicious cars which would follow us. If I speeded up so did they, if I slowed down they did too. I had planned to take another route from next Saturday. But as we went there today on a Friday afternoon, and not early Saturday morning, I reasoned that any possible followers would not expect me.

On arrival at Rodeo Grande on any normal Saturday we would greet Cristina, the administrator. She is a petite, attractive forty-four-year old woman. She has been with me since she first came to Rodeo Grande eighteen years ago as a university student, doing her practical. Her twelve-year-old son Matias is my godson. She sometimes brings Isai, her fifteen-year-old nephew with her. The others of the team were Cipriano, the short, rather stout, head cowboy. Amarilis is our eighty-four year-old cook, who has a dry sense of humour. She has been with me since I bought the ranch in 1977. Maria, a tall thin widow, is her assistant. Miguel and Daniel the house boy and gardener respectively are in their thirties. This was our group.

There were also five cowboys, a tractor driver, two night guards and three farm workers, but my relationship with them was more remote.

The first event was breakfast. We sat at the table on the wide balcony on the first floor. The ranch speciality was fried plantain slices with cheese, plus bacon and eggs, fruit juice and coffee.

After breakfast we would kit up to ride with hats, boots and whips, plus face cream and insect repellent.

The cowboys brought the horses from the paddocks to the garden and collected the saddles and bridles, which are kept on racks in the saddle room in the house. Kate has a pink saddle and bridle which Cristina had especially made for her in the nearby town of Vinces. The rest of the saddles and bridles were the normal brown color. Most are western style with a pommel to allow roping of cattle. Mine is the only English saddle. I had bought it from a saddler in Bedale, Yorkshire, forty years ago.

We would all mount and begin the three-hour ride to see the cattle.

The house is a large structure. I built it in 1980.

It's constructed of concrete and bricks, with a red pantile roof. Two stories high, it has a partial third floor which forms an upstairs sitting room. There are six bedrooms.

The house is on stilts. We don’t use the ground floor except for a secondary kitchen for garden parties, and a store room now converted into an extra bedroom. I would park my car there in the shade and we climbed the stairs to the front door.

The reason for the stilts is that in the tropics it's cooler upstairs, there are less mosquitoes, it avoids flooding when the river behind the house overflows and importantly it keeps snakes out of the house.

It stands in a three-hectare garden of trees and flowering shrubs.

I am a dendrophile. I have collected a wide range of tropical flowering trees in the garden. There are pink flowering cana fistulas, purple Jacarandas, yellow buttercup trees, pink robles, red tulip trees, both red and yellow acacias, as well as breadfruit, mango, Saman, Norfolk Island pines and royal palms.

My pride and joy are the Toborochi, known as Brazilian capoc trees. I brought the seeds in a matchbox from Bolivia in 1980, when I had a business there. They flower in June with a mass of beautiful pink flowers.

There is a pretty little tree house, in a large Saman tree, which we built for Mati when he was a small boy.

We have two ostriches and six peacocks in the garden.

Peacocks can fly. When Kate and I were on holiday in Sri Lanka three years ago, we went to a game park and saw notices warning motorists “Beware of low flying peacocks ”.

Ours only fly when they have to move fast, perhaps with Snoopy chasing them, or when they roost in the Saman tree.

This always amused us as we would watch them from the balcony. Darkness comes around 6pm.They would gather under the Saman tree by the house and walk in circles. Then, as though they were cleared by air traffic control, they took off one by one with a great flapping of wings. I suppose it's a primal instinct to roost in a tree, away from predators.

When we ride on a Saturday, we leave the garden along a grassy track shaded by trees towards the corrals. Before getting there we had to cross the Babahoyo to Baba road which bisects the ranch. This is busy, so we have to wait for the gap in the traffic to enable us to cross with the horses and Snoopy. He is kept on a lead until safely the other side.

The road had been upgraded by the government seven years ago . Before that the traffic was slow, avoiding potholes, now it is fast.

We suffered a dreadful accident at this crossing five years before. Albino, who was our oldest cowboy, some seventy-five years old, was crossing it on his horse after dark. A truck with no headlights struck him and his horse, killing both of them.

We think about him every time we cross the road.

Once on the other side of the road we can let Snoopy off his lead. He races ahead of us to the corrals. When we get there we would find him happily rolling on his back in cow manure. A dirty beagle is a happy beagle.

There are two seasons on the ranch. A dry cool summer from May to November, and a wet, hotter Winter, from December to April.

We are now approaching Winter. It is getting hotter, but the rains have not yet started.

We ride chatting happily. As usual we divide into groups. I ride beside Cristina and Cipriano, followed a few paces behind by the cowboy nicknamed Español. He opens gates for us from his horse. Leaning over to unfasten the wire gate, pulling it aside and then refastening it behind us.

Kate rides with Mati and Isai. They normally spur ahead and canter, followed by Snoopy with flapping ears. We think of them as the children, though Kate is much older than the boys. They have bonded, and seemed to have so much to talk about.

One of their tricks is to find a wasp's nest hanging from a tree branch. They whack it with a stick and then, roaring with laughter, they set off at a gallop before the angry wasps attack them.

If we are following behind them they shout a warning, before we ride into trouble.

Friday 15th December 2023

Cristina and the ranch hands had just completed the cattle roundup this week. We do it in May, September and December. It takes three days to complete. The six herds of cattle are collected from their fields and brought one by one to the corrals. They are: the Big Herd, some four hundred cows and their calves, with fifteen breeding bulls. The Heifers are kept apart so as not to be mated before they are fully grown; The Pedigree Herd, where we breed our own commercial bulls; The Milk Herd, of thirty cows we milk daily and sell the milk in the local town of Baba. The Steers which have been weaned from their mothers and are fattening for market. We also have a herd of Buffalos. A total of eight hundred head.

Once in the big corral, the calves are separated from the rest into a smaller corral. Then they are released, four at a time, to where the cowboys, aided by Mati, lasso them and throw them to the ground for branding. At the same time they are counted. Indeed counting is the main purpose of the day.

As well as branding, the cattle are vaccinated for Foot and Mouth Disease and Brucellosis. They receive vitamin injections and are sprayed with insecticide against the pestilent small flies which plague them.

Only the calves are roped and thrown down to brand and inject. The older, already branded, cattle are walked through a cattle race. This is a narrow walkway fenced with metal tubes. There are raised platforms each side from which the cowboys can reach over to inject the cattle. The end man has a bucket of paint and puts a dab of green paint on the back of each beast.

This is a cheap and cheerful system to check if they have all been through. If we are missing cattle at the end of the operation (which we always are) we ride the whole ranch looking for those with no paint mark.

There are always a few cows with newly born calves, which they hide in the long grass or trees. They are missed when we round up, but we generally find them when we look for un-painted cows.

The cowboys lasso them from their horses. They still work the traditional way. They race after a cow and one ropes her around the neck. Then he winds the rope around the pommel of the saddle and pulls the horse up sharply. The cow is jerked to a halt. The second cowboy throws a loop of his lasso on the ground behind her. When she steps in, as she circles around, he pulls tight and between the two the cow falls on her side.

A third cowboy dismounts and walks up the stranded animal. He takes the lasso off her legs. He makes a running knot and replaces it. Then, once she is injected and painted, he removes the rope from her head. He returns to his horse and pulls the lasso which comes free of the legs and the cow can get back up. At that point all three need to be on horses as the angry cow will charge them.

We breed our own horses. Between horses, mares and foals we have seventy six animals. The cowboys only ride stallions or, more often geldings. Stallions can be very difficult to ride once they have been with the mares. They rear up and whinny to the mares. So it's easier to geld all but the breeding stallions. The mares are never ridden and colts are not broken in until they are three years old.

They finished yesterday and the number came out 100% correct.

We planned to have a celebratory dinner tonight, and ride tomorrow.

But we never got to ride.

The dinner is a longtime tradition, from the time my children were small. Amarilis cooks a stew of black beans with pork trotters and sausages. It is a great favorite of ours, which we wash down with a good quantity of beer or red wine. Then come floating islands, a pudding made of three types of milk product.

Today is Friday 15th December. Kate and I arrived at 6pm. Cristina was there by herself, her young lads are not included in the dinners. Cipriano, Fredy and his partner Omar had already got there. Fredy, as well as being an Agripac manager, is the ranch accountant. He had been present the last three days for the cattle count. He is the guy with the clipboard, and each batch of cattle can only be released from the race once he has counted them.

Omar is the manager of one of Agripac's shops. He joined us for dinner.

We began the night with beer to offset the heat of the day. We sat on the balcony, bantered and laughed, we were relaxed. The cattle count had been spot on, so a bonus has been earned by those involved. Counting cattle is rather more complicated than a normal company inventory. Boxes on the whole don't walk about, get lost or die. Then of course we have to deal with rustling. We employ two guards who ride the ranch at night with shotguns, but the ranch is large and from time to time we lose cattle or horses.

As the mosquitos began to get bad we closed the balcony doors and retreated into the house, and went upstairs to the sitting room on the top floor. This is decorated with memorabilia. There is a jaguar skin from Bolivia. It had been shot while attacking cattle on my partner Winston's ranch in the Beni province.

There is a zebra skin on the floor, a present from my sister Jane when she lived in South Africa. There is a colorful wooden screen from Guatemala, paintings from Costa Rica and an old wooden barrel made into a bar.

Today it's air conditioned, but there are still the ancient ceiling fans which I bought second hand from the Phoenix Club forty years ago.

The wine was opened and nibbles were put out.

At 8pm Amarilis indicated that dinner was ready. She brooks no delay. When it is ready we have to go to the table. But she won't eat with us, she prefers to eat in the kitchen with Maria, Miguel and Daniel.

They served the huge pot of stew and a large dish of white rice. We accompanied this with the ranch's speciality chili sauce. A particularly vicious one.

This will be our last visit to Rodeo Grande before Christmas. We exchange presents. My normal way is to put cash, or a cheque, in an envelope for each one.

Once dinner was over at ten o'clock, Cristina left for her house in Babahoyo, some fifteen miles away. She dropped Amarilis at her house on the way. Miguel and Cipriano got their motorbikes and left for home. Dani and Maria walked to their houses nearby.

So only Fredy, Omar, Kate and I were left.

I am the lightweight. By ten thirty pm I was falling asleep. I said good night to the others and went to bed. Snoopy followed me.

The others continued drinking and telling ghost stories.

Eventually Fredy and Omar went to bed.

So that left just Kate, the night owl.

As she has done many times before, she went for a walk at midnight. She walked through the garden to the football field. It is used from time to time by the ranch staff, and once a year for the finals of the Agripac championships.

She lay on the grass and looked at the stars. She thought she might stay out until dawn and see the sunrise at 6am.

But she got sleepy and at 1.00am walked back to the house.

As she was walking her mother called her from Colombia. Kate asked her why she was calling at this time of night.

Margarita told her that she was worried. She had had a premonition about her, she asked if she was all right, she had a sensation of danger.

Kate laughed it off. "No, Mum, I am safe. Nothing will happen to me at Rodeo Grande."

Meanwhile fifteen heavily armed men, dressed in fake police uniforms, stood in the shadows of the bamboo grove, watching her, waiting for her to return to the house, go to bed and switch off the lights.

I woke as she got into bed. She had partially undressed, she was only wearing her underwear. I kissed her, before falling asleep again.

An hour later I awoke and went to the bathroom.I didn't put on the light, so as not to wake her.

As I returned to the bedroom Snoopy began to bark hysterically. There was a startled cry from Kate. I rushed into the room to find the dark forms of several men there.

My instinct was to punch the nearest one. But that did little good. My wrists were quickly grasped and tied behind my back very tightly together with a plastic tie. I was naked, which is how I normally sleep, and that made me even more vulnerable. They threw a bed sheet over my head.

Snoopy was dashing about barking. I was scared that they would shoot or kick him. Somehow he survived.

It was all very quick.

They told Kate to lie on the bed face down and not look at them, although their faces were half covered with bandanas. They began to drag me out of the bedroom.

Kate screamed at them to take her too.

"He will die. He's an old man. He can't stand rough handling . Let me go with him to look after him".

The assailants hesitated, looked at their boss. He said to take her too. It would cause them less trouble than to leave her here as a witness.

We were both bundled half pushed, half carried from the bedroom, through the large hall and down the outside stairs to the car.

With the sheet over my head I could see nothing. Kate got a glimpse of Fredy standing with his hands in the air. Omar was lying on the floor with blood oozing from his scalp.

They didn't have a car there. I guess they had been left on the main road and walked in, so as not to alert us. They took my black BMW X5.

They pushed us into the back seat. One man got on either side of us. The driver couldn't find how to start the car and screamed at Kate, who showed him.

I was in agony with the plastic ties cutting into my wrists. I pleaded with them to take them off. I couldn't stop groaning. They told me to shut up.

They backed the car out from under the house and turned left towards the garden gate onto the road. There are heavy iron gates across the track in both directions, both the grass track and the paved road. They were locked with chains and padlocks.

The leader told the driver to smash the gates. He revved up and charged them. There was a loud crash and a jerk that tore into my wrists.

I screamed with pain.

The gates swung open and we raced onto the road and turned right.

We were doubled over on the seat with our heads pressed down to our knees, so we couldn't see where we were going. But I know the road well.

We took the bypass around Baba, continued a few kilometres and then pulled off the road into a lane in a banana plantation. They stopped the car and roughly pulled us out. My car was abandoned.

There was a double cabin white pickup truck waiting there. We were pushed inside and it immediately set off.

I shouted to them that they had made a big mistake. I am an ex-consul. This is going to cause them a lot of trouble. They told me to shut up. Kate said the same. She was afraid they would hit me. The man guarding me thrust two tablets into my mouth.

Whatever it was, it made me sleep. Thank God.

Kate later told me that we were transferred to another, brown, pick up truck before we arrived.

The change of cars was to avoid being tracked by cameras along the roads.

I awoke as the dawn came up at 6am. The car had stopped and we were bundled out. We were somewhere in the countryside. There was a cocoa plantation to one side and several coconut trees.

There were two small concrete houses with corrugated iron roofs. They had metal doors and windows. There were other men there, apart from our kidnappers. We were pushed inside one of the houses. It seemed to be a workers' dormitory. There were several grubby mattresses on the floor. The wooden bedsteads had been propped up to block the windows. There was a privy in an alcove to one side with a door off its hinges. Items of unwashed clothing hung from nails on the walls.

We were pushed down on a mattress and then, thankfully, they cut the plastic tie off my wrists with a rusty machete. The relief was terrific. I was even grateful to them. My arms by this time were swollen to double normal size and black. They were bleeding in places from the rough handling, each time we changed vehicle.

Kate asked them for hydrogen peroxide to wash them to prevent infection. They gave us a small bottle an hour later.

I was still naked. They threw me a pair of shorts, which though unwashed and smelly, I gratefully put on.

Kate needed to go to the privy. Four men were still in the room. I stood the door in the doorframe and held it there. The lavatory was a normal ceramic one with an exit pipe running through the wall, but was not connected to a water pipe. There was a large plastic tank filled with water and a plastic scoop to dispense it. But it was better than nothing. At least there was paper.

They began to question us.

"Have you got GPS chips inserted in your bodies?".

We quickly said no. We had visions of them slicing our arms with razors to check if they were there.

The leader asked me.

"What is your son's telephone number?"

"I don't know. You have taken my phone. I have the number on it. I can't remember it. "

They turned to Kate.

"Do you know where he lives?"

"Yes" she replied

They debated among themselves.

They told her to stand up and they took a photo of her.

After this they left the room, chaining the metal door behind them.

We lay down on the mattress. "Did they touch you in the car, My Love?" I asked.

She was only dressed in underwear and completely at their mercy.

"No, Honey. One of them put his hand on my knee, but I cried and pleaded with them to leave me alone, and they did.

We were both exhausted. We hugged each other and soon fell asleep.

We were woken about midday. They had stolen our watches, as well as the phones, so we had to judge the time of day by the position of the sun.

With a rattling sound the door was unchained, four masked men came in. They threw a bundle of clothes and a pair of sandals at Kate. They had got the size right by the photo.

"Get dressed, you are leaving".

She stood up and put on the clothes. It was a grey coloured track suit. She put on the trousers. They told her not to put on the top.

The leader produced a coarse cloth waistcoat sown with small pouches. He said it was an explosive vest. If she went to the police he would know, and explode it. He pointed out a small flashing red light which he said was the detonator.

He put it on her, over her brassiere and wound clear plastic tape around her several times to fasten it to her body.

Then she could put on the tracksuit top.

"Where is she going?" I asked

"To your son. To take a phone from the boss."

"I will do it and come back", she said "wait for me. Don't fight them. We will survive this."

" My love when you get to Nick. Remind him of Lien."

"Yes."

"We will survive this and go to White Desert together, Honey. I promise you".

We kissed briefly before they pulled us apart and took her out of the door and into the waiting truck,

It drove off.

Now I was on my own.

How much worse it is to be on your own. While we were together we could hug and comfort each other. Now I was alone with my thoughts.

What I had told them about being an ex-consul is true. I had been the honorary British Consul in Guayaquil for thirty five years, until I retired in favour of my son Nick, in 2016.

I knew how the chain of events would run. Someone from the ranch would call Nick. He would call the British Embassy in Quito. There is an emergency, out of office hours, phone number.

The Ambassador would call the Foreign and Commonwealth Office in London. It was Saturday, but there would be a duty officer.

Someone in authority would contact the recently elected Ecuadorian President, Daniel Noboa.

Because it was of international interest, the President would instruct the police on the importance of obtaining my release.

The UK press were bound to get on to it. There would be headlines such as 'Ex-Diplomat kidnapped by gangsters in Ecuador'. Which in turn would increase the pressure on the FCO to do something about it.

Finally, I am a constituent of the Prime Minister Rishi Sunak in Richmond, North Yorkshire.

I had never met him personally but he has been to my Coverdale business, The Forbidden Corner. There are photos of him with the manager Leo Morris, Nick's best friend and my adopted son.

And then there is Lien. My good friend Lien. We have known each other since he was working with the British Council in Ecuador, some forty years ago.

After leaving the Council he is now an insurance broker.

The policies he sells include Kidnap Insurance.

I had taken out a policy for Ceci and the three children, Nick, Diana and Alex, over twenty years ago. Then, as they married and had children, their spouses and children were added. Finally just this last year I had included Kate too. Nick knew Lien and about the policy.

Hence my instruction to Kate to remind him. Though he needed no reminding. By the time she got to talk to Nick, Lien knew all about the kidnap.

There is an important clause in the policy. It involves a link to a rapid response unit.

This organization is made up of people who have served in the armed forces or police.

They come to the assistance of the family of any insured person who is kidnapped.

They are experts in negotiating with the kidnappers.

Locally, there is a branch of the Ecuadorian police called UNASE, which specializes in kidnap rescues. They too will make contact with Nick.

That's what I thought would happen.

And indeed it did.

When I originally took out the insurance policy it seemed to me a bit over the top.

Ecuador at that time was an island of peace.

For over fifty years I have travelled the country visiting our shops, staying in small hotels on the Coast, in the Sierra and in the Oriente (Amazon) without a thought for personal safety.

I have stayed overnight at Rodeo Grande on my own so many times.

I used to let the dogs out in the night and leave the door open for them to come back in.

On the night of the kidnap, the men got into the bedroom before we, or even Snoopy, heard them. I suspect that the front door wasn't even locked.

Something I would never do in Guayaquil. But the countryside is safe. Or so we thought !

Ecuador is sandwiched between Colombia and Peru.

Colombia has had its seemingly permanent civil wars. For many years this involved the Conservatives and the Liberals. The recently released film "One hundred years of solitude", based on the book by Gabriel Garcia Marquez shows the continuous fighting between them.

Later it evolved into the state against the FARC, who touted Marxist values. Next came the Paramilitary who fought against both sides. By this time ideology had long gone. The fight was between drug dealers and the prevention of drugs. Colombia is a massive grower of coca, from which cocaine is processed.

The notorious drug lord Pablo Escobar came to fame as the biggest supplier of cocaine in the World, until he was killed by the Colombian army in 1993.

Perú had its own civil strife between the government and the maoist Shining Path guerillas, which lasted from 1980 to 1992. Eventually the leader of the Shining Path, Abimael Guzman, and most of his leaders were captured by the police.

Today Peru is much more stable. But it is still a big source of coca.

Ecuador adopted the US dollar as its currency in 1999. It's attractive for drug dealers to have easy access to the dollar. So began its problem with the narcos, which not only continues, but is still growing today. Coca is not grown in Ecuador. But it's through Guayaquil that most of the cocaine from Colombia and Peru is exported, by sea or by air to US and European consumers.

There had once been a problem for the narcos. Ecuador signed an agreement with the USA in 1999 for the US air force, and the DEA, to maintain a base at Manta, a coastal town. They flew missions to detect drugs being exported by air or sea.

They could only be gotten rid of by political means. The narcos found their man in Rafael Correa. He was elected as a left wing President of Ecuador in 2006.

It was rumored at the time that he had backing of FARC money. That was never proved. But a subsequent event shows that it was likely.

Rafael changed the constitution in 2008, making it illegal for Ecuador to host bases for foreign troops. Then in 2009, when the current contract expired, he ejected the US military from Manta. The door was now open for the narcos to increase their shipments through Ecuador.

Of course the decision was disguised in terms of human rights, national honour and other blarney. But the job was done.

From then on the amount of cocaine captured by the police each year goes on rising until recently it hit three hundred tons. The rule of thumb is that for every ton captured, ten get through. So Ecuador gifts the World 3,000 tons of cocaine a year!

There was an incident on 1st March 2008 which confirmed to myself, and many others, that the FARC was backing Rafael.

That was Operation Fenix. The Colombian armed forces raided a FARC camp at Angostura and killed Raul Reyes, the second in command of the FARC, and twenty two of his men. They found laptops with a lot of incriminating evidence, which has still not been released to the public.

It was just a fight between Colombians. True, but Angostura is in Ecuador!

Rafael made a huge fuss about it, breaking off relations with Colombia. How dare they intrude on Ecuador's sacred soil. Strangely his government made not the slightest excuse for the FARC having a base inside the country. The Colombian government knew about it. It must be supposed that the Ecuadorian police and armed forces knew about it. After all they patrol the border to prevent drug smuggling.

Eventually the quarrel was patched up by the OEA (the Organisation of American States). But it left a general suspicion about Rafael’s contact with the FARC.

Another related event took place in November 2021. The government of the day, under President Guillermo Lasso, installed radar on the Montecristi hills behind Manta. The aim was the same, to detect planes or boats transporting drugs. The radar was protected by a military unit. Eleven days after it was installed it was destroyed in an explosion. There is an ongoing trial of ten soldiers blamed for negligence. But who exploded the bomb has never been established. Who the beneficiaries are is clear, the narcos.

There has hardly been a rush to replace the radar. There was a long wrangle with the insurance company over the $7 million dollar cost, but as of today there still is no radar there.

That is the state of affairs as they stand now. Who are the players?

There are four main international groups.

El Cártel de Sinaloa (Mexican).

El Cartel Jalisco, Nueva Generación (Mexican).

La Mafia Balcánica (Italy, Albania y Kosovo).

Frente Oliver Sinisterra (Colombia).

They operate in Ecuador through ten local drug gangs. These resulted from the fracture of the once-dominant Choneros, who split into the Fatales, Aguilas, Gangsters, R7, Chonekillers, Lobos, Lagartos, Latin Kings and Tiguerones.

They fight among themselves to control territory, and to control the prisons. Not a day passes without newspaper reports of bodies found, many of them of people with criminal records.

As well as dealing drugs they have a sideline in kidnapping and extortion.

Many Agripac customers have told us they have to pay regular amounts of money to prevent their family being harmed. It has got so bad that a legion of small businesses have closed altogether. Farmers have decided not to plant, if they have to share the proceeds of the crop with the gangs. Ecuador's economy is paying a huge price for insecurity.

Now I need to go back to Kate's experience, which she told me about after my release.

She was driven four hours to Guayaquil, bundled up on the floor of the pickup truck. She recounted that they passed three toll gates on the road. Where there are always police, but no one even looked into the car.

She carried the phone to give to Nick. The man with the gravel voice kept calling her on it to give instructions. She had to let him know where she was and what she was doing, from the time they released from the car until she had delivered the phone to Nick. She had to take a photo of the taxi plates, a photo of where Nick lives. Everything she does has to be reported. Otherwise he will explode the belt.

As a precaution, the men she was with have removed the detonator from the belt while she is in the car. They don't want it exploding by mistake.

There are cameras on the highways too. But when the police tried to follow the trail of the car from Rodeo Grande looking at the cameras they lost track when we changed cars. Of course, on the return journey no one was even looking for her.

When they got to within fifteen kilometres of Guayaquil they put Kate out of the car. They gave her $40 for a taxi and told her to go straight to Nick's house. If she went to the police they would explode the vest. The car drove on, and then reversed to where she was. A man got out and put the detonator back in the belt!

She must not look at the car as it drove away.

She had been cramped for four hours and couldn't at first stand up. She sat at the side of the road. By now the sun was past its zenith, it would be about 4pm. Being Saturday, there wasn't much traffic. Certainly there were no taxis passing by. But she had to get to see Nick and then hopefully they would take her back to look after me, as they had promised to do.

There was nothing for it but to walk towards Guayaquil.

She walked for an hour and then came across an old, battered pickup truck loaded with plantains. The driver was eating in a kiosk. She told him that she had been the victim of an express kidnap (where people are taken to a cash dispenser and made to extract cash) which are all too common. It was better this than the true story. He sympathized and agreed to take her further into the city where she could get a taxi.

While she was with him the phone rang. But she didn't answer. There was no way that she could tell him who she was with, what he was wearing and the car's number plate. The driver would have put her out immediately.

The old truck was painfully slow, but eventually as they passed the Guayaquil Penitentiary on the Daule road, she saw a taxi rank. She thanked the pickup driver, gave him $10 and took the taxi to where Nick lives. She dutifully took a photo of the taxi plates.

She arrived at the walled enclosure where he has his house. The taxi could not go in. So she paid the driver and spoke to the guards at the gate. She asked them to call Nick. They did, he agreed she could come in.

It's about half a kilometre from the gate to his house. She walked it and found him waiting for her, with Almu, in front of the house.

She told him that she had an explosive belt on. With that Nick told her not to come any closer. She must return to the tennis court at the gate. He would ask the UNASE agent in his house to call the bomb squad. So poor Kate walked all the way back to the gate. By this time it was getting dark. But it was still very warm. She was sweating under her tracksuit top and explosive waistcoat.

She sat on a seat by the tennis court, which was luckily empty. After an hour four agents of the bomb squad arrived in a police van, dressed in heavy protective overalls. They asked her to remove her tracksuit top and inspected the waistcoat. They said it might not be real, but they were taking no chances. They gave her a pair of wire cutters, instructed her how to cut the red wire, cleared everyone fifty metres from her. They retired behind ballistic shields, and told her to do it. So as in the films, she took a deep breath and cut the red wire. Nothing happened. The police asked her to cut the green one.

She did, and again nothing happened.

At last they approached her and removed the wretched waistcoat. Kate protested to them that if they took it off she wouldn't be allowed to return to look after me. But they obviously couldn't leave it on, just in case it really was explosive. She replaced her tracksuit top, and for the third time walked the distance to Nick's house. Now that she knew that she couldn't return to me, she realised that had always been their plan. She had been made to cooperate with false promises. They didn't want her back with me to give me courage. Quite the reverse they wanted to scare the hell out of me to make me more amenable to their demands.

She and Nick could now talk. He remembered Lien's telephone number in the early hours of the morning when he had received Fredy's call from Rodeo. He had called him at once. Now there was already one rapid response operative in his house and another was on his way from Texas.

He had had no contact with the kidnappers. But that was because Kate had the telephone to give to him. She handed it over, without taking a photo of his house or the compound. She was not going to do their dirty work.

The police wanted to interview her. She sat with the UNASE agent for two hours while she recounted her story several times. He seemed to want to trip her up on some detail, as though he suspected that she was involved in the kidnap. He repeated time and again "Why did you want to keep the explosive belt on?" He said that no one in their right mind would return to a kidnap venue. She repeated that she wanted to be with me.

He couldn't understand that.

Finally he was through with her. Then the rapid response operative took over and questioned her again, but rather more sympathetically.

At about midnight she was allowed to go home. Heavily armed police drove her there. Before she was allowed to enter our penthouse, on the fifteenth floor, they checked it thoroughly to see if it was safe. Then they left her.

Her mother was already there waiting for her. She had been contacted by Janina, our travel agent friend, who had arranged her tickets from Ibague to Bogota and Bogota to Guayaquil. They cried and hugged each other.

Margarita wanted to hear all about the kidnap, but Kate only wanted to shower and sleep. She felt dirty after lying on the filthy mattress in the hut. It was twenty four hours since we had been taken from Rodeo Grande. She went and took a long shower, revelling in the hot water, shampoo and soap, as though washing away the horrible day.

Then she took her sleeping pills. She didn't want to talk, not even to her mother. She looked for comfort in sleep.

She slept all day Sunday.

On Monday morning Janina came and the three of them talked. Now Kate could tell her tale more calmly.

She was worried about me and the ransom. Nick had told her that she couldn’t help. He would negotiate the ransom with the advice of the professionals. He said that as she had arrived in an explosive vest the police were treating the case as terrorism and not just extortion.

To make payment impossible they had blocked Agripac’s bank accounts.

Kate was desperate. If no money could be paid, how long would the kidnappers wait before dumping my body somewhere for the police to find?

They would make an example of pay up, or its dead meat.

She went to her bank. She had money in a deposit account. But it was on a year’s fixed deposit. How could she get it out immediately? The branch manager recognised her from the TV news and knew what she wanted the money for. He could see that she was desperate. He said he would talk to his superiors, she should come back in two hours’ time. She went home.

On her return the bank informed her that she could make the withdrawal but that she would have to sacrifice a year’s interest. She agreed to do it.

She called Nick and offered to donate her money. She said that even though the company bank accounts were blocked, if each one of the family could put in what they had in the bank plus hers they might get me out. Even though they couldn’t get near the five million dollars demanded, the kidnappers might accept a lesser sum. At first he accepted the idea. He would consult with the advisors. But then he called her back and said no, he sounded stressed. He didn't need her money, he was doing the negotiation and would do it his way. She tried to persuade him. But he said no. He was following the instructions of the advisors. They had a lot of experience. The money would be paid and I will be released. But the process of negotiation must run its course.

She returned to her mother crying. If the family would not accept her money she was sure that I would be killed.

Janina was with them. She came up with a strange suggestion. She knew of a witch. She was famous for predicting the future. She would take Kate and Margarita to visit her.

They went in Janina's car. It was a long way, right across the city, until they arrived at a modest building in a poor area of town. It appeared to be a local shop selling bread, eggs, coffee and fruit. They entered and Janina asked for the witch. They were shown to a room at the back of the shop, behind a black curtain. They entered and met the lady. She was a negress, about fifty years old. She was dressed in a colourful blouse and skirt, she wore a black turban on her head. She had long fingernails, each painted a different colour.

She asked them to sit down on the wooden stools there, and tell her what they wanted to know.

Kate told her about our being kidnapped last Saturday. She wanted to know if I was still alive and if so would I be released. She was worried that the family would not pay sufficient ransom.

The witch handed each of them a Havana cigar which she lit and they all smoked. She charged them $15 for each cigar including hers. She said she had been able to talk to spirits ever since she was a young girl. She would ask them about me. Then she smoked her cigar and was silent for a long time.

From time to time she spat out tobacco juice into a glass of water.

She seemed to be in a trance.

Then she spoke. But in a deep voice, a man's voice.

She said she could see vegetation, she could hear the sound of trucks and motorbikes. She saw several young men. Then she said she could see an old man. He was stressed, he had high blood pressure. She would ask an angel to comfort him.

Kate asked her if I would be freed. She said she couldn't see that. But I was alive at this moment, she could sense it. But the future just looked white. All she could see was a very long journey, and there were documents to sign, lots of documents.

They all asked questions, but it seemed that the trance was over. Her voice was normal again.

They left.

Kate thought about what she had said. The very long journey. Could that be White Desert?

But she would never go alone. So I must be freed to go with her. She clung to that thought. But what were the documents?

So back to me. There was nothing to do except lie on the mattress. After Kate was taken away a guard brought me a plastic bottle of water. He asked me if I was hungry. I said yes. He returned with a plate of chicken with rice. I tried to eat but it tasted rancid. I left it.

He came for the plate and asked why I hadn't eaten it. I told him I didn't like it. He said there was nothing else except a coconut, would I like that?

I said yes, and he brought one in. He hacked it with a machete and handed it me to drink the coconut water. It tasted so good. Then I handed the shell back to him. He put it on the floor and with a swipe of the machete cut it in half. He gave me the halves with a spoon and I ate the coconut flesh.

He said, "We mean you no harm. We are just farm workers here. But we daren't let you escape".

I said I understood.

He asked if there was anything else I needed. I said yes, some healing cream for the wounds on my arms. I had applied hydrogen peroxide several times but needed something to heal them.I was scared it would get infected in this filthy place.

I needed a toothbrush and paste too.

All of which he produced later that day.

It crossed my mind that I could hit the guy on the head with something when he delivered food. But even if I knocked him out there were two or three others outside. They slept in the next door house. I could hear them talking together. Even if I managed to escape them where was I to go, dressed only in shorts? I had no idea which direction to take. And if I got violent they would too.

So I stayed quiet.

Saturday ended. I slept on and off both day and night. There was nothing else to do.

I wondered if Kate had got to talk to Nick. But she would not be able to tell him where I was.

I had no idea either. Because of the sleeping pill I had lost track of time. I thought I was only two hours from Rodeo Grande, not the four that it was. I tried to work it out. I know Ecuador well from my visits to my shops and customers' farms, over the last fifty years.

It was quite cool at night, and there were no mosquitos, so perhaps I was in the foothills of the Andes, say Echeandia, a small town near Ventanas, about an hour from Rodeo Grande. There was a cocoa plantation and coconuts, so we were at no great elevation.

Beds had been upended against the windows to block the view. But there were narrow strips that I could look out.

There was a dirt road outside. It seemed that it led to a quarry, or some such destination, as the sound of heavy trucks was a constant, though I couldn't see them. There were also motorbikes which came and went, one of which sounded like a heavy machine, by the thump, thumping of the motor. The same sound as the Royal Ensign bikes we had seen in Nepal. But I had never seen them in Ecuador. It had once been a British brand, but now they are made in India.

For the rest of Saturday I was left in peace. But on Sunday I was woken by the rattling of the chain on the metal door. A man came in with a bandana across half his face and thrust a telephone at me.

"The boss wants to talk to you".

I took the phone from him and said Hola.

"Escuchame, said a gravel voice. Escuchame". So I agreed to listen to him. What else could I do?

He went on to say that they wanted five million dollars for my release. The sooner they got it, the sooner I would be released.

I said that there was nothing I could do to help them while I was in captivity. They had to talk to my son. He said that he would put me in contact with Nick and I had to tell him to pay the five million dollars.

I agreed to do it. All the while crossing my fingers. I knew that the asking price was never the one paid. Lien had told me about many kidnaps, in Ecuador and other countries of Latin America.

Whatever the asking price was, the going rate was about two hundred thousand dollars. We were insured. We could pay it. But there was another factor that worried me. Kidnappers have a nasty habit of cutting fingers or ears from the victim, to encourage the family to collaborate. That did scare me. It had happened to a kidnap victim only the week before in Quevedo, in Ecuador. I didn't know whether it was the same gang who had me.

After a while the phone was again thrust at me. I was told to talk to Nick. It was done by two phones being held together. I was told to talk only in Spanish.

"Hello Dad, how are you?".

"Hi Nick, so far I am fine. They have not mistreated me. We will have to pay to get me out. Take advice on this and we will get there. I love you Nick. "

"I love you Dad".

Then the phone was taken back. I guess Nick had to be reassured that I was still alive before making payment.

I was left in peace for some more hours, on my diet of coconuts. Then I heard a vehicle arrive. The door opened and a middle aged man and woman, both with half their face covered, came in. I was told to sit back to back with them so I wouldn't look at their faces, even though they were masked. They began to question me.

"How much cash do you have in the safe in your office?"

A strange question. They seemed rather amateur. As far as I knew it was only narcos who piled up cash in recesses of their houses. I had watched the TV series on Pablo Escobar, the notorious Colombian drug lord.

As a businessman, I have a lot of bank debt, and very little actual cash.

"I don't know, I guess about a thousand dollars".

They seemed surprised. "You must have more cash, maybe a hundred thousand dollars?"

"No way. My business is largely credit. I have a lot of money owing to the company, but they don't often pay in cash. I get bank deposits, cheques, credit cards, but not cash."

" But you have a lot of shops. You sell to small farmers and they pay in cash?"

This is true. We do have some cash sales. I had to think of something before these two felons got annoyed and went for my fingers.

"Yes, we do have cash sales. About a hundred thousand dollars a day, but it is deposited in the company bank accounts."

"You have to give it to us. We need a half a million each week. If you give us that we won't ask for five million dollars, we will let you go for two million."

"Thank you. But I can't do it from here. You will have to let me go so I can organize it."

"But you promise to do it?"

"Yes", again the crossed fingers. Then they became more friendly and asked if there was anything I wanted. I said yes, a bottle of red wine. They asked which wine I liked. I replied Doña Paola. They said they would get it for me tomorrow. With that they left.

I had promised to do it, but in fact I could never keep that promise, even had I wanted to. For one thing it is illegal to give money to terrorist groups. Agripac bank accounts would be frozen until I was released. After that I still couldn't pay it. I am the owner of the company, but I would have to ask others to commit a crime. My family would oppose paying when I am already free. Then there is the logistics of it. We have two hundred shops. Each one deposits daily in a nearby bank. To ask them all to send cash to the head office would expose us to risks of the money being stolen en route. Finally I am not even sure if we really get that much in bank notes. Most payments are by cheque or cards.

All in all it is a very hollow promise. But strangely they believed it.

I had asked for Doña Paola for a reason. I do indeed like it. It's a Malbec wine from Argentina. We drink it at staff parties when I tour the shops. I am famous for it. Wherever I am now I hoped that if they asked for Doña Paola in some village shop it might just spark with one of my employees. Dona Paola ? That's what Colin drinks.

But it didn't happen.They returned on Monday and gave me the bottle.

They kept insisting on the half million.Which day could I deliver them the first one ?

By Friday?

I said no. It was already Monday and I was still locked up. I needed five days to get that much together. They seemed in a rush. I said if they let me out today I could have it by the following Monday. They said they would talk to the boss, then they left.

Later I was told that I would be released at 6pm today. I was excited. But it didn't happen. I was still there on Monday night.

I was asleep that night when sometime in the early hours I was woken by the chain rattling in the door.

Without putting on a light a masked man barged in and thrust a phone at me.

"The boss wants to talk to you".

I took the phone. Hola.

"I have given orders for you to be killed", he screamed at me.

"Why ?"

"You have caused me a lot of trouble. That son of a bitch of a President has ordered the police and the army to eliminate my group. They have arrested nine of my people. But they are just the little guys. Why have they arrested them? They have done nothing wrong. He went on in the same vein for some minutes. When he stopped I said

" So what do you gain by killing me? Instead of extortion the charge against you becomes murder. I am an old man with only a few years to live anyway."

The phone went dead.

I had had my moment of bravura. Now my hands were shaking. I was facing death. At any moment the door might open and the hitman come in. Telling him that it would be murder was silly. How many murders are already attributed to him? Probably dozens.

I have heard that at such moments people review their lives. I certainly did.

I couldn't pray to God. That would be cheating. I had denied his existence since I was at school.

If I were to die now, what would people think of me? I had not been entirely good or bad. Like most people I was a mix of the two. On my way up to business success I had pushed others aside. There had been girls who wanted to marry me. I selfishly refused to marry until I had made a success in business, or at least got started on that road. There were business partners that I had pressured to sell out, until I owned the business entirely.

Most importantly there was my family who I had hurt when I went with Kate.

I am very ashamed of that.

I have done some good deeds too. Many people have thanked me for my help or kindness over the years.

So where do I stand in the balance of good and bad?

It is the opinion of my fellow men that I value. I don't believe in my soul going to heaven, or to hell. Just the memory that I would leave behind here on earth.

Would my legacy be the 'founder of the family fortune?' or 'the man who broke up his family?'

The hours passed. My normal coconut was delivered for breakfast.

Perhaps the hit man was delayed?

Was he on his way?

I was left to dwell on this all day.

Then I got another call.

The same gravel-voiced man. He said that I had offered to pay half a million in cash each week for four weeks. When would I deliver the first one? He would give me a phone that I could use to contact him when the cash was ready.

I repeated that he would have to let me go so I could fulfill my promise.

He said he would let me go tomorrow morning.

He rang off.

So it appeared I was worth more to them alive than dead. A great relief. But while I was in captivity, something else could go wrong to warrant my death.

Some time on Tuesday one of the kidnappers (I didn't count my immediate guards) came to tell me that I would be released at midday.

I thanked him but said I needed some clothes to leave in. I couldn't go only in this pair of stinking shorts. He said they would get me something to put on.

I was animated. Perhaps I would get out intact, with all fingers present.

Once out I would leave the country. Get out of their reach. There was no way I was going to honour my promise of the money. A promise made under duress does not count.

I sat and listened for the car that would take me to freedom. Trucks came and went all day. But I stayed in my cell.

About five in the afternoon one of the gang came in to say there had been a delay. A car was coming from Guayaquil to take me, but would not get here before midnight.

Once again my hopes were buoyed up.

When freedom beckons one is very much aware that you are still in their power. They may never let me go. They may even carry out the threat to kill me. I wondered how they would do it. A bullet in the head would be the least painful. Hopefully it wouldn't involve the rusty machete. On the other hand they might just settle for a finger or two, to remind me of my promise. They had gone on about being men of honour. A promise made was a promise that had to be kept. Or else!

When they finally came for me I asked them the time. It was 10.30pm. They threw me a pair of loose-fitting overalls and sandals. I gratefully put them on.

I was led out of the hut and put in the back seat of a pickup truck. One man got in beside me and thrust my head down.

"Don't look".

I couldn't look, but I could feel the bumpy track. It was half an hour until we got to a paved road. I could see the clock on the dashboard between the seats, it was 11:00pm.

The man beside me asked the driver where I would be dropped off. I didnt hear his reply. Then the driver called on his phone. He was talking to a woman. I could hear them.

"Do you remember where we had coffee, by the side of the road? Yes, that is it".

He rang off.

"Was that the police you were talking to?" I asked

"No".

But it had to be someone who would in turn talk to the police. I would be left somewhere for the police to collect me. That was the normal way.

We didn't go far on the paved road when they pulled into the side. There was a wooden kiosk there, closed for the night but with fairy lights around the porch. There were two guard dogs who growled as I was taken from the car and made to sit on a stool there.

"Wait here. The police will come for you in an hour. Don't forget what you promised us, or we will get you again. We are the biggest organization in Ecuador we are the Tigerones (Big Tigers)".

They got back in the car and drove off.

I sat and wondered where I was. The road was quite busy with cars, trucks and buses. I thought about flagging down a car. But at this time of night who would stop to pick up a stranger?

The only clue to my whereabouts was the buses. They had their destination lit up on the front. I saw one that said Quito. But that could be from anywhere. Quito, the capital, was several hours drive from the Coast.

Another bus said Chone. That was a better clue. Chone is in Manabi province.

But I still didn't know.

I heard the sound of people laughing in a bar half a kilometer down the road. I imagined that it was a chongo. That is the name for bars outside the city limit where prostitutes are tolerated. It occurred to me that I might get mugged. But what was there to steal? I had no money, watch or phone.

The night was quite pleasant. It was cool and there were no mosquitos.

I stood up to stretch my legs, but the dogs began to bark. So I sat down again.

I expected the police to come after an hour. I kept looking for cars slowing down. But in vain.

It was 1am when they arrived (I asked them the time). A red pickup passed me then stopped fifty yards past the kiosk. Five plain clothes men got out.

"Are you Colin Armstrong"?

I replied yes. They said they were from the police unit UNASE.

I squeezed into the back of the car with them. They drove off. After a few kilometres they stopped the car in a small town. They explained that there was a phone signal here and they had to call their captain to tell him they had me.

"Where are we? "

"Rocafuerte".

So we are indeed in Manabi. Not only that but another few kilometres away was one of my bigger warehouses and shops.

One of them called the captain. Then we all got out of the car and they posed with me in the center as they took a photo. For good measure I was given a police cap to put on.

I thanked them all and the captain for my 'rescue'.

Then we drove on, we passed my shop, which was obviously closed. I had been so close for four days.

We took the road towards Guayaquil. The policemen chatted to me. One knew the Agripac head of security, who had formerly been a policeman. Another knew my friend Trevor who has a security business.

They asked me about my captivity. I told them it was the Tigerones. They said they were the most active in Manabi.

We arrived at a village where, despite the hour, there was a cafe open for truckers. They suggested we get a coffee. I said fine, but I couldn't pay. They laughed and said they would give me the coffee.

We all got out and sat at a table. Then a marked police car pulled up. Two uniformed officers got out and joined us in the cafe. Once again we all posed for photos.

After the coffee they told me that these two officers would take me to Guayaquil. The others had to return to their base in Manabi.

I thanked them, shook hands with each of them, and got into the other car. Here there was more space. The pickup had six people, this one only three. They sat in the front and I had the back seat to myself. I fell asleep.

I woke as we approached Guayaquil. They told me that we had to pass by the police headquarters so the doctor could examine me. I protested that all I wanted was to get home. But they explained that they needed a doctor's report to make the case against the kidnappers. So I accepted it.

We were greeted at the police station as heroes. It was now 3.00am but everyone on night duty came to shake my hand. The doctor was friendly and asked me to take off my shirt to show him the damage to my arms. He took photos. Then he examined me and declared that apart from the arms I was in pretty good shape. I could then go home. I was driven there by four officers. The guards at the gate of the enclosure welcomed me back. They called the house. We drove in and Ceci, Alex and Diana (who had just arrived from Los Angeles) were waiting for me at the door. It was 4am on Wednesday 20th December.

We all cried and hugged each other.

There was the obligatory photo on the doorstep with the policemen and then we were left on our own. I badly needed a glass of wine. We opened a bottle and I told them my story. They are full of praise for Nick who they said had spent four sleepless nights waiting for calls from the kidnappers.

Once he heard that I was out he had finally gone to bed. He would come and see me in the morning.

We talked and drank wine until daylight. Then I went to get a couple of hours of sleep before I had to be debriefed by the UNASE officer and the response agents.

It was 9am when Nick came to the house. I was already up and dressed. I hadn't eaten last night so I needed breakfast.

He told me about the payoff. He had finally reached an agreement with the gravel-voiced boss of the gang. He had negotiated very well, it was a small fraction of the original asking price. I must get him to do Agripac purchasing!

A security man from Agripac had taken a suitcase with cash to an address given and left it there at 4pm yesterday.

So they had gotten payment 6 hours before I was released. It occurred to me that they might have reneged and kept me. But I guess it's a business, and there is some honour among thieves. Then again they were hoping for the rest which I had 'promised' them.

There was another very odd demand that they had made before releasing me. They wanted me to hold a press conference on TV on which I would make a statement that I had been well treated and that the nine men arrested should be released. This seemed very bizarre. Either way I was not going to do it. How could I have answered questions about being kidnapped after stating that we were all good friends?

I did my debrief as well as I could. But I couldn't pinpoint where I had been kept. Anyway by now it had probably reverted to a farm workers' barracks. I had not seen any of their faces, so I couldn't match up with photos that I was shown.

I learned how the nine members of the gang had been caught. One of them had foolishly taken my phone when they drove back to Guayaquil. There is a GPS tracker on it. The police were able to trace it to a house in the suburbs of Guayaquil. They raided the house and captured the nine, plus a quantity of arms and explosives and the saddles stolen from the ranch. That was what had so upset my gravel-voiced persecutor.

Nick told me that all our families in Ecuador now need security protection.

Josef Shalev, the Israeli owner of the security company Provica, that Agripac uses, said that he would need time to put it in place. He suggested we all leave the country until he had it set up.

Nick booked tickets for us all, including Diana and her family in Los Angeles. We would all go to England and stay at Tupgill and Ferngill, our houses in Coverdale, North Yorkshire, for Christmas and the New Year. Our tickets were booked on KLM for tomorrow, Thursday 21st December.

I wanted to go to see Kate, but I was told that it was dangerous. Though why the Tigerones would want to take me again just after releasing me was not clear. Perhaps another gang? So I was confined to the house today by my family.

Thursday morning I got up before the family at 5am. There was a security man stationed outside our house. I asked him to get a car and driver from the company. My car had been impounded by the police, anyway it was badly damaged.

The car arrived at 5.30am and I snuck out of the house before the family stopped me.

First I wanted to see Kate. We hadn't even talked since we parted on Saturday. I had no phone. Anyway I had no idea of the number of her Spanish phone, the only one she had left.

We drove to the apartment block. I took the lift up to the 15th floor where we have our penthouse.

I had my own key and opened the door. Even though it was just 6am she was awake. She was with her mother in the sitting room. I know Margarita well. She has three children including Kate. As to her age, well shall I say, she is a lot younger than I am.

Once more we all hugged and cried. We interrupted each other to tell our stories. There was a knock on the door and

Janina came in. We had another round of hugging. She is a very close friend of ours. She is an attractive blonde lady. She is in her forties and has two daughters of sixteen and seven years old. I had met her through Kate ten years ago when she worked in a travel agency. Now she owns her own travel company.

We sat down and I told them that I was leaving this afternoon for the UK.

Kate and her mother already have their tickets to return to Ibague tomorrow.

When would we see each other again?

Kate and I had a plan for the biggest holiday of our lives in January. But more of that later.

I couldn't stay too long as I had to go to the office, collect my laptop, passport and whatever else I needed to work from outside the country. For however long was necessary.

I have to be at the airport by 4pm.

I got to the office in the security car by 10am. The guards waved cheerfully to me and came to shake my hand.

I got out of the car, walked across the patio and into the office block. The receptionist sitting there gave a scream then ran and hugged me. Then another girl and another, until I was surrounded by the office staff. The men stood back until the tide subsided and then came to shake my hand. It was an emotional moment, I couldn't help crying.

Eventually I pleaded that I had to rush and went up the lift to my fifth-floor office.

Jorge, who helps me in the office, disconnected the laptop from the large desk screen.

I rummaged through my desk looking for my diary, passport, credit cards, Euros, Sterling and everything that comprises my travelling desk. We packed them into a large briefcase.

I had no idea when I could return to Ecuador.

We got to the airport in good time for the KLM flight to Amsterdam. We checked in Ceci, Diana, Alex, two of her children and myself. Alex's husband Javi would come on Saturday with their other child. There was no space for all of us on this flight.

There was a moment of panic when the lady at the check - in desk asked Alex for the legal paper which she needs to travel with her children, without her husband.

This is the law here, to prevent one parent taking a child out of the country without informing the spouse.

Alex called Javi at the office. He in turn talked to Alfredo Jr, our legal counsel, who called a notary public. If Javi can get the paper legalised within an hour, Alex and the kids can travel. He just made it. Sighs of relief. Also Alex has to sign for Javi to take their remaining son.

Nick and his family had left yesterday for Madrid on the Iberia flight.

Diana's husband Steve and their three boys will fly from Los Angeles to Amsterdam on Saturday and then to the UK. It was quite an operation to move all 17 of the Armstrong family.

Once we had passed immigration and were on the platform of the airport, first one, then another stranger, came to shake my hand and say they were so glad that I had been released from the kidnap. It had made the national newspapers. There had been many kidnappings this year, but mine made news as a well-known former consul.

We boarded the flight and the purser came to say the same thing. He kindly asked if there was anything he could do for me. I said I would be very grateful for a glass of champagne, which of course they give you anyway in business class.

The flight was uneventful and we arrived at Schiphol the next day at 1pm local time.

We made our way to the shopping area in the airport. We had plenty of time to wait as our onward flight to Teesside (Durham) airport was at 5pm.

The ladies did some shopping. I saw a shop selling Omega watches. I had lost my Cartier watch in the kidnap and decided to replace it, hoping my insurance would cover it.

Once done, we went to the Business Class lounge and had drinks until it was time to go to the gate.

It's only a one-hour flight to Teesside. The airport is very small but much more convenient than the larger one at Newcastle, and only forty minutes from home.

Leo came to meet us, and as we needed two cars our friends David and Monica came with their car too.

After hugging each other we got into the cars and drove home.

We will all stay in Tupgill. It's got six bedrooms so no problem there.

Ferngill is Nick's house. He, Almu (Almudena) and their three children will spend Christmas and the New Year in Madrid. Then Nick and his son Willie will come to see us on the second of January.

It was great to be back in Tupgill. We dumped the bags in our respective rooms and met in the large kitchen where we opened a bottle of wine. Leo had filled the fridge with food, so Ceci and the girls prepared supper for us all plus Leo, David and Monica.

Leo had bought a pork pie for me, which I ate with Colman's mustard. That was all I wanted. The taste of Yorkshire.

We went to bed about midnight. But I couldn't sleep.

I got up at 1.30am to check all ten outside doors were locked. I had visions of the Tiguerones (UK chapter) stalking me here.

I went to my study in the house and, carefully drawing the curtains shut, set out my laptop. But annoyingly I had forgotten to get the systems lads in Agripac to program it for use overseas. I sent them a message so they could program it remotely by Team Viewer. But there is a five-hour time difference to Ecuador, so it would be afternoon before they did it.

I settled for reading my book The Dumas Club, by Arturo Perez Reverte.

But by 4am I was falling asleep. I went back to bed and slept until 9am.

I had the Times delivered to the house. So on getting up on Saturday morning (the 23rd December) I collected it from the front door porch. I flipped through it and there it was on page 37.

"Police Focus on Drug Gangs after Kidnap of British man, 78".

I had heard from Leo that there had been several articles in the press. Reporters had tried to get interviews from both my sisters Jane and Catherine, who live on the estate, as well as from Leo.

I sat down and read it.

On the whole it was fair. It seems that the reporter had gone through a copy of my book Behind the Forbidden Corner, which I had published in the year 2000, to get background on my life, the family and the Forbidden Corner.

He pieced together the incident using Fredy's video of the scene of the crime. Though it was ascribed to a woman, Fredy was hysterical and his voice raised in tone. He had walked from room to room filming the ransacked house and the blood on the sheets that was erroneously thought to be ours. It was Omar's blood. He had been hit on the head.

The report mentioned that I had been having an affair with Kate for some months prior to the kidnapping (in fact it has been ten years), that the local police had originally thought she might have been involved, but they later declared her to be a victim.

He said that she had documented our travels around the World on Instagram. These included holidays to Japan, India, Egypt, Dubai, Kenya, Tanzania, Rwanda, Jamaica and on Queen Mary II.

For good measure he included a photo of us in front of the famous Hollywood sign.

I had just finished reading it when a lady knocked on the front door. I answered it and she handed me her card. She was a freelance reporter from one of the tabloid press.

She asked me if I would allow her an interview, so that I could give my point of view. But I said no. There was nothing that I could say that would reflect to my advantage. I certainly didn't want the gossip to go on, with all the pain it had caused to my family.

Some of the newspapers had really gone to town on the subject of an ageing ex-consul with a young girlfriend. The Telegraph's headline was "The expat the cartel and the kidnap plot. The bizarre story of how a British Consul ended up in the hands of Ecuadorian gangsters". Using lots of her instagram photos, they showed us in many settings, including one of us both in evening clothes on board the Queen Mary II last July, of Kate wearing a bikini and me bathing trunks in Dubai, and at a fancy dress party in Montego Bay (I was wearing a naval uniform, and won the competition). There were photos too from a yacht we hired in Montego Bay for her birthday last October. We had taken ten friends with us. There was her mother, sister, brother, Fredy, Orlando, Omar, Janina, Paola, Nichol and Andrea.

There was also a photo of her having been freed from the explosive waistcoat and of myself standing between two policemen wearing a police cap, the night that I was released.

I was described as a millionaire playboy. The yacht party was described as an orgy!

I politely declined to give them more ammunition with which to persecute me.

I had been with Kate for more than ten years. We had met at a casting to choose a model for the Agripac calendar in August 2013.

We became a couple some months later and have enjoyed over 40 holidays together in exotic places around the World. They totalled some 500 days, almost 17 months.

But I had always returned home to Ceci. It had been very awkward both the leaving and returning. But by mutual consent we kept our marriage alive. Neither was it easy with Kate. She complained when I left her to return home for dinner with Ceci, or when I couldn't stay the night because Ceci had returned unexpectedly from her beach house.

But now came the day of reckoning. My affair might be overlooked when it was an unspoken secret. Her friends avoided the subject. For my part I had abandoned most of my friends when I began with Kate. Time with them was time I preferred to spend with her.

But now the newspaper reports made it impossible to overlook.

The emotion of my return to the family was now cooling. At Tupgill I sensed foreboding that we had to talk about it as a family. My three children were the first to broach the subject. Diana and Alex directly, and Nick by phone and Whatsapp from Madrid. There were statements like 'You have to choose'. 'It's not fair to Mum'.'You have let the family down', 'You have damaged our family name'.

They insisted Kate was involved in the kidnap, even though the police had discarded the idea.

Why had she wanted to return to captivity, once she had been released?

Why had she been reluctant to remove the explosive belt?

I said it was because she loved me and wanted to be with me and protect me. Without the explosive belt, she could not return to my place of captivity.

I told them that she had insisted on being taken too when I was kidnapped from Rodeo. They were going to leave her.

The family thought it was all very suspicious.

I argued that I had given her an apartment, clothes, cash and jewellery. What on earth would she gain from sharing whatever ransom money was paid?

They didn't want to hear.

Kate had to be the bad guy in the story.

Ceci meanwhile had a dreadful cold and was not feeling at all well. She reproached me silently.

So Christmas came. We had a truce (much as happened in the trenches on the first Christmas of the First World War). Christmas is the time for children. We had six in the house. They played the piano, and sang carols by the large Christmas tree standing at the foot of the stairs, we dressed in Santa hats, we hung up stockings and went to bed in the expectation that Santa would come down the only chimney that really was a chimney, in the sitting room. The house had underfloor heating and we never lit the fire, but we had asked the architect to make it, just in case.

In Ecuador Christmas is celebrated with a dinner on the 24th. But we reverted to the English tradition of a lunch on the 25th.

The children are the first up on Christmas Day, well apart from myself. I had got up at 5am so that I could call Kate from my study. It was midnight in Ibague and she was there with her family. We chatted for a while but there was a lot of background noise, so we wished each other a Happy Christmas and rang off.

When I was a child, Christmas involved a church service. We were frogmarched to church that morning by mother and father. The presents under the tree could not be touched until we returned. The vicar seemed to drone on for ages, while we fidgeted.

But today our local parish church of Coverham is a redundant one. It is preserved and opened for a few services a year. The lady vicar has five parishes, but the main church is the ancient Middleham one.

The world has moved on and we are in a post-religious age. Ceci still attends Catholic church, but the rest of the family limit attendance to baptisms, marriages and funerals. What my mother used to call Hatch, Match and Scratch.

Though we had abandoned the church we didn't abandon the churchyard. It is a very peaceful place. At one side of it my family is buried. Starting with my paternal grandparents, Eleanor (Nellie) in 1945 and Bob in 1956, then my mother Margaret (Tiggy) in 1974, father Gerald in 1980 and aunt Doris (Do) in 1992.

Peter Conway, my sister Jane's son, is buried there too in 2018. Peter lived in South Africa all his life, until the last year when he was in England. After graduating from university he joined the army and was involved in the war between South Africa and Angola. Later he worked in military intelligence and rose to the rank of colonel. But there was another side to his life too. He was a Hell's Angel. He drank a great deal and took drugs. He died aged fifty.

In the last year of his life I encouraged him to write his memoirs. They are called 'Thy will be done', published in 2018 by Lionel Ross's i2i Publishers in Manchester.

It's a fascinating story about a bad boy. But it gives a vivid description of what went on behind the scenes both with the Apartheid and then ANC governments of South Africa. There were also the international ramifications of US and European military involvement in African countries.

Peter had been involved in the 2004 plot to overthrow the president of Equatorial Guinea.

Ex-SAS soldier Simon Mann led a group of mercenaries. The plot was discovered and the mercenaries arrested. Many important figures were named, including Mark Thatcher, as having financed the attempted coup, which appears to be an attempt to control its oil production.

I walked to the graveyard with both my sisters Jane and Catherine on Christmas Eve to place wreaths of holly on the graves.

The days between Christmas and the New Year I spent with my laptop checking the company sales and approving credits, as we approached the end of the year.

I went walking on Middleham Moor with my sisters, or sometimes just alone. Some days we went for pub meals together, on others the family went shopping in Northallerton or Harrogate, and I prepared a sandwich in the kitchen. In the evenings I watched opera DVDs in my study by myself.

I guess we were no longer comfortable together.

New Year's Eve came. We went to a New Year party at the Bell Barn, the large banqueting hall of the Saddle Room restaurant, part of the Forbidden Corner.

We took the grandchildren there at nine pm and toasted the Old Year in champagne. Dinner was served about ten pm. But I couldn't get into the spirit of it. Before midnight I pleaded that I was tired and went back to the house, over the protests of Ceci, my children and the grandchildren too.

"You can't go yet, wait for the New Year."

But my heart was in another country. I went to my study and called Kate.

She was in Cartagena with her family, where there were still five hours to go until midnight. She was walking on the beach with her sister Luisa and her mother.

After a while my son-in-law, Javi, came to ask me to return to the party for the New Year. Later my other son-in-law Steve came to say the same. But I was determined to be talking to Kate when the moment came in England, if not in Cartagena.

It seems now very callous of me to do that. But at that moment it was what I wanted to do.

It got to midnight UK time. We wished each other a Happy New Year and rang off.

2024 has arrived. What will it bring?

Will I still be with Ceci and my family at the end of the year? Or will Kate and I be living together as man and wife?

Will it be a good year for the family and for our businesses?

Indeed will I be alive at the end of the year? I will be seventy nine then. Well into the ballpark where people say a final goodbye.

In my family both Bob and Do made it to ninety-five years old. I hope I will be the third.

Nick arrived from Spain on 2nd January with his thirteen -year old son, Willie.

He first talked to his sisters and then we had a family meeting, though without Ceci, who was still suffering from a bad cold.

We didn't progress at all. They stuck to their position that I had to choose between Mum and Kate. I didn't want to make a decision, before I really had to.

But it couldn’t be put off much longer.

I had told Ceci that I was going on holiday with Kate. We will meet in Amsterdam on Saturday 6th January. She furiously replied that it was irresponsible of me to leave the family for my girlfriend so soon after the kidnap. She cried and pleaded with me to stay.

I felt very ashamed of myself.

But I couldn't do as she asked. When Kate and I had been separated on the first day of the kidnap I had promised her that if we survived we would go to White Desert together.

Now I must fulfil my promise.

We had planned the holiday almost a year ago. It was the most expensive holiday that we had ever done. It was put together by our good friend Chinmay of Explorations company. We will fly from Amsterdam on 7th January to Cape Town. Then after three days there we will take a charter flight along with eight other guests to Wolf's Fang airstrip in Antarctica. We will stay in a modern artificial igloo for a week and during that time, weather permitting, we will fly to the South Pole.

So the break was made. I told Ceci that I loved her and always will. I was very sorry to leave her, but if I must choose, then I would go and live with Kate. We both cried and hugged each other. We are going to be fifty years married in October. We have three wonderful children, nine grandchildren and we had built both Agripac and the Forbidden Corner together. How cruel fate can be?

You don't plan to fall in love. It just happens. I loved Ceci, but I was in love with Kate.

Just as in Verdi's opera, it is La Forza del Destino.

We met at Starbucks in Schiphol, as we always did. My flight from Teesside got in an hour before hers from Guayaquil (she had returned from Cartagena the day before).

It has become a tradition. Schiphol is enormous and crowded, where to meet?

"See you at Starbucks, My Love".

I was nursing a cup of milky coffee when she came up behind me and put her hands over my eyes. We hugged and kissed.

Dragging our suitcases, we left the airport and took a taxi.

"Where to sir ?"

"The Hotel L'Europe please".

We must have stayed there twenty five times. Amsterdam was our normal gateway to Europe. We would stay one or two nights and then fly to Madrid or wherever.

We arrived at the hotel in twenty minutes. We were immediately recognised by the uniformed doorman and porters, who greeted us like old friends, which indeed we were.

The man on reception beamed at us and sent us a glass of champagne while I filled in the forms.

"How long will you stay with us this time, Sir?"

"Sadly just one night, tomorrow we are going to Cape Town, but we are booked for two more nights when we return on the 20th January".

We had booked a junior suite, as always. It gave a bit more space to spread out our suitcases, well my one and Kate's three! It was one that overlooked the River Amstel and the opera house beyond.

"May I book you in for dinner tonight in La Marie Restaurant?"

"Yes, thank you. That would be lovely. Say 7pm"

Of course being treated as such valued customers demanded good tips. But that is fair.

We went to the room and changed. Kate had been flying eleven hours from Guayaquil, so insisted on a shower.

Then, when she was bathed, groomed and dressed elegantly in a long black dress, and myself in a blue suit and tie, we went down to the lobby at 6pm and found an empty table. A waiter immediately came to us.

"A bottle of Krug and a plate of oysters sir?"

I looked at Kate and she smiled. They know us well here.

By 7pm both the oysters and champagne were finished, and we were shown to the table in La Marie.

There was a Colombian waitress we knew. She came to say hello.

Kate was still a vegetarian at this time, she chose a Waldorf salad. I went for king crab as a starter and then breast of wild pigeon.

We had an excellent bottle of Puligny Montrachet.

The holiday has begun.

The KLM flight to Capetown was at 10:30 am on Sunday 7th January, so we left the hotel at 7.30am for Schiphol.

Just like the flight to Guayaquil it takes 12 hours. Normally I read a book on flights and Kate watches movies. But having finished my book I watched, for the second time, a film called Focus with Will Smith and beautiful Margot Robbins (alias Barbie). A tale of professional thieves, but it had a happy ending.

We got to Cape Town at midnight, with the one hour time difference from Europe. We were met at the door of the plane by a lady with a sign saying White Desert Tours, and our names. She escorted us through the diplomatic lane at immigration, we collected our luggage.

Then she delivered us to our driver with a smart limousine. Half an hour's drive brought us to the wonderful Ellerman House Hotel.

We were very tired by this time and were grateful that the check in had already been done for us by the tourist agency. We were shown straight to our room. It was a suite, with bedroom, bathroom a large sitting room and a balcony overlooking the sea. We could hear the sound of the waves on the shore.

We changed into pyjamas, got into bed and promptly fell asleep.

Monday 8th January

We were awake and dressed by 9am and went for breakfast.

I had lived in Swaziland for a year, doing International Voluntary Service in 1966, when I was twenty one. The breakfast menu had an option of boerewors, the tasty South African sausage.

I remembered it fondly and had to try it again. It was delicious.

After breakfast we explored the hotel. It really is magnificent, terraced down a cliff front with the rooms overlooking the sea. There were several bars and restaurants which we would try during our stay.

White Desert had arranged that we have a car and driver at our disposal while in Cape Town. We asked him to come to the hotel after breakfast.

I had last visited Cape Town, and then only for a couple of days, in 1967. So my memories of it were pretty vague. I wanted to see it again and to show it off to Kate.

We asked the driver to take us to the Cape of Good Hope, and once there we got him to take our photos with the sign saying that it was the most southerly point of the African continent.

Both my sisters had lived in South Africa. Jane lived and worked in Johannesburg for forty years, and Catherine occasionally in Fish Hoek near Cape Town. We decided to go there and send her photos. It's not a very big town today, but she said that it had grown a lot since she was last there.

Then we went on to Simonds Town. There is a beach where you can see penguins. Though they are very small ones.

Kate was excited, they were the first penguins she had seen in the wild. We watched them surfing the waves to land belly first on the shore and then stand on their feet and waddle inland.

We are going to see the much bigger Emperor penguins in Antarctica.

We drove back to the hotel via Table Mountain. As so often happens the cable car to the top was not working because of strong winds. But still the view of the city, with the docks and sea beyond was fabulous.

We then headed back to the hotel through the centre of the city. We were impressed how majestic and clean it is. We know two African cities, Cairo and Nairobi, which are not at all attractive. So Cape Town stands out.

My father, Gerald, had once made a cruise on a P and O Lines ship to South Africa in the nineteen thirties. He had stayed in the Mount Nelson Hotel. I asked the driver if it still existed. Oh yes, he said. It's l considered the best hotel in town, if a little dated.

Rich people go there for afternoon tea.

We drove past the very elegant portico entrance, but didn’t go inside.

We got back to the hotel at 6pm and went to the bar on the terrace. After drinking two sundowners, we went to the restaurant for a wonderful fish dinner with white Stellenbosch wine.

The next day we were asked by White Desert to come to their boutique in the center of the city to collect our Antarctic clothing. We drove there at 11am.

We had been in touch with them for several months over clothing lists. We had bought most items online. But there was a lot we had to ask them, as well as trying on ours for size.

We found that our fellow travellers were already there. There were only ten of us. There was a Panamanian man in his seventies and his forty-year-old son, both called Jaime. They immediately started talking to us in Spanish.

There was a Russian couple in their thirties, an elderly American with a middle-aged Chinese woman (we never worked out their relationship), and a young American couple on their honeymoon.

We were served sparkling wine to encourage us to buy. And indeed we did buy far more than we needed. There were items of clothing which had battery-powered heaters in them.

I asked if we would need them. If you feel the cold it would be wise to take them. So we did.

I had already ordered a heavy jacket, but we were shown the top-of-the range Mammut one, at only a thousand dollars, so I took that too.

Basically it's all about layers of clothing. You wear three pairs of socks, three pants, three tops, and three gloves. Then there was a beanie hat, and two pairs of boots one heavier than the other (to wear separately not together).

Once dressed in our kit, we went two by two into the ice box. This had glass walls and was kept at minus 10 degrees. Of course we clowned about to amuse the others. But the clothing worked perfectly, we didn't feel cold.

We had been instructed to bring two soft suitcases each. One for the hold luggage, one for the cabin.

Now they packed them for us. We will fly to Wolf's Fang, five hours by jet. One hour before arrival we will change into our Arctic kit to prepare for leaving the plane. The temperature will be minus ten degrees.

To avoid changing in the tiny bathrooms we were told to wear our thermal underwear beneath our civvies on the plane. Then we can do the change in the cabin.

They took our hold luggage from us. They will put it on the plane. We left with our hand luggage.

Of course we all wanted to know when we were going. In the programme it was on the 10th January. But now we were told that because of weather conditions, we would leave tonight, the 9th.

We returned to the hotel and sorted out what else we needed to pack into the hand luggage. Then we left our large suitcases in the hotel, to be stored until our return in a week's time.

At 4pm we took our car to the airport. As it was a charter flight we were quickly through the formalities, though as we were leaving South Africa, our passports were stamped.

We were taken by bus to the plane. I had imagined that it would be an executive jet, but it was a normal-sized commercial plane. It was explained to us that though we were a group of only ten people there were a lot of support staff for the mission who came and went.

The weekly plane was the only transport for them, and to carry food, fuel and supplies.

We were surprised to see that the business class section had seats very widely spaced apart. I suppose it was so that we could put on our heavy clothes in comfort.

We took off at 6pm.

Food and drink were liberally served during the flight. An hour before landing we all took down our carry-on bags and began the process of dressing for Antarctica, laughing as we began to look like the Michelin man.

We landed at Wolf's Fang airstrip at 11pm (though the local time was 9pm. Antarctica works on GMT).

It was daylight, it never goes dark in January.

The tourist industry for the Antarctic only works for two months of the year, December and January. That is when the temperature is the highest and daylight twenty four hours.

There was great excitement on the plane as we waited to step on to Antarctica. We had looked out of the plane window when we began to encounter icebergs in the sea. Now everything was white.

Just as the witch had predicted.

We descended one by one with guides helping us step on the snow, so that we didn't start the tour on our backsides.

There was a snowmobile waiting to take us to Echo Camp, about fifteen minutes away. We had asked about the camp and been told that we would be sleeping in igloos. But they quickly added that they were modern synthetic igloos, heated and well insulated. They include a half bathroom, but no shower. For that we would have to go to the central, much larger, igloo where we would have our meals and drinks.

There were just six double bed igloos, the two Jaimes had one each. We were allotted ours and carried our kit inside. But we were much too excited to go to sleep. We dumped our stuff and headed towards the social area.

There we found our fellow travelers in the bar. We peeled off the outer layer of clothing in the hall and joined them.

Everyone was animated. We had finally got to Antarctica. Most of us had booked the tour last January. We had had a long time to look forward to it. The process had begun with the down payment. Then we were asked to do a medical to see if we were fit enough to stand it, where I discovered that I was the oldest of the group.

There was another stage payment, then the ordering of clothes, the final payment was made in October and lastly, before leaving home, there was a zoom conference with White Desert to answer questions.

Now we are finally here.

We talked with the others, comparing notes.

We were surprised when the Russian man asked us if we were the people who had been kidnapped. We said yes, and then of course had to recount a brief version of it for them all.

We had been asked the same in Freddy's Bar of the L'Europe Hotel.

We were getting used to fame!

We went into the dining room. The food was excellent and the staff very attentive. Is there anything I can get for you? Yes, in my case Tabasco sauce.

Kate had told our friends in Guayaquil that when she got to Antarctica she would dance in the snow in a bikini. We all thought she was crazy. At minus ten degrees!

We walked back to our igloo and I was preparing to go to bed when I saw that she had taken off her clothes and put on her tiny black bikini.

"You are not going out in that?"

"Yes I am. I told you I would do it and I will. We will never come back to the Antarctic again."

She asked me to film it.

Then she opened the door and walked onto the snow.

Admittedly we had had a lot to drink. So I stood outside the door and filmed her as she ran, pirouetted, and danced in the snow, laughing all the while. After five minutes she returned to me. I asked her to check that I had got it on film. She took my phone and said yes I had it.

Then as we looked up we saw Jaime, the younger Panamanian, watching us from outside his igloo. We waved to him and went inside.

She had not quite escaped unscathed. Her feet were burned with the ice. But it wasn't too serious.

We finally got to bed and to sleep.

The igloos, though warm, were very cramped. We have a lot of Antarctic clothing and there was nowhere to hang it, so it stayed in the cases on the floor.

We got up for our first White Desert breakfast at 8am. We put on what we considered the least we needed to cross the fifty yards of snow to the restaurant. In fact, there was no wind, it wasn't that cold.

We greeted our new friends.

The service was excellent and a full breakfast was served.

The staff was young and friendly. Most of them were there for the fun of it, rather than as a job. The opportunity to see Antarctica for free.

After breakfast they announced that today we would go to see the penguins. That surprised us, we thought we would have a day or two to settle in before we went.

We had to return to our igloos and get appropriately dressed for a much colder area.

The plane would be leaving within an hour.

That was when we found the difficulty of dressing in a limited area, from cases strewn across the floor with layers of clothing we had never previously put on, and finding which garments were his or hers, as they all looked the same. Add to that we had to put together all the battery-operated heaters. Each item of clothing had a different one!

So the hour passed and there was a knock on the door. All the others had got their act together and were waiting in the snowmobile to go to the airstrip.

We were still battling with layer two.

We were urged to hurry up. There's only a small window of opportunity with the weather, and the pilot was eager to get going.

We decided not to use the electrically heated stuff. We managed all the rest plus the heavy boots and joined the others.

When we got to Wolf's Fang we found not our Boeing jet of yesterday but an ancient DC3, with skis. It is painted red, white and blue. I guess it will be easy to locate if it crashes in the snow. We were assured that the plane was constantly updated, but it didn't look it. We clambered aboard. The seats are very different from yesterday's comfortable ones. They were close together and very narrow. The fuselage is low, so I can't stand upright. Added to that was our bulky clothing. We began to strip off our outer layers and stow them in the overhead racks. But of course there is not enough space. There was extra storage of nets at the back. But as everyone's gets thrown in, recognising your own is a problem.

The toilet is at the back of the plane. We were told that it was not heated. And you certainly noticed. It was freezing, especially when you had your trousers down. We didn't linger.

It definitely isn't a comfortable plane.

There was a three-hour flight to where the penguins were, with a stop on the way to refuel.

They served us snacks including biltong, which is like jerky, dried meat which you chew. But the taste is good.

Once we landed on a snow-covered airstrip we found ourselves on a large flat area near to the sea. We left the plane and once again got into a snowmobile to reach where the penguins were.

We had been told that only half of them were still here. They come to breed and as soon as the young are feathered they return to their natural habitat, the sea.

But there were still many thousands of them. They were spread out over a large area. We were instructed not to get too close to them. They have their young with them and will get stressed.

They are the largest of all penguins and stand about four feet high. They either walk upright or lie on their bellies and paddle along with their flippers. It was wonderful to see them.

It was much colder here, minus twenty degrees, with a wind blowing from the sea. We pulled up our collars and wrapped scarves around our faces.

We appreciated the three layers of clothing and began to miss the battery-heated stuff.

We took lots of photos and videos, but sadly there was no chance of a selfie with them.

We stayed about two hours and then returned to the snowmobile to the plane.

On getting on the plane I reached into my pocket for my mobile phone. It wasn't there.

I searched all the pockets of the three jackets I had on, but nothing.

Then I discovered why. The outer jacket had a false pocket. You could reach through to the pocket of the jacket below it. So I must have put the phone in that and it went straight through and fell into the snow. We had no idea where it could have happened. So there was no point in trying to look for it.

Bleakly, I told the guides about it. They in turn told the snowmobile driver, who promised to keep an eye out for it when he went with another group.

But it seemed a remote possibility of finding it. If it snowed in the night then no chance. I had most of our penguin photos on it, and more importantly to me, the video of Kate dancing in the snow.

I told her she would have to do it again. But she wasn't keen. Her feet were still hurting from the snowburn.

So we returned to base.

We met in the bar for drinks before dinner. It was announced that we are going to the South Pole tomorrow. Once again there were groans at this. We had come to see the penguins and the pole. But we were getting all the best bits up front. There would be four days in camp afterwards.

Once again it was weather related. Either go tomorrow or risk not going at all.

So we go tomorrow.

It wasn't an early morning start. We had lunch and then packed a bag for the one night out at Dixey's Camp. We left on the DC3 at 4pm.

Once again it was an uncomfortable flight but this time with five hours flying time to Dixey's Camp, the refuelling stop.

We duly landed there and remained in the plane while it refuelled. The captain and copilot got out and left the door open. It was freezing. We began to retrieve our heavy coats from the rack.

We saw that they were standing on one wing and appeared to be struggling to fix something. That really gave us confidence. A broken plane five hours from base!

The refuelling was taking a long time. The captain came back on board.

We expected to get under way. But we didn't.

He was unable to start the motors.

He announced that there was a technical problem. We will sleep the night here, on the way to the Pole, rather than on the way back, as was planned.

This was to let the pilots rest and not go over their statutory flying hours.

By this time it was 11pm. But of course it is still daylight.

We trooped out of the plane and walked towards the small wooden hut at the side of the strip. There were tents either side of it. Tents? Yes ordinary canvas tents. The temperature here was about minus thirty degrees because we were at 2,000 mts altitude and there was a strong wind blowing.

We took our photos by a signpost which read:

'Dixie's Camp, 83.3 degrees South, 20 degrees East. The Most Remote Camp on Earth…probably.'

The signs pointed to the International Space Station, 400 km. To the South Pole 737km, to Whichaway 1458 km and to Wolf's Fang 1317 km.

We got to the hut, which was our restaurant, and were very pleased to find a wood-burning stove in it. Two men handed out glasses of whisky as we huddled around the stove. That cheered us up. Jaime the younger had the bright idea of sitting actually on the stove. Until we smelled burning plastic!

A hot stew was served to warm the inner man (or woman).

Finally at 1am they announced that we should get some sleep as we had to be up at 5am tomorrow to continue to the Pole, if of course the plane was working. There were two latrine huts. We queued to use them. There was no facility in the tents. There was no heating in these huts either!

They handed out sleeping bags, which each couple took to their tent. There were two wooden beds in the tent. We were shown how to lay out the sleeping bags, which were very special Arctic ones, and told to take off only the outer layer of clothing. We were given blindfolds for our eyes, as the tents let in the light. The igloos at Echo have blackouts on the windows.

We did as instructed and surprisingly were snugly warm.

I had been dreading this night. When I had read the brochure months before, I realized that there was going to be a problem. I normally have to get up a couple of times in the night to go to the loo. There were five hours before we left the tent for breakfast and the adjoining toilet, which was a hundred meters away from the tent. It had even been suggested that I could use a bottle to pee into. But we hadn't got around to getting a suitable one.

So what would I do? I slept for a while and woke up when I heard Kate move. I opened my eyes and saw her go to the flap of the tent, where she proceeded to pee into the snow. Well of course, that was the solution. I did the same.

Friday 12th January

South Pole day.

We were woken up at 5am. We quickly replaced our outer clothing and tramped through the snow to the hut. There we had a hot breakfast and heard the good news that the plane was now functioning.

We clambered back into the plane for the last two hours to the Pole.

The excitement built up as we approached it. We had our heaviest gear on. It would be below minus thirty degrees as we will be at 3,000 mt elevation, but because it is the Pole it feels like 4,000 meters. In fact, when we got out of the plane, as there was no wind, it felt warmer than Dixie's camp last night.

So what do you see at the South Pole? There is a very large brown building, the Edmundson/Scott Centre for scientific research. It's owned by the USA, but open to all scientists. We were told that up to one hundred and thirty people lived and worked there. But for the two hours we were there we saw no one. What we did see were piles of equipment under wraps out in the open behind the Centre. It was explained that supply planes could only get here in the brief Summer months so they have to stockpile food and equipment for the other ten months.

We have come as tourists, and we want to see the Pole itself.

We saw the flags of the Antarctic Treaty countries in a circle. We were led to them by the guide and took photos of each other. We asked one of the others to take photos of Kate and I holding the Union Jack (Colombia isn't a signatory).

But confusingly, this is no longer the South Pole. It used to be the site when the flags were put there, but the geographical

Pole moves a little each year. It is now some fifty yards away, marked by a single sign. We went to it and walked around it. In doing so we walked around the World.

Of course, we all wanted to get our passports stamped with the South Pole logo. There was an office to do this. We trooped over to it. But it's disappointing, just an empty hut. There is no official to stamp your passport. Each of us took the stamp and did it ourselves.

But at least we have it.

It reads 'South Pole Station. United States Antarctic Program. Jan 12 2024'.

There is a second, larger, stamp. It's very worn and difficult to make out the words, but it has a plane with skis. South Pole, elevation 9,300 feet. And a map of Antarctica.

And that's it. There is no T-shirt, no gift shop, no cafe and no decent lavatory.

The South Pole marketing department has a lot of work to do.

Tourist groups are only allowed to remain at the Pole for two hours. When our time was up we boarded the plane and, with a short stop in Dixie's camp, we made it back to Echo camp.

We had done it. That night we all drank more than we should have. This led to my falling on the ice while walking back to our igloo and hurting my arm.

It is a self-inflicted wound, as Kate told me!

There is only a wash basin in the igloo and two loos. Two? Yes two. The rule is that one is for liquid only, the other for solids. This is to do with non-contamination of the Antarctic. The solids are shrink-wrapped in aluminum foil and carted back to Cape Town for burial.

Try as I might, it's very difficult to achieve this separation of residues!

We have now gone several days without a shower. We decided to try the ones in the restaurant block.

There were just two of them, luckily neither was occupied. I relished my nice warm shower and stood for some time under it, though there was a sign saying that water should be used sparingly, as it comes from melted ice.

When we emerged I asked Kate how hers was. She said it was wonderful. The best cold shower she had ever had. OMG, an Antarctic shower!

The Antarctic holiday is seven days. We arrived on the 9th and will leave on the 16th. So we still have four days to fill. The guides at Echo Camp sorted us into the fittest and those not up to much. Kate was in the first group. I was in the second.

But on the first day we were both together on a walk from the camp to see the incredible snow drifts. One thinks of the Antarctic as all snow. But close to the camp, at this low elevation, there are mountains of rock too, but no vegetation. We put chains on our boots for stability and had sticks to support us. Then we walked with Lucas, the guide, for about two kilometres. Wind is a constant factor in the Antarctic and blows the loose top snow into fantastic shapes around the rocks. Today was bright and sunny, and not at all cold. We began to discard our heavy jackets and tie them around our waists, as we warmed up with the exercise.

The next day was slightly more difficult.

We had to wear helmets and were harnessed together with a rope, as we descended into a crevice in the snow. It was a steep and slippery descent but on reaching the bottom the colours of the ice were amazing.

This was near to Wolf's Fang airstrip.

We had been deprived of WIFI since we arrived five days ago. So when we were offered a chance to go to the visitors' hut where there is a connection we were all keen.

That day was very cold and it was bliss to get inside the heated hut. We separated and took chairs around the room to reconnect with the World.

Correction, we had all been deprived of a connection except the Russian, Dimitry, who had a satellite phone. That was how he had looked us up on Google and found out about the kidnap. We wondered if he had checked out all our fellow passengers. We wondered indeed who he really worked for!

We had all told our backgrounds during the sessions in the bar. He said that he owned a chocolate factory in St Petersburg. It's as good a story as any other.

Finally when the snowmobile was about to go back to Echo camp we were taken to the ice bar nearby.

It was hollowed out of solid ice. We went down slippery stairs and there was a bar serving vodka. There were ice seats, ice tables and an ice bar. It was fun for a while, but even with our heavy gear on it was freezing.

Then we went back to the camp bar for our now very friendly drinks, and then to dinner and bed.

The next day, Monday, we slept in, as we had been warned that the weather would be too bad to do any activity in the morning. We only got up for lunch at 1pm.

The guides announced that today would be more adventurous. There would be a long hike up a mountain which involved abseiling down again. The participants wore crampons and helmets and were roped together. Kate went. I opted out.

I spent the day putting my diary up to date and reading a novel, partly in the bar, and partly in the igloo. It is nice to have a day off.

Kate and the party returned at 6pm. They had had an exhilarating day and were in celebratory mood. It was our last night in Echo. We stayed in the bar until after midnight.

Tuesday 16th January

Today we are to have lunch in a tent five kilometres from the camp. We were advised to put on our warmest clothes, it would be very cold. We went there in the snowmobile. The tent was halfway up a mountain, with wonderful views of the snowy hills below us. We ate sandwiches and drank soup.

Once again the fit were divided from the also-rans. Kate went with them. They were given crampons, helmets and ice axes. They would be roped together and would climb a sheer ice face.

As she told me afterwards only she and Dimitry managed to get to the top. But then Kate is very fit and in good condition from her interminable gym, Pilates, pole and aerial silk lessons.

Dimitry is obviously a very fit man.

Once they had left for their ice climbing we others went back to camp.

I wanted to walk. Jaime, the elder, walked with me.

He is a very interesting man. A lawyer by profession, he had been Panamanian Ambassador in Washington. He was a travel addict and had visited most countries around the world. His next ambition is to leave the World in a spaceship, and he has already booked a voyage with X, the Elon Musk space company, for two years hence.

He told me that the price had been outrageous, so he said no. Then they reduced it to a mere one million, five hundred thousand dollars …and he accepted.

He said that his son was very interested in politics and was a member of a political party in Panama.

But I was less keen on him. He seemed to have a rapport with Kate, which annoyed me.

We had to pack our bags and leave them outside our igloos by 6pm. Then we had our last meal in Echo. We left for Wolf's Fang at 8.30pm. The plane was late arriving from Cape

Town, so we sat in the warm airport hut and communicated with the world.

We finally left Antarctica at midnight.

But before we left I had a pleasant surprise. One of the guides approached me and gave me my phone. Against all the odds it had been found five days after I lost it in the penguin colony. It had lain in the snow at minus twenty degrees. But it still worked.

I recovered all my photos, not only of the penguins, but also the video of Kate dancing in her bikini!

Wait until I show this to our friends!

We were met in Cape Town airport by White Desert people who sent us to our respective hotels by car. We had not slept much on the plane so wanted to catch up on sleep. We went straight to our room in the Ellerman House Hotel and to bed.

I woke after a couple of hours and called reception. I needed two things. The first was a barber. I was feeling unkempt. The second was a dentist. I had suffered toothache most of the time on the holiday. I had assumed that it was due to the cold, but it still hurt now.

Both the barber and the dentist were found and came to the hotel.

First the barber and then a mobile dental clinic. The young lady dentist took an x-ray and said I would need root treatment for the tooth. There was no time to do it before we left Cape Town so she prescribed me Nurofen to keep the pain at bay. I would have to get it seen to in Madrid.

Before leaving Cape Province I wanted to take Kate to see Stellenbosch. We still had our car and driver, Faruz. So on Thursday we made the trip. White Desert people had booked the Graff restaurant for lunch.

We left Cape Town on the Johannesburg road. It's a motorway and took us past the less attractive side of the city where there were small houses crammed together, each with a TV antenna. Even though it was three lane highway we ran into a traffic jam, which wasted an hour of our day. I used the time to chat to Faruz. The last time I had been in South Africa, fifty-six years ago, it had been under the Apartheid government.

I ask him what has changed. Surprisingly he replied,

"Very little has changed. The white people still have the money and live in the best part of Cape Town. Black people flock in from other parts of the Republic and get whatever jobs they can."

Faruz was of Indian descent, they and the 'coloureds'of mixed race, form the middle class.

Stellenbosch was as pretty as I remembered it from my one brief trip there. It's a town noted for houses with lovely Dutch gables. It has charming parks and gardens. It's now a university town. It was good to see students of all races walking and chatting together.

Graff is beyond the town. We were running a bit late for our lunch reservation so Faruz called them. There was no problem, they would wait for us.

We drove out of town down a long valley flanked by mountains on the sides of which there are vineyards on the lower slopes and eucalyptus plantations higher up.

We left the main road and took a smaller one which wound up the right side of the valley.

Then we came to imposing gates at the entrance to an estate. The word Graff was embossed on the stone pillar.

Faruz explained to us that Graff is a famous name in diamonds in South Africa. This is the private estate of the owner of the family business, Mr Graff.

Apart from his private house he has a hotel and restaurant. It's a bit like my house Tupgill in Yorkshire, surrounded by the Forbidden Corner which is open to the public.

The estate has the most magnificent views across the valley.

Faruz delivered us to a hostess. He had something he wanted to do, so declined our invitation to lunch. He would wait for us in the carpark. She showed us to a table, shaded by trees on the garden terrace restaurant.

The food and Stellenbosch wine were delicious, but above all the setting made it special with a view all the way across the valley. There were birds in the trees and gentle buzzing of bees. The day was not too hot and there was a breeze. I think it was one of the meals I have most enjoyed anywhere.

Of course, in this frame of mind I fell into the trap laid for me by the owners.

As we left the restaurant and made our way back to the car park, we passed a cellar with a large circular window where we could see wine barrels piled up. Then quite extraordinarily, there was a high-end jewelers shop. Of course, it was Graff.

Kate seized my arm,

"My Love, I have been a very good girl. Will you buy me a present?"

The wine flowed through my veins. We went in. We were the only customers.

There were lots of showcases. We looked at them idly. I really didn't have anything in mind to buy her. But she was attracted by a display of very pretty watches. The lady assistant, who had looked rather bored (I expect she had many lookers and few spenders), now perked up and asked us if we would like to see more.

Kate did.

So we sat at a desk and watches were brought to show us. When I saw the prices I was beginning to panic. They were expensive. But as she explained they were masterpieces, and just look at the tiny diamonds encrusted in them. That was where the value was. We got the choice down to two that we liked. Then, as always to clinch the sale, we were told that there was a 15% duty refund on it. She would give us the form and on leaving South Africa we must get it stamped. Hey presto, the cash will be transferred to my bank account.

So we bought a very pretty watch with a large round dial which was decorated with tiny jewels made into flowers. The rim of the dial is covered in small diamonds. It has a white leather strap.

That evening was our last in Cape Town. We asked the hotel to recommend us an Italian Restaurant. They obliged, and we went to Il Leone. It was on the promenade which flanks the bay. It was full of people talking animatedly in loud voices. Very Italian. The food was excellent, and the wine too. In a mellow mood we talked about the holiday.

We discussed writing a book recounting the kidnap, the holiday and our life together.We have so much to tell. And perhaps things that are better not to tell!

I have already written four books about ourselves, under a pseudonym. But Kate didn't like them. She said there was too much sex, and worse I mentioned another girl, whom she thought that I had an affair with. Two books got into print, the other two got no further than my laptop.

She convinced (bullied) me into withdrawing the two from sale. I did it and the remaining forty books were returned to me by Lionel Ross the owner of the publisher i2i.

I hid them in Tupgill. But when she was there with me in May 2023, she discovered them and made me burn them. We made a bonfire in a field and she gleefully threw them on it, one by one, and smiled at me as she watched them burn.

So much for free speech!

Before we left the hotel for the airport we had to sort out our Antarctic clothing. I didn't want to cart it all back to Madrid, especially the battery-operated stuff, which we had hardly used. The hotel offered to take what we didn't want and give it to some charity. I imagine that it happens with every returning Antarctic traveller. I sorted through them and made a pile of mine, Kate much less so. Then she began to retrieve what I wanted to discard.

She said that one day we might go to the North Pole. But I was sure I never would. One Pole had been interesting, two was a Pole too many.

We finally agreed that I would take my expensive Mammut jacket, the boots, gloves and some other kit.

We left for the airport at 9pm. We said goodbye to Faruz, who had shown us so much, and of course gave him a good tip.

We went to the duty-free desk, and the lady there asked us to fill out a long form including UK bank details, which I didn't have to hand. So she stamped the Graff invoice and said we must fill out the forms and send them back to customs, she gave us the address.

We went to the so-called business lounge. But it was just an open area of seating, and rather scruffy.

The KLM flight left at 00:35am.

We flew back to Amsterdam and returned to the L'Europe Hotel for two nights.

We know Amsterdam well. After changing in the hotel, we walked to the Bijenkorf department store in Dam Square. There we bought an attractive sailor suit outfit for Kate. And, for my benefit, we went to Agent Provocateur!

After shopping we walked to Rembrandt Square to one of our favorite restaurants called Indrapura. It's Indonesian food. They serve multiple small dishes of spicy food, the best one containing lobster. They have vegetarian dishes too so we both enjoy it. We knew the waiter who attended us. He is from Nepal. We talked to him about our holiday there in March 2022.

It was another wonderful holiday organized by Chinmay. We went for ten days which began in Kathmandu. While there we took a helicopter ride up Everest. We reached six thousand metres, just above the famous Everest base camp, where we landed and walked about in the rarefied air. We saw the peak of Everest three thousand meters above us.

Another day we flew by helicopter again (the roads are appalling) to Pokhara. We went paragliding for the first time in my life, and then to the Gurkha museum. The Gurkhas, who originate from this area, have been part of the British Army for two hundred years. This dates from the time the British Raj attacked them and got a bloody nose. They are such good fighters it's better to have them on our side.

From Pokhara we flew once again by helicopter to Chitwan, where we went on a safari to see rhinoceros and crocodiles.

Just as on safari in Tanzania, they made a lovely surprise for us. At the end of an afternoon when we had seen a female rhino and her baby close up, we took a canoe down river back to the camp. Then as the sun went down we landed on the river bank. There was a table set out under a palm tree with two chairs and a bottle of champagne. The guides left us alone. We toasted the holiday happily and watched the glorious sunset.

Altogether a memorable trip.

The next day in Amsterdam, we took the hotel buggy (easier than a taxi as they can use the bicycle lanes) to the Rijks Restaurant, at the side of the famous museum. We had a date to meet our good friends Hans and Marianne Boon. Hans is a consultant for shrimp feeds for Agripac. We struck up a great friendship seven years ago and see each other socially, apart from work.

They live in Utrecht. We stayed in a hotel there in May last year. Hans took us to the Delft Porcelain factory where, after the tour, we bought plates and mugs with the Miffey rabbit design. We drove to see Holland's famous windmills and a fishing village where we ate eels. That night we dined at the famous Hemel and Aarde restaurant. The following day we returned with Hans to Amsterdam and went to the Rijksmuseum for a guided tour.

The problem with guided tours of art galleries is that you don't get to see much. Our guide today was an elegant Argentinian lady, wearing a wide-brimmed hat. She had so much to say about each painting that in the two hour tour we only saw a dozen paintings.

Ceci and I were once on such a tour in the Prado. We left the others to it, and did our own tour. Much more satisfying. If you want more information, you can always buy the guide book.

We flew to Madrid with seven suitcases. Kate had brought three from Ecuador, two of which we left at the L'Europa while we went to Cape Town. There we acquired the Antarctic clothing, and also some shopping.

So arriving in Madrid we had to take two taxis. Annoyingly the airport taxis are very small. They can manage a maximum of four cases. But on the other hand the fare to the centre of the city is only thirty-three euros, a far cry from a Heathrow taxi, of a hundred pounds to the center.

We returned to our Madrid flat. We have had it for five years now, and though small, it's very convenient for shops and restaurants.

My toothache had returned, despite the Nurofen. We called a dentist and got an appointment. He took an x-ray and declared that it was an infection. He couldn't extract the tooth until the infection was cured, so I was prescribed antibiotics. Really, I was rather relieved that I didn't have to go through an extraction yet, so putting off the evil moment.

The dentist's surgery is a long way up the Castellana from our flat. We went there by taxi, but decided to walk back. It was a pleasant day, quite mild for January.

It was a lot further than we had reckoned. We walked and walked and came to the Corte Ingles on the Castellana.

There is no way that Kate would walk past the Corte Ingles, so we went in. We luckily got through the high-end fashion shops which fill the ground floor, without her finding a must have.

We headed towards the electronics area. She had wanted a new iPhone 15 for some time. So we bought that and then of course looked at the latest Galaxy 23 for me. It is rectangular with square corners, rather than the usual rounded ones. It has a bigger screen than mine, so we took that too. Then we looked at a computer screen for the laptop. I have trouble seeing numbers on the screen even with reading glasses. In my Guayaquil office I have a large desk screen, but I can't travel with it. So we bought one for Madrid.

With all this to carry, we had to take a taxi home.

The fridge was empty after our being away since November. But there is an excellent deli in the street nearby. We went there and stocked up on basic necessities, such as champagne, wine, bread, cheese, ham, smoked salmon and caviar.

We ate at home and watched the opera Carmen on DVD, which is a favourite of ours. It stars the beautiful mezzo soprano Elina Garanca, tenor Roberto Alagna and soprano Barbara Frittoli.

I have a large collection of opera DVDs. I used to buy them from the music department of the Corte Ingles. But the last time I went to look for them, not only don't they have opera DVDs, but they don't have DVDs at all! Astonishingly they have gone back to vinyl discs which I last bought when I was a teenager. So the world progresses!

It was towards the end of January that we had dinner with Rodrigo and his wife Sylvia at the Coquette Restaurant. Rodrigo is our lawyer in Madrid who had originally helped us purchase the apartment. Once again we have become close personal friends. We had not seen them since the kidnap, so with that and Antarctica, we had a lot to talk about. We stayed until after midnight and then walked home.

The kidnap has consequences. We now need bodyguards when we return to Guayaquil. Josef Shalev flew to Madrid to talk to us.

He said that our penthouse is no longer safe. We should move out of it and temporarily rent a place in another area of town. We will both need protection each time we move from the flat. He insisted that I buy an armoured Toyota to replace my smashed BMW. I will drive it and be followed by a pickup with two of his armed guards. The guards will leave me at the office in the morning, then take Kate to wherever she needs to go, and collect me at 5pm to escort me home.

We agreed to do this. But, he said, he needs to recruit more operatives and buy the support vehicles. We cannot return to Guayaquil until early March.

Josef is an old friend. We invited him to La Maquina restaurant on Jorge Juan Street.

Two days later he returned the invitation and we went to the James Joyce Irish Pub, which has the best fish and chips in Madrid.

We got in email contact with an estate agent in Guayaquil and after a few days found a flat we liked from photos. We will rent it for a year, and then see what happens. We asked the same agent to sell our penthouse on the fifteenth floor of a downtown building. We thought that with the proceeds we might be able to buy a house or a flat. We don't want to live in rented accommodation longer than we have to. There are obvious limitations on what you can do to it.

Using my new computer screen, I struggled to put together the tax reclaim form for Graff. I got everything photocopied and sent the email to their address. The money will be transferred to my UK bank account. Or so I hoped.

There was another sequel to the kidnap. We were contacted by our lawyers from Guayaquil.

They have been in touch with the state prosecutor regarding the nine men who had been arrested in Guayaquil. They were all in prison and their case will go to court for a preliminary hearing on 8th February. Were Kate and I prepared to testify against them?

If we did not then the state case would be damaged, and they would probably be released from prison.

Our first reaction was to say no. We are the victims, we didn't want to have to re-live the case. Anyway, we can’t return safely to Guayaquil to appear in court.

We were told that we didn’t have to be there physically, we could do the court appearance on Zoom.

We talked it over. If we didn't do our civic duty, as many didn’t, then the mafia is winning the game. Their people escaped justice and could carry on kidnapping people.

With some trepidation we decided to do it.

We were instructed how it would go. There would be the judge, the prosecutor, the secretary of the court and the lawyers for the criminals. For criminals they were. There was no doubt about it. The GPS on my phone had led the police to their lair in a low-cost area of Guayaquil. They had recovered, apart from guns, the saddles and bridles taken from the ranch.

On Thursday 8th February we were waiting in the apartment for the call to begin the Zoom. It would be at 9am Ecuador time, 3pm Madrid time.

We received the call and opened Zoom.

The lady secretary of the court read our names and noted that we were present. Then there was a very long process while she read out the names of the accused. Each one had a different lawyer to represent them. We saw the lawyers, one or two of whom were dressed in suit and tie, whereas the judge and prosecutor wore open-neck shirts. It's a profitable business defending the guilty.

From time to time the camera showed the prison where the accused sat on a bench dressed only in boxer shorts. We could see them, and presumably they could see us. Though we didn’t recognise any of them. It had been dark, and they had worn masks.

As the proceedings droned on, the secretary named the defending lawyer for each one. She stopped, looked at her list and then declared that one of the accused was dead. Why and how was not explained. We supposed that he had been eliminated, perhaps by a rival gang, or even by his own mates, if they thought him the weakest link.

We had been on Zoom for more than an hour when one of the lawyers protested that a court-appointed defence lawyer had not turned up. That violated the human rights of the accused, so the proceedings should not continue.

The judge accepted it. The court would reconvene next Wednesday 14th.

We closed the screen.

We were both nervous after the appearance. Looking at the accused upset us. They scowled at us, as though to threaten us not to give evidence.

Worse, we were not yet finished. We had to go through the whole thing again next Wednesday.

There was a problem here too.

We planned to go to England on Monday 12th February. We will stay in London for two nights and then take the train to Leeds on Wednesday. We have a meeting there.

Leeds is where my UK solicitors have their offices. For some time I had been struggling to put my English estate into trust. I had taken advice from a tax consultancy that this government, or a future one, might tighten up the rules on capital relief of inheritance tax on family companies. At the moment it is exempt. But as one never knows in advance the day that you will die, the rules might be changed.

We had applied to put the Forbidden Corner Ltd into trust. The revenue body, HMRC, replied yes. Now we had to sign the relevant documents and do the deed.

The meeting with the solicitors was for 11am and then we would have lunch together.

The Zoom meeting would be at 3pm. Perhaps we could borrow a meeting room with a screen?

But before we left for London we had planned to meet Kate's younger sister Luisa, who is studying psychology in Madrid, and her boyfriend David.

They suggested we hire a car on Saturday and drive out of Madrid. They knew of a very pretty village called Patones de Arriba. It took about an hour and a half to get there. We arrived in the village of Patones, from where we had to walk to Patones de Arriba on foot.

We parked the car and set off. The day was cold and we all wore coats, but as we walked we heated up and wished we hadn't dressed quite so warmly. The track ran straight up the hill, crossing the winding road from time to time. It was hard going. I was the one they had to wait for. I was surprised that Luisa's little pomeranian, Blue, was doing so well.

When we got to the foot of the village, we thought we had made it. But no, the village itself wound upwards another hundred metres. The houses are built of rough stone,as one might expect of shepherd's huts.

The view from the top must have been spectacular but by the time we got there the clouds had come down and we couldn't see anything, so we went into one of the many small restaurants for beer and an excellent lunch, before returning to the car.

It was still early, so we decided to go to the nearby Madrid Safari.

This was great fun. We bought paper bags of carrots at the entrance. As we drove through the park camels, deer, zebras and large, hairy goats came to the car to beg for them. They knew the game. The camels would stick their heads inside the car and slobber all over us.

Kate was driving with myself in the front seat, Luisa and David behind. I got fed up with the camels and closedmy window, but Kate from the drivers side kept opening it again and roared with laughter as I fought off the camels. At one point there were two heads inside the car.

They lined up across the road and would not let us pass. Eventually, all the carrots were gone and they attacked the next car.

It was a well-stocked park. Although it was February the animals didn't seem to feel the cold. There were elephants, giraffes, hippos, zebras, antelope, and even a pride of lions.

They were in another area, separated by a chain link fence and cattle crossing, from the herbivores. For extra safety a warder herded them away from the crossing in a jeep.

Before leaving the park we went to the reptile house where there is a large collection of snakes, including the long, thick South American Anaconda which I had never seen before. They can grow up to six meters long. The biggest here was nearly five meters. They are very impressive when they uncoil and move around the glass-fronted cage, with raised head. They are reputed to be able to eat a calf, which they open their throats to swallow and then digest slowly over a week.

We got back to Madrid at 7pm and headed to a sushi bar to finish the day.

Luisa and David told us that they are planning to go to Finland to see the aurora borealis next week. Kate immediately offered them our Antarctica clothing.

I said I would lend David my Mammut jacket.

After they returned from Finland they split up. I thought that I would never see the Mammut again.

The next day, the 12th of February, we drove to Barajas airport and left the hire car at the Hertz depot at terminal 4. The Iberia flight was on time and two hours later we arrived at Terminal 5 of Heathrow. We took a taxi to the Ritz Hotel. We had been regular guests at the Ritz Hotel in Madrid, before we bought our apartment. Now we would see what the London one is like.

I had once taken my family to lunch at the Ritz Hotel in the magnificent dining room. It was the day of my investiture of the OBE from Her Majesty the Queen at Buckingham Palace, on

17th July 1996. The same evening we saw the musical Les Miserables.

Today we arrived at the hotel door at 3pm. The top-hatted, frock-coated doormen were very friendly, asking our names, taking the bags and ushering us inside. We quickly filled out the registration and were shown to the room. We had not taken a junior suite, just a deluxe room, as we saw they were forty square meters. For two nights that would be ample, as we had only two pieces of luggage. In fact, it was a lovely room with a large bathroom.

We ordered a bottle of champagne to the room, it was delivered by a Nepalese girl.

We had been checked in by an Italian man, and two ladies from Madrid behind the desk, hearing us speak Spanish, had said hello. A very international hotel.

There was something I wanted to do today. For many years I have bought my shirts from Budd in the Piccadilly Arcade. They are made to measure and being good quality they last for years, before fraying collars and cuffs brings them to an end. They come with plastic collar stiffeners, but these tend to get lost if I forget to take them out before the shirts are washed. I have had silver, mother of pearl and plastic ones. But at the moment I can't find any of them.

We walked from the hotel down Piccadilly to the arcade.

There are two assistants who have been there for over thirty years, Mr Rowling and Mr Butcher. We went in and I asked if they were there. They always recognised me, even after several years of not visiting, and would address me as Ambassador, to which I always replied no, Consul.

But today neither was in the shop. There was a young lady who attended us. I bought three sets of mother of pearl collar stiffeners, and at Kate's urging, another black bowtie.

Then we walked back, past the hotel to Fortnum and Mason. I love the shop with its tail-coated assistants. We really didn't want to buy anything. I guided Kate towards the chocolate counter where there was a fantastic collection of many flavours. But she protested that she was eating too many sweets. So we left.

Next door is Hatchards bookshop. This is a Mecca for me. We wandered around. I was looking for new titles from my favourite authors, Bernard Cornwell, Robert Harris and Ken Follett.

I didn't find anything new from them, but there were other books which attracted me. I bought six.

Then we walked back to the hotel, freshened up and went to the lobby bar, where we were attended by a Colombian waitress.

We had booked dinner in the famous Ritz Restaurant. But sadly it is now Michelin two star.

I say sadly, because so many Michelin restaurants disappoint us. They tend to have only one option of a tasting menu. There are ten rather tasteless dishes, served with an excess of explanation as to their provenance and preparation.

But we drank delicious Corton-Charlemagne wine and listened to a pianist, who of course played 'Putting on the Ritz'.

Before going to bed I asked the hall porter if the series The Crown was authentic.

The young Princess Elizabeth, in army uniform, is celebrating the end of the war. She danced in the Ritz basement with American soldiers. He assured us that it was a fact.

Today the basement is the Ritz Club.

The next morning Kate wanted to sleep in. So I got up alone for breakfast at 9am.

I returned to the Ritz Restaurant, they can't spoil breakfast. There was a wonderful menu including kippers, smoked haddock and kedgeree.

I had the kippers with several cups of tea, and toast with honey. Then I wandered into the lobby, found a comfortable chair and read the Times from cover to cover, before going back to the room. Kate was by now in the shower.

Yesterday had been my treat, today was hers. She wanted to buy a dress (it always starts in the singular tense, but finishes plural).

She suggested that we go to Harrods, but I wanted to show her somewhere different. We went to Harvey Nichols, which had been my mother's favourite dress shop.

They showed her any number of dresses. I found a seat and did my emails. I was only required to look up from time to time to give my opinion. We bought four diaphanous long dresses, two in pink and two black. They really did look good on her, but then again what doesn't?

It was lunchtime so we went up to the fifth-floor restaurant. The seafood platter was the speciality. We had a bloody mary each beforehand and a bottle of Portuguese vinho verde with the meal. So we were pleasantly mellow as we returned to the hotel at 4.30pm.

Tomorrow we have to get the 8am train from Kings Cross to Leeds, so we decided to pack all but essentials now.

Once done, we returned to the Ritz cocktail bar at 6pm, and then walked to an Indonesian restaurant called Toba in St James Market. It wasn't as good as Indrapura.

I have always enjoyed trains. My early life was marked by trains to boarding school and back each term.

For many years in the summer holidays my mother sent me by train to stay with my bachelor uncle Stuart, who owned the Manor Farm at Rockbourne in Hampshire.

I would spend my days with his gamekeeper Philip Hood (he had a brother called Robin Hood). I took my twenty-eight-bore shotgun with me. Philip built a hide and put out decoy pigeons. Then he left me there all day with a sandwich for lunch. I shot hundreds of pigeons. They are a plague in the corn fields, and are classified as vermin.

I once took a dozen dead pigeons back home to mother to make a pigeon pie. She was not at all impressed with them. They were immediately thrown out.

Uncle Stuart was a great cook and host. He used to cook dinner himself, dressed in his striped butcher's apron, while his guests sipped cocktails in the large kitchen of the Manor House. I met many interesting people while staying there, including the painter Augustus John, who died in 1961 at nearby Fordingbridge.

In fact, I took trains everywhere until I eventually got my own transport. The first was an old BSA motorbike which I bought when I was seventeen and a farm pupil in Mevagissey, Cornwall.

My first car was a present from Aunt Do, when I was twenty one and at Writtle Agricultural College, doing a management course. She had a way of explaining her gifts. She said that her shares have had pups, meaning a rights issue. So she would give them to me. It was enough to buy a second-hand, green Morris Mini Cooper. I got more fun out of that car than any other I have had.

Just for the record, it is possible to do it in a Mini Cooper!

We got to Kings Cross in good time. The station is a wind tunnel and freezing as always. I gazed at the board indicating the departures, while Kate bought us coffee. All trains go North from here, and seemed to duplicate each other. You have to look and see where they stop. The express trains have very few stops between London and Edinburgh.

We found that the 8am Leeds train leaves from platform seven.

The train leaving platform 10 3/4 for Hogwarts didn't appear to be running today.

We had been given very precise instructions from Leeds station to the solicitors' offices. He said that it wasn't worth taking a taxi, it was only a hundred yards walk to Wellington Place.

But Leeds City station has four exits onto four different streets. We emerged hauling our two suitcases, and two pieces of hand luggage, only to find we were in a building site. No sign of Wellington Place. We asked a passerby and were told to return to the station and come out a different way. We did, and again couldn't find it. By now the cases were feeling a bit heavy to pull. We rang the office and were told there was yet another exit.

Finally we made it. The meeting was for 11am, so we were half an hour late.

We left our luggage in the office lobby and went into the meeting room where the others were waiting for us.

There were three people waiting for us. There was a lady tax expert, Orlando our solicitor and Gary the accountant.

We waded through the details of setting up the trust. It all seemed very complicated, but we got an agreement on the way forward.

Then we went for lunch.

I had asked Orlando if we could borrow a meeting room for 3pm.

That was arranged and the TV screen was set up for Zoom.

The same sequence of events took place as the last time. But in the intervening week they had moved ahead with procedures, so they were soon ready for our testimony. I went first. At that time I didn't have my hearing aid. I said my piece but there were interruptions from the prosecutor and one of the defendant's lawyers. I couldn't hear clearly what they said and asked them to repeat it. The judge asked crossly if I spoke Spanish. I replied yes, but I am a bit deaf. Kate tried to help me but the judge ordered her to leave the room. Finally my ordeal was over.

Then it was Kate's turn. She made a much better fist of it. She told her story in detail, and answered the questions clearly.

By five pm we were free to leave. A great relief. It was over. We were not required to do any more.

We thanked our hosts and left the building.

We found a taxi to take us toTupgill, about forty miles away.

What a delight it is to be back home. Because it is still home to me, it always has been. I have spent my life leaving it and returning home. First to boarding schools, when I was 8 years old, then university, then holidays from work in Malaysia, Mexico and Ecuador.

Leo came to the house and we shared a bottle of champagne, before moving to the Saddle Room restaurant next door. We all had the seafood platter with a bottle of good Albariña Spanish wine. Kate by this time was eating fish to supplement her vegetarian diet.

The following day we met up with my sisters Jane, Catherine and her daughter Emilie. They had not met Kate before. I introduced them and they got on very well. They thanked her for looking after their little brother. They told her that she keeps me young.

Their big news was that Catherine (we call her Kate too) and Emilie were going to return to Australia. Emilie had lived there for many years since she had married an Australian. Kate had spent several months living with them over the last few years. Emilie has two children, Daniel and Sophie, who are now grown up and working. When Emilie's marriage finished last year both she and Catherine returned to England. Luckily a cottage on the estate was free and they moved into it, next door to Jane's cottage.

But they had not settled. They missed their children and grandchildren and the friendly Aussie way of life. Coverdale is very quiet after that.

They will leave in May, and made us promise that we will come and see them again before they leave.

The weather is mild for February, so we kitted up with coats from the large collection in Tupgill and walked on Middleham moor together chatting. I had not seen them since the Antarctic trip so we had a good story to tell.

We only stayed two days in Tupgill and then on Friday we returned on the train from Darlington to London.

This time we decided to try the Savoy Hotel.

I had upgraded to get a room with a river view. It is lovely,we can see the London Eye across the river and the constant river traffic.

There is a theater advert done in lights we can see across the river. It shows the 2002 film based on the book by Oscar Wilde, The Importance of Being Earnest, starring Colin Firth, Reese Witherspoon and Judi Dench. I would love to see it one day.

We had not pre-booked the famous Savoy Grill and sadly it was full, so we had dinner in the River Restaurant. Kate had caviar and lobster, me oysters and a Dover sole. We washed it down with a bottle of Corton-Charlemagne.

On Saturday we had arranged to meet with Lien and his wife Rita for lunch at Franco's in Jermyn Street at 1.30pm. We hadn't seen them since the kidnap, though I had talked a great deal to Lien by phone.

He said that he had some loose ends he needed to clear up with the insurers. The first was that the UK National Crime Agency had been involved in the kidnap. They wanted to interview us before closing the file. We haven't time to see them in London so he arranged for two agents to come to Madrid and interview us on the 22nd of February.

The other was a pleasant surprise. We were insured for the amount paid to the kidnappers. As the policy was in my name personally I will receive the refund. Additionally they are prepared to reimburse me for the costs of getting the family out of Ecuador, and other out-of-pocket expenses. These were quite considerable as we had to buy last-minute tickets just before Christmas, when the fares are astronomical.

So I would recover this, plus the cost of the new Omega watch to replace the one stolen.

They also offered to pay for a short holiday which we need to calm our nerves.

I suggested it could be this trip to England. So the cost of airfares and both the Ritz and Savoy hotels will be paid for, plus the Harvey Nic's dresses. Not bad going.

The next day we returned to Madrid.

Over the years we have been good customers of Tiffany the jewelers, especially at their Madrid shop. We had made friends with the managers, Manuel and Tina. Now they kindly offered to give us a free trip to Dubai for three days, where they would launch their new collection.

We have been three times before to Dubai, as it's on the way to many places, if you fly Emirates. We first went there for three days before flying to Egypt. Another time on our way to Sri Lanka and finally when we went to Thailand.

I had reservations about accepting the invitation. We were not able to buy anything significant this year. Once before they had invited us to Milan, and to the Scala to see a modern version of Rigoletto. But it ended up with us buying an expensive brooch.

It is said there is no such thing as a free lunch. So I supposed we would be expected to buy something this time. We told Tina that we can't buy anything as we are looking to buy a bigger flat in Madrid. But she said it wasn't the case. It was just a thank you for being good customers over the years, and because we are your friends.

We left for Dubai the evening of the 22nd February, after being interviewed all day by the NCA officers from London. We had to repeat our stories individually, with many interruptions and repetitions. They seemed to want to catch us out on some detail. But eventually they were satisfied and left us.

We could now pack for Dubai.

We arrived there on the 23rd, and took the car and driver provided by Tiffany from the airport to the Mandarin Oriental Jumeirah. It was our third time at this hotel.

On the first trip to Dubai we stayed at the seven-star Burj Al Arab Hotel in a duplex room. It was not only very expensive but also far too big. We trailed up and down stairs in the room all the time.

Once we checked into the Mandarin Hotel we were given the Tiffany program for our stay.

It began with a massage and wellness program in the hotel, but as we had a siesta after we arrived, we missed it.

That evening at 7pm there was a welcome cocktail at the Tiffany Mansion. Our transport was waiting for us at the hotel to take us there. It was the most palatial house.

The guests were greeted by their hosts, us by Manuel and Tina, and taken for a preview of the new collection. It was very fine indeed and involved a jeweled cockatoo brooch standing on a very large, expensive opal.

There was a cocktail party on the roof garden of the building. It was a lovely night with a breeze. We were treated like royalty and introduced to their overseas directors and to wealthy customers.

After two hours we left with Manuel and Tina to Il Borro restaurant.

We were joined there by three more Tiffany people from other countries.

To fill in the free time between official events we had an interesting program. The next day we were driven to the Police Academy and given a half hour helicopter flight over Dubai. We were escorted by a Mexican lady, Lourdes, who is resident here. It's the best way to see the city. Lourdes told us what each area was and pointed out buildings, and the famous palm tree-shaped island. We filmed it as we went.

On returning to the Academy we asked her to video us as we walked away from the helicopter with our hair blown about by the wind from the rotors.

We had time to fill in before dinner so we went to the Dubai Mall. It's enormous, you can easily get lost. But Kate has a knack of finding what she is looking for. In this case Chanel. She asked me to buy her a dress, as a consolation prize for not getting any Tiffany jewelry.

That evening we dined informally with Manuel and Tina and laughed together over the many happy memories we had. Though I also recounted a very sad one. We had been together in Tiffany's shop in Madrid on 8th September 2022. There was a TV in the shop and the breaking news was that HM Queen Elizabeth II had died. I was overcome with emotion and couldn't help crying. I had met her twice. Once when I received the OBE in 1996 in Buckingham Palace and again in 2011 when I received the CMG from her in Holyrood House.

Apart from that I had proposed the loyal toast thirty five years in succession when I hosted the Queen's Birthday Party at Rodeo Grande.

"The Queen. God bless her".

Sunday 25th February, today is the main Tiffany event. This is the reason we have all been brought to Dubai.

I got up at 8am and went for breakfast with my old Peruvian friend Jorge Cepeda. He now lives in Miami. We do business together and keep in touch. I got a whatsapp from him yesterday and asked him where he is. He replied Dubai. What a coincidence. So we met for breakfast at the hotel. He has good customers in Dubai and comes here frequently.

Kate didn't want to get up so early, she said to give him her love.

Then we dressed for the show.

Kate wore a pretty floor-length pale blue and white dress with shoulder straps. I wore a grey suit and tie.

When we got there we were again met by Manuel and Tina and escorted to a private viewing room. Then the show started with one beautiful piece after another being brought to show us. There was a wonderfully worked necklace of butterflies in diamonds. Then another of emeralds. She loved a tiara of white gold and diamonds. But, as I pointed out, there is nowhere she could wear it, unless she was presented to King Charles III!

There were several more lovely pieces of jewelry including the cockatoo.

After she had tried each piece on, they said they would leave us alone to choose which we liked. We sat and looked glum. There was no way that we could rise to the occasion. They returned and we explained once again about not being able to buy anything this year. They said please don't worry. There will always be another year.

Shortly after that we left. The program included a visit to the Museum of the Future with a lady guide. This was an incredible building, built like a wheel standing upright. Inside there are glimpses of what the future could be like. There were flying taxis over Dubai and incredible vehicles, as well as sensory experiences.

Afterwards we returned to the hotel and ate in the Japanese restaurant. It was very good but the saki was horrendously expensive. We met an American expat at the bar, and after a great deal of saki, we became firm friends. We told him all about the kidnap and our holiday in Antarctica. He said he has a music business. We promised to keep in touch.

I can't even remember his name now.

On Monday we flew back to Madrid. The flight was in the evening. We had one more Tiffany invitation. This time to have lunch in the Blue Box restaurant in the Dubai Mall. We went there and surprise, surprise, it was Tiffany blue. The first time we had seen a Tiffany restaurant, (there is no breakfast in Tiffany).

We were on our own, just the two of us. The menu was cauliflower soup, smoked salmon and caviar, but sadly no wine. It was still very enjoyable.

We returned to the hotel at 3pm. We had time to fill before we left for the airport at 8pm. We had already checked out of our room. Kate had bought a bikini in the Mall. She went to a cloakroom and changed into it. Then with a shirt covering it for decency, she walked with me through the lobby to the beach.

It was quite cold but she went into the sea while I nursed a beer in a deck chair and filmed her.

Back in Madrid, we had four days before we were to return to Guayaquil. We really were looking for a bigger flat. If we are going to live for more of the year in Madrid then we need more space. I want an office to continue my work. Kate needs somewhere to put her pole. Our friend Sylvia, an estate agent, is helping us. She took us to see five possible ones. The small (big) problem is the price. Sylvia said that ours had gone up 50% in value since we bought it in 2018. But then so has everything else in the centre of Madrid. So even with selling ours we would need to put a lot of money up front. We had talked to Rodrigo, our lawyer friend, and found out the facts of life of buying and selling property. On selling we would have to pay the agent's fee of 4% plus capital gains tax up to 25%. On buying the new one there will be value added tax of between 6% and 10%, depending if the building is new or second hand. Then of course there are legal fees.

Given that this was a difficult year, and I was restricted by covenant from taking dividends from Agripac. It was looking like a pipedream.

Return to Guayaquil

We have been given the green light to return to Guayaquil. An armoured Toyota SUV has been bought, guards assigned, a flat in a safe area rented. We left Madrid on 2nd March 2024.

I didn't take much luggage, the flat is quite small, and I have a lot of clothes to pick up from Ceci's (it used to be our) house. So I left a lot of my clothes in Madrid.

Kate did the same. She has to move her large wardrobe out of our penthouse, as we have put it up for sale. Only a fraction of it will go into the new place.

We were met at Guayaquil Airport by my assistant Jorge with my new Toyota Fortuna. It's a beast of a car, large, high with seating for seven, but that leaves no room for luggage. The engine is huge so even with all the extra weight it has excellent acceleration. The test will be when (if ever) I take it to the Sierra, and see how it copes with that.

We have been assigned two bodyguards. They followed us in an armoured pickup truck from the airport to the enclosure where the rented flat is located.

I had asked Jorge to buy a few bottles of wine for our first night.

The flat is in a block ten stories high, within a walled enclosure with eight armed guards at the gate. We are on the second floor. It's rented for a year. After which we need to decide if we are going to buy somewhere in Guayaquil or simply live in Madrid.

We are disappointed with it. It looks very different from the estate agent's photos. The walls of the sitting/dining room are painted black. There are heavy black curtains on the floor-to-ceiling windows to the balcony, which overlook the communal garden, swimming pool and the river beyond.

Trying to open them, the curtain rail collapsed and we had the curtains on the floor. We don't like them anyway so we packed them up to return to the landlady. We also removed the fly screens which slide parallel to the windows. They have a habit of coming off their rails too. We carted them down to the lockup in the basement garage.

The fridge was not working, there was no hot water and no WIFI. We didn't like the furniture either. Kate said that she would return it to the owner and bring ours from the penthouse. We had thought to sell it furnished, as a lot of the furniture was made to measure when we moved in there six years ago.

Kate declared that she was not sleeping here tonight. She wanted to return to our penthouse. But we couldn't do that. We had been told that it wasn't safe, and moreover, our bodyguards had gone home. We were not supposed to move without them.

I comforted her, we opened a bottle of wine and I promised to sort out the problems tomorrow.

But tomorrow is Sunday.

We called the landlady and went through our complaints. She was sympathetic. She would get everything fixed during the week. But she said she had rented it furnished and she had nowhere else to put the furniture if we didn't want it. So we relented on that point.

We called our guards at 10am and drove to the penthouse. We were both sad to be leaving it. It is on the fifteenth floor of a tower block with a wonderful view of the city.

But we have to be realistic. We began to sort out what we could fit into the new place. We will take the piano and a few pieces of furniture. We put out some of her clothes to go there and others to be boxed up and go into store. We have collected all sorts of things over the years as souvenirs of our travels. They only have value for us, but we couldn't bear to be parted from them. There again some went to the new flat, some to store.

Then Janina arrived.

We had luckily left a bottle of wine in the fridge. I opened it and we drank to old times and of the many parties we had enjoyed here.

There was a call from the porter in the lobby. Carlos, the Rodeo Grande driver, is here with Snoopy. He had been left on the ranch while we were abroad.

We were very excited to see him. He looked very well, if a little fatter. In the way of dogs who have been left alone for some time, he wasn't very excited to see us. But he did recognise the apartment and seemed pleased to be back.

I had not told the family that I was back in Guayaquil. I don't know why, I guess because they are so antagonistic towards Kate.

Now I got a Whatsapp from my daughter Diana. She had been staying with Ceci while I was away but was returning to Los Angeles tomorrow. She said she was sorry not to have seen me.

So I had to reveal myself. I replied that I had got back yesterday and would come to the house to see her this evening.

She replied at once that the family is having dinner tonight in Alex's new house, which was close to Ceci's. Would I like to come?

I asked Kate if she would mind. She said no problem, Janina will stay with her, I can go and see my family.

At 6pm we drove back to the new flat. I left the girls there and went on to Alex's place with my guards in tow.

It was a very pleasant evening. Ceci, Alex, Javi, Diana and Nick were there. We chatted about the Antarctic trip and I showed them photos, of course not the ones with Kate or her dancing in the snow!

They asked about the new flat, they had heard about our renting it. I said we were not fascinated, but it was only for a year and then hopefully we would buy something.

The next day was Monday. I woke early and showered in cold water (something that I have hated ever since it was compulsory at prep school). Then I tried to find something for breakfast, but the fridge was empty. There was no WIFI so I had no connection with the guards. Eventually, they knocked on the door. They had been waiting for me for an hour in the car outside, while I had been fretfully walking up and down the apartment waiting for them. It was a new relationship.

I drove to the office with them following me and got there at 8am. I found the new safety procedures in place. There was a face recognition control on the door into the office block, a further one in the lift to my fifth-floor office, and one more on my office door. They had set it up with a photo of me, and luckily I was recognised.

I had been away since 21st December, ten weeks. The longest time I had been out of Ecuador in fifty years. There was a lot to catch up with. Despite being in touch with the office while away, I don't have a printer in Madrid and so had many balances and documents to print out and file.

I put together the receipts for the insurance claim. They had accepted our flights from Madrid to London and back, both the Ritz and Savoy hotels, restaurant meals in London, and the train fare to Yorkshire. They inquired where we had stayed in Yorkshire, which was in my house. As I couldn't claim for that, they did accept our spending in Harvey Nicks. So we got the dresses paid for.

Annoyingly, the South African Customs replied, after two months, that they did not accept photocopies of documents for my claim, they wanted the originals. I got them together and sent them off by courier to Pretoria.

In fact, I never did receive the VAT refund.

That happens far too often. Sometimes we get the Air Europa flight back from Madrid. It leaves at 1.30am. By which time the customs office in the airport is closed. Recently we showed our purchases to a customs agent in Barajas and she wouldn't accept the claim on the grounds that the shoes had been worn. Where is that in the rules?

At least with jewelry and watches you can't tell if they have been worn or not.

Every so often colleagues would come in to welcome me back. I had lunch in the company canteen which we call Bandurria. Maria Doloreswho manages it, gave me a big welcome. She is eighty-four years old and has worked with us twenty-six years. She came with her team of caterers when we first opened Bandurria, and is the only person in Agripac older than me.

At 5pm my bodyguards, who had looked after Kate all day, returned to escort me home.

When I got there we compared notes. She said she had enjoyed having protection. She had gone to the supermarket, and they had helped her carry the bags to the car and then to the flat. She had had her hair done. One of the guards stood outside the salon. The other ladies there were intrigued. It made her feel very important. The fact that Pedro is a handsome guy didn't go unnoticed!

We ate bread and cheese that night as the gas contract had not yet been signed, so we couldn't cook.

Her pole dance teacher Karen had come with her husband Frank and installed both the pole in a spare bedroom and the aerial silk from a hook over the balcony.

Frank, a handyman, offered to paint the sitting room walls white. We decided on just the wall opposite the windows. He set to it and that day got the first coat of white paint on. It needs four coats, but even with one, when it was streaky, it looked so much better. The room is lighter. We have brought over a few pieces of our furniture from the penthouse and that makes a difference. There is a limit to what we can do, as it isn't our property, but we are starting to bond with it.

Kate was upset that the place was not even clean when we arrived. There was a layer of dust on everything. The landlady said that she would send a maid over to help get it clean. Yaneth, our daily maid, came too with her niece Emilie. Together with Kate's help, it was soon sparkling.

to offload expensive product at a discount, or even at a loss, in order to replace it with cheaper stock.

The country is in recession, and agriculture is threatened with the Niño current, which could cause widespread flooding. Add to this the insecurity problem of criminal groups demanding protection money. Many farmers just don't plant. Sales have collapsed.

This depressed me.

As HM the Queen once remarked when Windsor Castle caught fire: It is my Annus Horribilis.

School holidays in Guayaquil are from February to April.

This coincides with the hot wet months, when traditionally families would go to their beach houses, where it is a lot cooler. It's certainly not the best time to go to England.

Nick, Almu, Alex and Javier, plus their children, went there at the end of March this year.

Alex went to Tupgill, Nick to Ferngill.

After all, if you live in a hot country then a little cold weather can even be welcome.

I had been a director of Ripon Race Company since my father died in 1979, he in turn had taken over from my grandfather, Bob Armstrong, when he died in 1956. Now I have handed it on to Nick. As the name suggests, the company runs Ripon Racecourse, where horses are raced in the summer. In memory of Bob we named a race The Armstrong Cup. This used to be run the first Monday in August, when we were in England. We would invite sixty friends and host a lunch in a box on the stands.

Nick persuaded the other members of the board to change the date to April 18th this year, so that he can host it. He invited his friends and both my sisters, and maintained the tradition.

The family donated a huge silver cup in 1957, which is competed for each year. The name of the winning owner and horse are inscribed on the base. The prize money is given by the race company and the Horse Racing Levy Board.

All four of them work in Agripac, so for the month of April, while they were away, I was working without them, and that kept me busy.

Which is what I needed to take my mind off problems.

But that didn't help Kate. She was bored with not being able to move about freely or go to Rodeo Grande. So to do something different we asked our protection squad to arrange cover in Quito for the weekend of 5th to 7th April.

It's only a forty-five-minute flight. We were met at Quito airport by the Agripac manager, our good friend Jaime Garces. There were also two bodyguards from Josef's company. It was 7pm when we got there so we drove straight to a restaurant, followed by our escort. We had a lot to chat about, it was an amusing evening. Then Jaime dropped us at our hotel near the airport.

Quito stands at 2,850 mts above sea level and I can't sleep well there. I run out of oxygen and get terrific headaches. The airport is on a plateau 300 meters lower. There I have no problem.

The following day Jaime and the bodyguards, took us to the Mitad del Mundo, the Equatorial line which runs just North of Quito. I had been there many years before, but Kate had never seen it.

There is a monument which you can go inside and guides point out Ecuador's history and culture. There are many cafes and bars to cater for the tourists.

We spent two hours there and took photos of each other straddling the line.

So this year we have touched both the South Pole and the Equator.

Jaime kindly invited us back to his house for a barbeque lunch with his wife Ximena and daughter Juli.

We ate, drank and laughed until darkness fell. Then our escort drove us back to the hotel.

On Sunday morning Kate wanted to go shopping. Our bodyguards drove us to Tumbaco Mall. She loves sports clothes, and has loads of them, but she always needs something new. We went into Marathon Sports and bought some stuff, and then to Nike, which to me was exactly the same range of kit, and bought more. Then we went to Studio F.

We always enjoy this shop. We had first seen it in Cartagena, Colombia. She had joked that this is where putas (prostitutes) shop. They make the most amazing clothes to show off a girl to best advantage. They have jeans which uplift backsides, and other sexy items.

I describe it as a clothes shop designed by men for women, for men.

We had found a branch in Madrid, now there is one in Quito too. Wherever we go they are always busy.

After which it was back to the airport, and a flight to Guayaquil.

Our trip to Quito was only a short break, but better than nothing.

We are not allowed to return to Rodeo Grande. But one Friday in April Fredy brought Cristina, Mati, Isai, Cipriano and the driver Carlos to our apartment, so we could get together. It was the first time we had seen them since that night in December. We recounted happy times, especially the days when we were taking photos for the Agripac calendars, with all the crew there.

Our apartment block has a shared garden and swimming pool. There is a barbeque area too. We went down there.

Fredy is a great cook. He had bought steaks, sausages and potatoes. He prepared lunch for us which we ate with beer and wine. The young lads spent most of the afternoon in the pool, and before they left Cipriano and Carlos borrowed trunks from me, (they stretched them seriously) and went in too.

It was great to see them all again. But there was a cloud over the gathering.

We had not been back to Rodeo since the kidnap, four months ago. We missed the riding and the good times we had enjoyed.

I wonder if we will ever return. We are still traumatized by the kidnap. We will never stay the night there again. That had been a big part of the fun. If we went again we would be heavily escorted by guards, and only for the day. Looking over our shoulders all the time.

I couldn't make any decision yet, but perhaps we will never return.

The 21st April 2024 is an important day for Ecuador.

Daniel Noboa, the young dynamic President, had taken a political risk when he announced a referendum two months ago. Today the population of Ecuador will vote on it. There are ten questions, mostly regarding reforming the police and armed forces to enable them to combat the drug gangs. The most important question of all was to approve extradition of convicted drug lords to the USA.

The importance of this cannot be overstated. When Colombia tried to pass the same law in the 1980s, Pablo Escobar declared war on the state.

Ecuador's prisons are in the hands of the drug gangs. Many judges are corrupt. Anyone arrested has a good chance of going free again. Or if not free, they can operate from prison.

What they all fear is being tried and convicted in the USA, as recently happened with Chapo Guzman, the leader of the Mexican Sinaloa cartel. He got a thirty-year sentence. He will never return to Mexico.

Previous attempts to pass this law have been defeated by politicians in league with the gangs.

Today the measure passed.

Before the end of April Laura Marcos delivered my portrait. She had spent six months working on it. It is quite large, about a metre square. She went into great detail and kept visiting me in the office to get the facts right. She took lots of photos to work with of my desk, the bookcase behind it, the spinning globe which Kate gave me, the color of my jacket, my awards of the OBE and CMG, my face and hands. To my mind she had painted my eyes too blue. I always reckoned that they were green. But both Laura and Kate said they are blue. So blue it is.

Finally, the portrait is finished. She helped me remove it from the frame where it is stretched, and roll it up to fit inside a cardboard tube. It is to go to Tupgill House with Kate and I in May. I am determined to leave something of myself in what is a family museum, alongside a painting of old Bob, and photos of father, Do and other family members.

I took a photo of it and showed it to Kate. She said she liked it. I was not so sure. My face has too many wrinkles. I looked in the mirror and didn't see myself like that. But it cost ten thousand dollars, so I am stuck with it.

We have been back in Ecuador less than two months and are planning to leave again. We want to go to Tupgill, once the family has left. I had promised to see my sister Catherine and her daughter Emilie before they leave for Australia on 25th May.

We have booked appointments both with the eye hospital and with a dermatologist in Madrid.

I have been following the cancer treatment as instructed by Dr Jose Maria. We were supposed to continue it for six weeks, but as we are to leave on 7th May, we would not be able to fulfil the six weeks before we saw him again. We left it until just before we departed to make an appointment. We were to get a very pleasant surprise. I removed my shirt and sat on the operating table. He put a magnifying glass to his eye and looked at the wound without saying anything for several minutes. Then he smiled and said he considered it ninety per cent healed. He congratulated me on having put up with the pain and completed the course. We could now stop using the aggressive cream. He would prescribe a gentle healing cream.

We had thought that we were winning the battle, but to have it confirmed was the best news possible. We will get a second opinion from the Madrid dermatologist.

We told him that we were going on holiday next week. He said, no problem, but don't expose your chest to the sun. Meaning me of course.

You can't stop Kate from exposing hers!

Kate wanted to do something more than just go to Tupgill and then to our place in Madrid. Her sister Luisa had recently been to Morocco, and said that she loved it. Could we go?

OK, why not. I sent a message to Chinmay of Explorations. He put me on to Anthea (call me Aggie) who deals with Africa. We began a text conversation. I am wary of staying too long in the same hotel so said that we would go for just four days to Marrakech. She suggested hotels. The best was La Mamounia. As always we chose the most expensive option. But it does look special. It has history too. Winston Churchill used to spend part of the British winter there from 1935 for several years.

Aggie suggested she book us a suite overlooking the swimming pool. She put together a program. We will fly from Madrid on the 20th May, it's just two hours to Marrakech. We will be met by their Morocco agent and driven to the hotel. There is a program for each day there.

It looks fascinating.

So we paid in advance. We just needed cash for shopping and tips. She advised us to take euros rather than pounds or dollars, as they are accepted everywhere.

Morocco had been a French colony and French was still widely spoken, along with Arabic, and of course English.

Janina called us excitedly. She has received her British visa. We had talked of her coming to stay with us in Tupgill, but until she had the visa it was only talk. Now we could plan. We will fly from Guayaquil to Amsterdam on the 7th May, stay the night of the 8th there and fly on to Teesside on the 9th.

She will go first to Barcelona to see her cousin, then she will fly to England. Which airport should she use? I remembered I had once flown from Barcelona to Leeds/Bradford Airport. It is only an hour from Tupgill. She will arrive at midday. That was before us, as we get into Teesside at 5pm.

I called Leo. He will send a taxi to collect Janina. I asked that the driver have a card with her name, as she doesn't speak much English.

On the 7th May we flew on KLM from Guayaquil to Amsterdam. We stayed in L'Europe Hotel once again.

After checking in, we walked to Dam Square. Kate wanted to go to a strange Gothic shop where we have been several times before. It is very weird. It's decorated with witches and broomsticks. The gothic dresses are all black, but surprisingly they look very attractive on Kate. They are not expensive, the downside is that the black dye they use is not fast colour. It will stain a white handbag. Despite this we bought three dresses.

After leaving this shop we passed a cafe selling marihuana. We went in and bought a couple of smokes and two beers. I have never got high on it as I don't inhale, but it gives a pleasant sensation.

Then we walked to Indrapura again. We are birds of tradition. After another good dinner we walked back to the hotel.

We had to circumvent a street protest in favour of the Palestinians. These are happening all over Europe as the Israeli/Palestinian war in Gaza rages on, with ever more casualties on the Palestinian side.

Reaching the hotel we went into Freddy's bar for a nightcap, or two.

These were my undoing. During the night I got out of bed to go to the bathroom. I didn't put on a light so as not to wake Kate, and in the dark I fell over a suitcase cutting the inside of my right elbow badly on a piece of furniture. Despite my startled cry Kate didn't wake up. I felt my way to the bathroom, closed the door and put on the light. I was appalled by the amount of blood. I thought of calling the reception for a doctor or nurse. But on reflection I didn't want it bandaged, as removing the bandage would be painful with the skin sticking to it. My skin is so thin that it would tear.

The solution was to wrap a towel around it and return to bed and try to get some sleep.

In the morning I got up with the daylight at 5am and returned to the bathroom. I peeled off the bloody towel. I couldn't use the shower as that would hurt, so I ran a bath and soaked it in, with my right arm propped on the edge of the bath. I dabbed at the wound with a sponge and managed to clean it up considerably. The wound isn't that big, but it is on the inside of my elbow where the veins are prominent. It seems to be bleeding less now. I will survive.

I dressed and put on a shirt. The sleeve immediately was stained red, but with a jacket over it it didn't show.

When Kate woke I told her about it, then we went down for a late breakfast .

I was gaining confidence. Though it hurt, it wasn't noticeable.

At the airport to pass security I had to remove my jacket.

There was immediate concern. "Are you badly hurt Sir? Do you need a doctor?"

I replied "No thank you, I fell in the bathroom. I am on my way home and will see a doctor there". With that they let me pass.

Teesside airport has bad memories for Kate. She came to visit me in Tupgill in May last year and had been detained for two hours in immigration, while I fretted and fumed outside. I asked to be allowed in to help clarify the situation, I even appealed to them that we were colleagues with my being ex-consul of the FCO.

But of course UK Border Control is the other house, the Home Office.

Eventually they let her in with a promise that she would leave in three days, which of course was when we were leaving anyway.

The problem is that Kate had been denied entry to the UK at Heathrow in 2016. We think someone tipped them off to make trouble for her. She had a visa and was going to stay with me at Tupgill after a few days in London. She was interviewed and when they rang Tupgill the housekeeper said she didn't know her. She tried to call me in Madrid, but I didn't pick up.

I was in the opera at the time, and phones are prohibited.

They made out that she was lying and deported her back to Madrid.

For the last two years Colombians haven't needed a visa to visit the UK. Now I see that sadly they have been reimposed.

Since the May 2023 incident she has entered the UK twice with no problem. Once when we arrived at Heathrow and once onboard the Queen Mary II.

But memories are long at Teesside.

This time, as we were together, I didn't anticipate problems.

But once again she was asked to wait. The few passengers quickly passed. A friendly agent apologized and said he had to check on her. Would she be staying with me?

Yes at the Forbidden Corner, did he know it?

"Yes indeed, my children love it."

It took half an hour. I asked why it was only Teesside that had to check each time. He said because of her record she would always be questioned here. That's annoying as it's the nearest airport to Tupgill.

So we got out, collected our bags and met Leo and Janina who had both come to meet us.

Leo drove us home in my Range Rover. He and I talked in English and the girls in Spanish.

We left our suitcases in the bedroom and went straight to the kitchen with Leo and Janina, where we got stuck into the wine, cheese and pork pie.

When we finally went to bed I peeled off my shirt. There was some blood on the sleeve, but not too much. I put that shirt and the two others with blood stains into a washbasin and filled it with cold water. Tomorrow they will be washed and I was sure there would be no marks left.

We stayed a pleasant five days in Tupgill. We had come to say goodbye to Catherine and Emilie before they left for Brisbane. In fact we spent a lot of time with them and Jane. We went walking on the moor, ate together in the Saddleroom restaurant and the Forbidden Corner cafe.

I showed them my portrait. They were polite, if not enthusiastic.

I had to get it framed. There is a shop in Leyburn which does this. We took it in, removed it from its tube and laid it out on the floor. Wendy, who served there, said that it was bigger than they normally dealt with. She would call her workshop to see if they could handle it. They said yes, so we paid a deposit and left it. No more tube to carry about.

Wendy, after asking where we lived, said she was going on holiday to South America tomorrow to Bolivia and Peru, to climb mountains in Bolivia and to see Machu Picchu in Peru. We talked about both countries which I know, and wished her well.

The frame will be ready in six weeks.

Then we went to Campbells, an excellent grocers and wine merchant. We stocked up on food and Burgundy wines, which are my favorites. We are having dinner at Tupgill tonight with Leo.

Finally we had a beer and snack lunch in the Bolton Arms Hotel.

While there, an elderly couple sitting at another table kept looking at us. Eventually they asked if we were the people who had been kidnapped in Ecuador. We said yes. They said they were so happy that we had been released. They had prayed for us.

Tupgill is a crazy house. It was designed and built by my great friend Malcolm Tempest over seven years. I let him have his wicked way with interior decoration and that resulted in themed bedrooms. There is the Medieval room, with knights in armour in the bathroom, the Chinese room, the Arabic room, the Tudor room and best of all the Indian room, which is mine. He even went to India and brought back a carpet, especially made for it, wooden Mughal arches and furnishings. On the arches are small plaques depicting scenes of people copulating, copied from an Indian temple. The bathroom features an enormous shower with tiles depicting a jungle scene. You can activate a sound system. The shower becomes a tropical downpour from three points, and you get the jungle noises to go with it.

The bathroom floor is a huge mosaic of a peacock. It had taken a skilled man several weeks to place the pieces, like a giant jigsaw puzzle.

Downstairs we limited him to fun themes in the toilets. One has a frieze showing the seven deadly sins and figures being carried down to hell by devils with three-pronged spears. We point out to visitors that the majority are women!

The other bathroom is decorated with a skull motif on the wallpaper. As an unsuspecting lady sits on the lavatory a sensor is activated, a trapdoor in the floor opens and a workman sticks his head up to ask if he can start work now.

Several ladies have bolted from there.

Leo and I took Kate and Janina to the cellar. It's connected by underground passage to the Mausoleum. This is the scary part of the Forbidden Corner experience.

Kate had already seen it, but we managed to frighten Janina with the lady in the mirror, the coffins with the talking dead and the hanged lady in white who screams.

We looked with Leo at where we will hang the new portrait. On the staircase there is a painting of my grandfather Bob, mounted on a white horse. The painting was done by a local artist when we finished rebuilding Tupgill in 2011. It's based on a photo taken about 1910, when the family lived at Eamont Bridge in Cumbria.

I will move Bob to one side and put my painting next to him.

There is another portrait on a nearby wall. It's of Thomas Lamplugh archbishop of York in 1640. We claim him as an ancestor.

Grandfather Bob married above his status, as it was thought of in those days, when he married Eleanor Lamplough (the spelling varies) in 1895.

She, on the other hand, stooped to conquer, literally.

The Armstrongs were short. Both Bob and Gerald were jockeys. The lamploughs were tall people. I get my height from that side of the family.

Jimmy Clark was my godfather (his mother was a Lamplough). He emigrated to South Africa as a young man and built a successful business. I stayed at his house when I first went to Johannesburg, on my way to Swaziland in 1966.

I had volunteered with IVS (International Voluntary Service) to do a year's secondment there. I worked with a cooperative of 200 small dairy farmers. My duties included collecting their milk churns every day and taking them to the nearby dairy. Also once a week I had to supervise that every one of the cattle passed through a dip in which insecticide was mixed. This is to kill ticks which spread the deadly redwater fever.

Uncle Jimmy was the source of support and good advice both when I was growing up, and when I started my own business. He died some years ago at the ripe old age of ninety-two.

Early on the 14th May, Leo drove us to Northallerton. Kate, Janina and I took the London train.

Kate and I were returning to the Ritz Hotel, which we had enjoyed so much. Janina was meeting her Ecuadorian cousin Joanna. They have booked an Air B and B flat.

On arriving in King's Cross, we went first to the Ritz. Joanna met us there. After we checked in we asked the hall porter where Shepherd's Market is. He said it is only a few minutes' walk away.

We walked there dragging their bags between us. It was not easy to find. We used GPS and found the address, or where it should have been, but it wasn't. We went to a pub, ordered a gin and tonic each and asked the bartender if he knew the address. He did, it was around the corner. The street numbering is a mystery here.

Kate and I left them to go to the flat and unpack. We walked back to the Ritz. We unpacked and then had a siesta until we met them again at 7pm in the Ritz bar.

I searched my memory for places where I used to eat in London, when I frequented it many years ago. One of the best was Bentley's Oyster Bar. It is close to the hotel in Swallow Street.

We walked there. You can either eat out in the street, which curiously is a covered area that practically closes off the street, or inside. It was quite cold so we opted for inside. We ordered an excellent Meursault white wine to go with the oysters and lobster. A wonderful meal, but it didn't leave much change out of a thousand pounds!

The next morning Kate slept late, so I went for breakfast alone at 9am.

The Ritz dining room is a splendid place with a high ceiling, tall windows and waiters in tailcoats. It seems to be a venue for working breakfasts. There are several groups who ate little and talk a lot. An Indian Babu came in with a young and pretty lady in an orange sari. She went to and fro to the kitchen and served him. It appears that only she is allowed to serve his food. The waiters didn't interfere. He is obviously a regular customer.

My mother had occasionally served kedgeree for breakfast. I hadn't had it for many years. It was on the menu, so I chose it.

I didn't like it. It was prepared with curry powder, and a bit too much of an Indian dish for breakfast. I was sorry not to have had the kippers or smoked haddock.

Afterwards I found a copy of the Times in the lobby and sat and read that, before returning to the room. Kate was getting dressed.

We wondered what to do today. Our friends had their plan to see London by Red Bus. It was the first time for both of them.

Shopping is not on the agenda, to Kate's dismay. A trip to Harrods is a step too far.

We decided to walk to Trafalgar Square and visit the National Gallery.

I have been there many years ago, Kate never.

It was a very pleasant surprise. For a start it was both free entrance, and not crowded, so no waiting in line.

We spent nearly three hours there, wandering from room to room admiring the paintings.

Most of the artists were not known to us, but none the worse for that. We had been to the Prado in Madrid and seen the famous Velazquez, Rubens, Rafael and El Greco paintings. We had been to the Van Gogh Museum in Amsterdam and the Louvre in Paris.

We are not experts, but we like what we like.

Eventually we were hungry, Kate had missed breakfast. We left the museum without much idea of where we could find something to eat.

We circled around behind it and found ourselves in Leicester Square. I had heard of it, but have never been there before. And surprise, it is filled with restaurants. Though most of them are Italian. We chose one and, as it was a warm afternoon, we sat outside under an umbrella. We both had fish and chips. I have always enjoyed it. Kate has developed a craving for it while in England. Her vegetarian days are coming to an end.

She had aperol spritz and me a beer.

Then we wandered on, hand in hand. London is full of tourists, and we became tourists too. We walked down Whitehall, past Horseguards and Downing Street. Currently it's home to Rishi Sunak, but there is an election on 4th July and it seems likely that Sir Keir Starmer will be the next occupant.

We got to Parliament Square and headed to St James Park.

There was an old man feeding the pigeons, squirrels, ducks and geese. We watched fascinated as they flocked to him each time he scattered food. Kate, dressed in her low-cut, long black gothic dress, hitched it up and climbed over the fence at the side of the path. She sat on the lawn on the other side and tried to attract the squirrels to her, pretending she had feed. The old gentleman kindly gave her his bag of food. Now they really did come to her. She wanted to feed the squirrels and a brown goose, but the pigeons were very aggressive, shooing the others away. She held out her arms and they landed on them. I stood on the path taking lots of photos. She attracted a crowd of people, she is the Dama de las Palomas (rather than the Camellias).

Eventually the bag was empty. She got up and climbed back over the fence. We thanked the birdman. Kate insisted that we pay for the food. I gave him ten pounds, and he seemed very pleased. Only then did it occur to me that he did this for a living.

Crossing the park we arrived at St James Palace and from there walked to the Ritz.

It was now 6.30pm. We were due to meet Janina and Joanna in the Ritz bar at 7.30pm. We had time to go to the room and freshen up. But before that I asked the hall porter to reserve the Veeraswamy restaurant for tonight. Once again it is an old favourite. It's in Regent Street on the corner of Swallow Street, in fact right next to Bentley's Oyster Bar.

Established in 1926, it's one of the oldest Indian restaurants in London.

We emerged from there at midnight, after an excellent meal and a lot of wine. We set off to walk back, Kate and I to the hotel and the girls to Shepherd's Market. But seeing a bicycle cab we hailed it to take them, as it was a longish walk, in their present happy state. The cab had an outsized speaker and was blaring music. The driver was an extroverted cockney lad. He declared that he was in love with Kate, and had her in fits of laughter when he propositioned her, saying that he has a big dick.

He was disappointed that she was not part of the fare, just Janina and Joanna.

We said goodnight and he peddled away. We could hear his music blaring for several minutes afterwards.

Tomorrow we will fly back to Madrid from Heathrow and they are going to Barcelona from Stansted Airport. We will see them again in Madrid. They will stay with us the night before they fly back to Guayaquil.

At Heathrow Terminal Five, after we checked in and passed security, there is a Harry Ramsden restaurant. I explained to Kate that it is the most famous fish and chip shop in Britain. So once again we ate fish and chips. It was very good too.

There is a WH Smith bookshop. I went in to get the Economist magazine. Then browsing the book selection I bought one called The Gentleman from Peru by Andre Aciman.

What a wonderful story it is, of love lost and found. It's mystical with time, not a constant. A book I will always remember.

Four days after we returned to Madrid we left for Marrakech.

The holiday was expertly planned by Aggie.

This is feature of Explorations. Their holidays are expensive, but top of the range. One is guided and looked after, which might take some of the excitement out of doing it on your own, but is much more comfortable. We got our first taste of this on arriving at Marrakech airport.

We were met at the door of the plane by a lady and escorted through the diplomatic line at immigration. When we saw the thousands of people waiting in line there we relished the service. They will surely be there an hour or more. I have always wondered why it is that immigration officers are never present in sufficient numbers to process the crowd quickly.

I didn't see how many booths were manned today. But I have been in Madrid and Amsterdam where there are say twenty booths, but only four officers.

We then collected our luggage and were taken to a waiting limousine.

Ibrahim, the driver, will accompany us for the next four days.

It took about half an hour to get to the hotel. We drove from the airport down wide roads into a surprisingly modern city on the outskirts, and then to the narrower streets in the centre. We drove alongside the huge ochre-coloured city walls, topped with Arabic balustrades. The walls are pockmarked with holes. Ibrahim explained that was for the scaffolding when the walls were repaired. But that didn't seem right. The holes were in no sort of order. It looked totally random.

Then we turned in through an enormous gateway in the city walls and shortly afterwards arrived at the impressive gates of La Mamounia Hotel. The car was checked by a uniformed guard, and we were allowed to pass through and stopped under a huge portico.

A porter took our luggage and another showed us to reception. The lobby and ground floor are impressive with high ceilings and Arabic arches decorated with mosaics.

It was dimly lit with lots of tiny lamps, giving it a romantic thousand-and-one Arabian nights effect.

We were shown to our suite on the third floor which is large and airy. The walls are decorated with intricate tiled wainscoting. The doors have beautiful inlays and each doorway is an Arabic arch. The bed is huge and covered in lots of pillows and cushions. The bathroom contains spacious twin washbasins and there is both a shower and a bath.

Thankfully there is ample room for all Kate's many lotions and cosmetics, without infringing on my space. The sitting room has a large sofa, two comfortable chairs and a balcony overlooking the swimming pool.

We immediately went to the balcony, as I guess most people do.

We could see the outsized swimming pool below us. To one side was a restaurant with tables with umbrellas over them. It was six pm. People were having drinks there.

Beyond the pool are palm trees stretching away into the distance and finally the city walls. We were told that the hotel grounds cover seventeen acres.

Incredible at the very heart of the city.

We quickly unpacked and I hung up my jackets and trousers, Kate her dresses, then we showered. Kate put on a pair of white shorts and top, and covered them with a long transparent shirt. She wore sandals which laced up her calves.

I rose to the occasion wearing my pink blazer. We went down to the poolside bar.

There are lots of cats around. We asked a waiter who said there are nine of them. They belong to the hotel.

We began the night with a couple of gin and tonics each and then moved to the dining room. In fact we walked to another part of the garden and once again sat outside. It is pleasantly warm. We were told that by July it would be too hot to sit outside, but May is a lovely month. There is a choice of four restaurants. We chose to begin with Le Marocain, traditional Moroccan food.

Lamb cooked slowly in earthenware pots is the famous dish. I opted for this while Kate had fish.

We drank Moroccan wine, which was surprisingly good.

The lamb was exquisite. It was served in oil and was full of flavour from the many herbs used to cook it. I sadly ate too much and spent part of the night in the bathroom. I had been to Morocco before and knew the form. Imodium came to the rescue.

Kate, who has a stronger tummy than mine, suffered no problem.

The next morning we got up at 9am and began our exploration of Marrakech. First we went down to the poolside restaurant and had breakfast.

It was so delightful sitting in the warmth with little birds coming to pick crumbs from the floor, and the table too, if you let them (where are the cats when they are needed?).

At ten o'clock Ibrahim was waiting for us with the car. Today we are to see Le Jardin Majorelle, created by the French painter Jacques Majorelle in the first half of the last century. We met our guide, Nourie, a man in his fifties, he wore the traditional long jalabiya.

There were a lot of tourists there already. The garden is more shady walks below tall trees and palms, than flowers. There are a number of water features flowing in blue-painted troughs and ponds. Apparently that color of blue was the artist's trademark. Today it's seen all over Marrakech on house walls.

Within the garden is the Yves Saint Laurent Museum. He bought the garden some years after Majorelle died, restored it and built his house there. When he in turn died his ashes were scattered in the garden. As it was our first day of the holiday we took far too many photos of each other with Nourie, and he took them of us. They were very repetitive, we only kept the best ten.

Our tour here lasted an hour and then Nourie took us to the El Bahia Palace which is a former home of the royal family. It's empty of furniture but has the most wonderfully decorated floors, walls and ceilings in Arabic tiles. There is a magnificent courtyard with tiled floor and fountains, surrounded with blue arches.

I found it fascinating, but as Kate soon lost interest, we didn't stay long.

The next item on the agenda was lunch. We drove through the centre of the city and stopped outside what seemed to be an ordinary house. Inside it was quite dark. We were shown upstairs. Kate held my hand to make sure I didn't trip over anything (a frequent event). We got to a landing, then there were more stairs and yet more, until we emerged on the flat roof where there is a garden and pergola. Nourie explained that this is common in Marrakech as before air conditioning families ate on the roof to take advantage of the cooling breezes. The food was mainly salads, but it was tasty and was washed down with Casablanca beer.

Nourie suggested that after lunch we go to El Badi Palace and Madrasa Ben Youssef, but Kate wanted to go to the souk of the Medina and buy something. So that is where we went.

Having Nourie with us was a great help. He is well known in the souk and chatted to each stall holder, thus we were spared the relentless pressure to buy that we had experienced the last time I had been to Morocco with Ceci and the family, nearly twenty years ago. We had hated it and quickly left the souk for more modern shops with fixed prices.

That trip was memorable, as that was where Steve proposed marriage to Diana. He did it in a very theatrical way. We were having dinner at a restaurant with a band playing and people dancing. He got up from the table and walked over to the band master. He asked him to stop playing for a few minutes as he has an announcement to make. The music stopped, the dancers walked back to their tables. Then Steve asked Diana to come onto the dance floor, he got down on one knee and asked her for her hand. Everyone applauded, and of course we cried.

Kate soon found a dress shop she liked and began to try them on. We bought two kaftan dresses, one pink, one white with red borders. I did my best at negotiating the price but probably paid too much. We are very happy with them. They look lovely on her.

We left that shop and walked down the narrow covered way in the souk dodging motorbikes as we went. We found a shop selling brass urns and bought an Alladin's lamp.

There was an elderly street musician sitting on the ground with an extraordinarily long, three-stringed guitar. He gestured for Kate to sit by him to have her photo taken. She did and he took a red fez and put it on her head. I thought she might object to this as the man was none too clean, but no, she enjoyed it. It's a great photo.

We emerged into the Jemaa el-Fna square where there are stalls selling fruit and sticky cakes. We were given figs at one stall, an orange at another, and offered snails at a third. We left the snails. They are very friendly people and gave us freebies even if we bought nothing from them.

Then we saw the snake charmers, or rather we heard the music first and headed their way. A man sat on the ground banging a drum, another stood and played a flute while a cobra reared up from a basket. A third man held a water snake in his hands and offered it to passing girls, all of whom refused to hold it.

Kate is made of sterner stuff. She has done this several times before. Once was in Jaipur in India, once on the Charles Bridge in Prague and once in Times Square in New York. The Indian snake was a cobra. The others were thick, heavy pythons. Each time the snake had been laid around her neck. They writhed all the time.

I sided with the wimps and refused to hold them.

Today's snake was only four-feet long and an inch in diameter. She put it around her neck and held the head in one hand and the tail in the other, while I took photos and made a video of it.

Then as we left the square we saw monkeys on chains. But they looked so sad. We didn't stop to see what tricks the poor things did.

The day's tour was over. We thanked Nourie with a tip and went back to the hotel with Ibrahim.

After changing clothes, Kate put on her pink kaftan dress and we went to the Churchill bar in the hotel. It's very small, only eight people can sit at the bar. We were told that it is the ideal place to chat to strangers. But we didn't, even though we occupied the last two seats. As in Dubai, we have to be very drunk to strike up casual friendships.

We each had a whisky and left to eat in the Asian restaurant.

Churchill is well remembered at the hotel. There is a Churchill suite too. It's the most expensive in the hotel. On seeing the price we decided that we would leave the great man in peace.

On Wednesday our agenda was for a tasting tour of the markets at 5pm so we had the rest of the day to ourselves.

We slept late and as we had missed breakfast we got room service at midday. Once again the birds arrived on the balcony to help us eat it. This time they were pigeons.

Then in the afternoon we tried the swimming pool. Kate put on a tiny white bikini, I donned my usual baggy trunks. To allow for Muslim sensibilities we covered up with dressing gowns and walked to the pool.

There were a lot of people taking a late lunch, but only one or two bathers. There was a little girl paddling in the shallow part and a man who swam length after length, which I supposed was his daily exercise.

hills and said that the women have to walk down to the streams in the valley every day to carry water back home. I asked if there was electricity. He said yes. Then I asked why did the village not buy a small pump and avoid the backbreaking work of carrying water.

He had no answer to this.

As we drove further up the mountain we came to a small town. He told us that this is the centre both for commerce, health and education. The villages have primary schools, here there are secondary ones. I asked if girls get secondary education. He said that there was no discrimination, but unless the girl has a relative in town to live with the conservative villagers would not allow her to attend school.

Marrakech stands at 500 metres above sea level. Here I measured the height on my phone and it is 1,200 meters. It now seems to be a more humid area, there are more trees and greenery. We drove out of the town and a few miles further on we arrived at the Hotel Olinto, Atlas Mountain Retreat.

This is an oasis of shady gardens with paths winding between pools. It has a wonderful view down the mountains. We compared it to the Graff estate in Stellenbosch.

This is where we had a splendid fish lunch with white wine.

It was built and is owned by an Italian gentleman. He has his bungalow to one side of it.

We stayed there for two hours and then made our way down the mountains and back to La Mamounia.

Friday was our last day in Marrakech. We will fly back to Madrid at 8pm. We began the day with breakfast by the pool. Kate wanted to buy more scented wood and a second burner to give to her mother. Ibrahim took us to the same shop to get it. Then we had to return to the hotel and check out by midday.

The plan for the afternoon was a tour of the city by motorbike and sidecar. We will be collected at the hotel at

2.30pm and after three hours delivered to Ibrahim, who will take us to the airport.

The motorbikes are old-fashioned Russian Urals, copied from the 1938 edition of a BMW. The engines thumped, just as I had heard the motorbike on the kidnap. There are two bikes, ridden by young men. Each with its sidecar for one person.

It was difficult to make conversation while we were on the move, with the noise of the engines and the wind, plus the helmets we had on. But from time to time we stopped and they explained where we were.

We began in Medina. This time it was others who had to jump out of the way as we roared through the souk. Kate's bike was in front. She turned around laughing, and took photos of me as I grimaced each time we almost hit someone.

We saw the city walls, and examples of the earthquake damage to mosques and older buildings constructed of mud bricks. Then we left the old town and sped through the new. Here the streets are wide and there are large houses with gardens. We passed the royal palace. The king, Mohamed VI, rotates around several towns in Morocco and has a palace in each one.

After a while we got thirsty and asked the lads where we could get a beer. They took us to a modern bar. We invited them to have beers too, which they accepted, and then we chatted about all sorts of things. They had seen our kidnap from Google, and we retold the story. They are Muslims but seemed at ease drinking beer. They described life in the city. Morocco, and especially Marrakech, has more tourists than any other country in Africa. So the people have adapted to Western habits. A big part of the population earns its living from tourism.

Time went by and then we had to find Ibrahim and the car. They knew where to meet him.

Once we arrived at the car we said goodbye to them, gave the appropriate tip and headed towards the airport. Here we said goodbye to Ibrahim and thanked him for all his kindness over the last four days.

Now, back in Madrid I have to face my eye operation. On Monday 27th May, I had my first appointment with Dra Martinez de Carneros. We walked to her clinic on Calle Velazques. There seemed to be a lot of people waiting to see her.

We announced ourselves at the reception and took seats in the waiting room. We wondered where we were in the queue. But there is no queue. We were summoned within five minutes. We saw that there was not just one but about ten doctors. Most are young, female, and pretty. They do the preparatory work of tests until the patient finally gets to see Dra Martinez herself. I was taken from booth to booth, sat on stools and gazed into machines. Some with letters I had to read, others with red and green lights. Kate stood behind me. After half an hour we met Dra Martinez.

She was very friendly, "Hi, I am Paloma Martinez".

She looked at the tests and then did one or two more herself. "You have very serious cataracts. You should have had them operated on long ago. I will operate on your right eye first on Thursday. The left eye a week later."

We left her and were taken to another lady doctor who took a blood sample and made a prescription of many eye drops to be used from today until the operation. We were given the address of the clinic which was in another part of Madrid, and I was instructed not to eat or drink twelve hours before the operation, which was scheduled for 11am Thursday.

Though we had been told that it is painless, I left with foreboding.

I have had few operations in my life, and am very scared of them.

The next day we went to see the other specialist, a dermatologist, Dra Maria del Mar Martin.

This was a happy diagnosis. I removed my shirt to show the skin cancer. She looked at it carefully and said "What cancer?

You don't have it anymore ". I was ecstatic. We had thought that it had gone in Guayaquil, Doctor Jose Maria said he was 90% sure. Now it is 100%. She made a prescription for creams to apply to the area to build up the skin, as it is very thin.

We left her and got a taxi back to our apartment.

Tonight we will celebrate. Jorge Cepeda is in Madrid. Also, Janina and Joanna have arrived from Barcelona. They are staying with us tonight and then flying home to Guayaquil tomorrow. Finally, Kate called her sister Luisa, who is studying psychiatry in Madrid. We all met at the apartment. I told them my good news and opened the champagne.

After several bottles, we made our way at 9pm to the restaurant Arde, which is by Alcala.

It was a fun evening with laughter and jokes.

I have known Jorge for more than forty years. We are both in the agrochemical business, we first worked for multinationals, and now we have our own businesses.

The day of the operation came. We had been instructed that today Kate, who was acting as my nurse, has to put eye drops to dilate the pupils of my right eye. She has to do this every half hour for three hours. At 11am we arrived at the clinic. We went to the reception and paid for the operation by credit card. Then we sat and waited for my turn to go into the theatre. From time to time an assistant shone a torch in my eye and then put more drops. The dilation was taking its time.

Finally, after kissing Kate goodbye, I was led into the theater, and put on a gown. The nurses were very chatty and talked to me as a needle was inserted in my hand and connected to a bottle on a stand. I had to be partially sedated. Then a drop of anaesthetic was put in my right eye.

I was put on a stretcher and wheeled into the operating room. There, they positioned me under the laser. My right eye was held open by a plastic mask. I was told it wouldn't hurt but I must not move my head.

It only took a minute. I envisaged needles going into my eye. But it was just a red light flashing. When the light turned green, that was it.

After that I fell asleep so I didn't see the second part of the operation.

It was described to me. I was wheeled to where Dra Martinez was. She and another surgeon used a machine to suck the broken particles of the cataracts from my eye. Then a lens was inserted by robot in the center of the pupil.

Finally, I was taken to a ward to rest.

I woke up about an hour later and walked back to where Kate waited. There was no patch on the eye, not even dark glasses. We left the clinic and went to a pharmacy to get the prescription items. Another list of eye drops, both for the post-op on the right eye and pre-op of the left one.

I woke the next day with my right eye blurred, but it gradually cleared during the day. Then after three days I began to notice the difference. By closing my left eye and looking only with my right one. The walls of the apartment, which I thought cream coloured, are white. A picture we have of Marilyn Monroe is so much more colourful than I had thought. It is a world of difference.

I now couldn't wait to do the left eye.

Apart from health issues, we had come to Madrid to look for a bigger apartment. The one we have is only a hundred and fifty square metres. It has three bedrooms but Kate has turned one of them into her walk-in wardrobe. So we have one room for us and one spare for guests. But its not so much extra bedrooms we need, as a bit more living space. If I am to continue working when we live in Madrid I need an office. She for her part wants somewhere to put her pole and aerial silk, ideally in a room with a high ceiling, as well as more space to hang her clothes and display her shoes and bags.

We had looked at some apartments the last time we were in Madrid with our estate agent friend Sylvia. She offered to show us more.

We went to visit our lawyer Rodrigo and told him about it. He suggested we talk to two friends of his who are renovating a building in Calle Hermosilla. It's a complete renovation, only the noble nineteenth-century facade is still standing, as it's listed. All the building behind it has been demolished. They will rebuild with two brand new apartments on each floor. There will be a lot of shared facilities as well. The basement will have storage space for each apartment. The first floor will be a gym and swimming pool. There will be five floors of apartments and the sixth will be a common garden, barbeque area and jacuzzi.

We met them the next day, the architect and the two developers.

They were very enthusiastic about it, claiming that it will be one of the best addresses in Madrid.

They told us the price, which was over our budget, but suggested that it could be negotiable. A big plus was that it didn't have to be paid for all at once. On signing the contract we would pay 10%, and then stage payment until the building was finished in March 2026.

They will send us details and a draft contract.

Now we were excited. We would have to sell our place first, but perhaps we could do that shortly before we were to move into the new one? Maybe we could negotiate to sell and remain there for a month or two?

We decided we will go and see it on our own. We were not far away as Rodrigo's office is in Calle Velasquez. We walked down Calle Hermosilla. We noted the shops as we went by. Where we live now has an excellent deli, a small supermarket, a Chino which never seems to close, and several good bars and restaurants.

Ideally, we would have liked to buy in the same street, but for the moment we can't find anything we like, or within the price range we are prepared to pay.

The shops in Hermosilla are mainly boutiques. Even before we even got to the building Kate had pulled me into two of them, so we were carrying several carrier bags by the time we arrived.

We did find a deli and two restaurants, one of which we sampled, it was good.

Then we arrived at the site.

It has a handsome facade, five large windows wide each with a small decorative balcony. There are tall trees in the street which restrict the light on the first two floors, so we preferred the fourth one. We had been given the choice of the first or fourth floors.

But there is no garage. Kate wants to buy a car, so we can get out of Madrid on weekends.

We could perhaps drive to nearby Toledo, or much further afield to other parts of Spain or even Portugal or France.

There are underground municipal car parks close by. But they seldom come up for rent, anyway it's not convenient if you have luggage.

That is the first downside.

Others were to come. We received the plans and contract. A feature of Spanish building plans is that you are quoted a number of square metres. But that includes your percentage of the shared areas of the building. As this one has an uncommonly large area for the gym, pool and rooftop, plus an internal garden as the lightwell, we would buy 400 square meters but occupy only 240 meters. So when they quoted a price per metre it seems about right, but on the actual living area it becomes nearly twice that!

Another problem is that it was a complete rebuild, and not a renovation. Because of this the VAT tax is 10% and not 6%. On selling ours we would be subject to 25% capital gains tax, plus the agent's fee. Then there are the usual municipal taxes and lawyer's fees.

We began to get cold feet.

Of course, we would have the same problem with any property we bought or sold.

Where we live at the moment we have a neighbour on the same floor of the building. Gloria, our cleaner, works for him too. I asked her if she had ever heard that he wanted to sell. She said no, but she would ask him. Apparently he would sell if we offered him a really good price, but equally he would like to buy ours.

Either way it could be interesting. If we are going to sell it's better a private deal as we avoid the 4% agents fee. If we bought his place then we don't have to sell ours. We knock down the wall between them and join them up. His is a bit smaller than ours, only two bedrooms, so say 120 meters. Between the two we would have two hundred and seventy metres, more than Hermosilla.

So we wrote him a note saying please come and have a glass of wine with us and we can talk about it 'You can make a price and we will either buy or sell.'

Many years ago my partner in Agripac had made me the same offer. It's brilliant. If I go too low he will buy, if I go too high he will sell. At that time I was so keen to buy that I probably overpaid.

The neighbour left on a trip to France without replying. But we have planted the seed. It's always good to know that you have a buyer, if you ever want to sell.

The next day was Sunday. It is hot outside. We went for lunch at Patio de Leones next to Alcala. We sat in the outside area under umbrellas. They have a system of water sprays into the air, which keeps it cooler.

Afterwards we crossed the road to the Retiro Park. This is a favourite place of ours. Being Sunday it is full of people. There are families with children, groups of young people and lovers two by two, both walking and lying on the grass, displaying bodies either white or tanned. We can smell marihuana. There are people on bikes, skateboards and roller blades. There are people walking dogs. This is where we will bring Snoopy when we live full time in Madrid.

To cater to all these people there are buskers playing instruments, street artists who will paint your portrait, and magicians. Years ago there used to be Africans selling knock-off high-end handbags. They would display them on a blanket, but at the first sign of the police they picked up the blanket with everything inside and legged it. Now we don't see them.

We walked up and down the many roads under shady trees. Kate doesn't like to get a tan on arms and legs only. If she is going to do it, then it must be done properly with only a bikini bottom on. Today is not the time or place for that.

There are several cafes where you can get a beer, soft drink or a sandwich. We made our way to one, drank a beer and watched the antics of the pigeons which plagued the tables.

The Retiro is open until late in the summer. Not so in the winter when it closes at dusk, about six o'clock.

Once, Kate was here with her Colombian friend Paola in the winter. They were rollerblading. They stayed too late and found that they were locked in. In desperation they called the police who said that there was a gate at Atocha which stays open late.

Retiro is a very large park, and Atocha, the railway terminus, is a long way away.

It was getting dark and was very cold as they ran to find the gate. Luckily it was still open.

I had laughed at this and suggested they should have called the fire brigade.

We had seen them block an entire street with two fire engines and twenty officers just to rescue a cat from a tree.

Surely they would have rescued two shivering girls.

Kate has spent a lot of time in Madrid without me. This was before we moved in together and I was still doing family holidays in Tupgill. She had always enjoyed the Retiro for running or rollerblading. She told me of an occasion when she met a very handsome policeman. He had been watching her and then approached her to talk. He asked her name and phone number. She was intrigued, but asked his age. He said twenty-six. She was then twenty-seven. That turned her off. She told him that she had never been out with a man younger than herself. He insisted, and she gave him her Instagram. He continued to pester her for some time to go out with him, but (as far as I know) without success.

When she told me the story she sighed, and said that he was so handsome in his uniform.

Since the kidnap she has thankfully stopped using a public Instagram. Before that, what began with a few friends got bigger and bigger with friends of friends until there were over a thousand contacts. I never looked at it, but from time to time she would show me chats of men asking to date her. There was even one who said he wanted to be her sugar daddy. How much would she charge him?

My right eye is now clear. We had returned to the clinic for tests and Dra Martinez pronounced my sight as 90% perfect. She gave us an appointment for the left eye operation tomorrow at 8am.

I am keen to get it done.

That night we went to an oyster bar. But on arriving home I had a violent urge to vomit. I rushed to the bathroom and got there just in time. It was horrible. The contractions went on and on, long after there was nothing more to throw up. Kate brought me a clean towel to wipe my face. Then she guided me to the bed and brought me a cup of tea. I still felt nauseous.

I got up several times in the night to vomit again.

We thought that one of the oysters must have been bad. But we had both eaten them and Kate was OK.

At eight am we called the clinic and canceled the appointment. I then slept for most of the day.

We got another appointment for the following week, so finally my left eye was operated on 13th June. It was getting close to the date we had booked to return to Guayaquil, on the 20th.

We returned to the clinic three days later for a postoperative check. Dra Martinez would have liked to see us again the following week, but that was impossible.

She said that even though my sight was now good I should buy a pair of reading glasses to help me read in poor light. She gave us a note and sent us to a shop owned by her sister. I was surprised to see the glasses were 'off the shelf' with 1.5 times magnification. They only cost forty-five euros. That is all I need.

We had another dinner of oysters before leaving Madrid. And the same thing happened. We now reasoned that I have developed an allergy to oysters. But it seems to be specific, I can eat other shellfish with no problem.

Silvia had shown us two more apartments. One was in Hermosilla Street close to the construction we had seen. It was recently renovated and well laid out, but had a common defect. All the places we had seen had between two to four windows onto the street. The sitting/dining room would be placed there. The bedrooms and kitchen would be behind them and be lit with light wells running from top to bottom of the building. Inevitably these looked out onto the wall of the next building. Sometimes the walls were brown with water stains, sometimes there were rusty air conditioners and even laundry hanging out.

It would be depressing to wake up and see this each day.

There was no solution to the problem as the wall in question belongs to the next building and the residents would hardly smarten them up just for our pleasure.

Over the years we have known Sylvia, we have enjoyed a particular restaurant together. It is called La Favorita.

Tonight was our last night in Madrid, so we invited her to go with us.

La Favorita is famous for opera. It's not a theater, just a restaurant. The waiters and waitresses serve at the tables. But from time to time a pianist plays and they put down their trays and sing popular arias.

Tonight it was well attended. We had booked our table in the principal room near the piano. The music is wonderful. The owner came to talk to us, he recognised us from our many previous visits.

When the show had finished we noticed that he called the soprano to come to the piano and talked to her and the pianist. They looked our way.

I thought I knew why, and I was right. She sang 'Oh mio babbino caro' from the opera Gianni Schicchi by Puccini.

I inevitably asked for this as an encore. And just as inevitably I cried.

What a lovely way to finish the evening, and our holiday in Madrid.

On arriving back in Guayaquil on 20th June we were met by Jorge with our car and two men from the protection detail.

We drove back to our rented apartment. Strangely this time I liked it better. I suppose I had got used to it. The initial problems have been sorted out. My shower now boasts a large electric water heater, which takes up a lot of space in the laundry room. I could run the shower for ages without exhausting the supply of hot water.

This time the fridge was full and Yaneth had left us dinner for tonight. We had sorted out the newspaper delivery, so I could read the Expreso every morning.

But Kate was not happy with it. She had bent my ear while in Madrid that it was a disgrace that a successful businessman of my age is living in rented accommodation.

I might put up with it but she wouldn't.

I was soon back into my office routine. I got there early each day to avoid the traffic. At that time of day it only took twenty minutes.

Daylight comes at 6.15am at this time of the year. There is only thirty minutes variation during the year, as Guayaquil is 2 degrees south of the Equator.

Before leaving the apartment I made my breakfast, fed Snoopy and read the newspaper, until I got a message that my escorts were waiting outside the building. A quick kiss for Kate, who sleeps somewhat later, and I went down to the basement parking lot. I drove my armoured Toyota, and the escort followed me.

I am glad to be back. I find work satisfying. It's not true to say that working at a distance is just the same. There are things one needs to do personally. I have to sign a lot of documents referring to bank loans. But the most important thing is to be seen.

I have been out of the country for four months this year. There were rumours that I had left the company.

So we made a plan to show myself to the troops. I went to three of our factories and waved to the people as I toured them.

I am not allowed to visit the two hundred shops we have, for security reasons. So we brought in the shop managers in three groups of thirty to the head office in Guayaquil, for three hours meetings aimed at raising morale, and sales too.

Then with Nick and the shop manager, Geronimo, we flew to Quito and drove to our regional office for two more meetings. Finally we flew from Quito to Cuenca for the final batch of thirty shop managers. Our security detail saw us off at one airport and received us at the next.

Another group to see are bankers. They want to be reassured that I am still fronting the company. Francisco, our CFO, began to make appointments.

I somehow believed that my very presence here would end the run of bad months. But it is not as easy as that. We continued to have low sales during June and July 2024. But the difference from the same months last year is getting less. I hope that from August to December we can recoup, before the year ends.

As I told my directors. I had seen worse.

It was 1999. At that time Ecuador still had the Sucre as the national currency. When I arrived in Ecuador in 1972 the exchange rate was 25 Sucres to the US dollar. That rate held for many years. But by the 1990s inflation and devaluation were taking their toll. The Sucre collapsed to 250, then 500, then 1,000 to the dollar. By 1999, when the President of the time changed the national currency to the US dollar, it was 25,000!

That was a huge problem for a company that has its earnings in Sucres, but its debts to suppliers and banks in dollars.

I had said to Ceci one day "My Love we are bankrupt".

But we weren't. We survived and rebuilt the company to a size ten times what it had been then.

Today I tell everyone that I will stay on long enough to see this crisis out.

Paraphrasing Churchill, I told them that 'this isn't the end of the crisis, not even the beginning of the end, but it is the end of the beginning'.

Shortly after I returned to Guayaquil in May this year we had an event at our Opera Club.

I had formed this club with the young soprano Viviana Rodriguez some years ago.

There is no opera house in Ecuador. From time to time a group of opera singers would be able to put on a production in one of the theatres. But it needed a lot of support. Sometimes the municipality would pay for it. At others it needed private sponsors. Opera is expensive to produce and ticket prices rarely cover the cost, especially so as it's not popular music.

Even the famous Metropolitan Opera House in New York, despite very high ticket prices, needs sponsors.

I am a fan of opera and we began with my holding lunches in the Union Club for the good and the great, to shake them down in support of the next production. Viviana and one or two others would sing at the lunch. We did raise money, but it was never enough, so I picked up the difference.

It got more and more difficult to ask for money. So we formed our own club. This consists of five or six principal voices, plus an ad hoc chorus. We have a pianist instead of an orchestra, and avoid paying for a theater as we have adapted our own in Bandurria, the Agripac company canteen, where we have built a stage. It seats a hundred people.

It still has a cost, but it's much less. We ask our guests for $20 each, which covers the opera plus wine and a snack. I still have to put in the difference.

This month's performance, on 11th July, is Lakme, by Leo Delibes. It's one of my favourites.

Sung in French, it's the story of colonial India where a British army officer falls in love with a Hindu goddess. She is the daughter of a Brahman priest who is violently opposed to British rule. Gerald, the officer, is torn between his love for her and his duty both as an army officer and fiance of the governor's daughter. The music is wonderful, especially two arias. One is The Flower Song, a duet between soprano and mezzo soprano. The other, the Bell Song, sung by the soprano.

Viviana decorated the stage with Indian themes, including a painting of the Hindu elephant god, Ganesh.

The singers wore colourful saris and Indian clothes.

It was a great success. We filled our small theater.

Over the years we have performed La Traviata, Lucy of Lammermoor, Don Pasquale, The Marriage of Figaro, The Girl of the Regiment, Elixir de Amor and La Serva Padrona. The next will be Rigoletto in October.

One day while I was in my office Nick came to see me.

"Dad, as you can't go to the Rodeo Grande now, do you want to sell it? We have been approached by Kleber, who bought our banana farm some years ago."

This came out of the blue. But indeed I had thought about selling it. The fact is that we haven't been back there since the kidnap on 16th December, five months ago. How much longer would it be out of bounds? We will never be able to stay the night again, so there would only be day trips. I have enjoyed riding a horse there for forty-seven years. But I have to be realistic. If I have a fall at my age, it would be serious. My horse is well-behaved, but should we get into a cloud of horse flies all horses go mad, rear up and prance about.

On the other hand, what about my staff there? They are friends. They will lose their jobs. I imagined that Kleber, who is one of the biggest banana producers in Ecuador, would plant a lot of the farm with bananas. There will be no need for cowboys.

I told Nick that I would think about it for a day or two.

That night I told Kate.

She agreed with me. It will be sad to leave it and our group of friends there. But it will solve a problem. We can buy a house here, and hopefully put something towards a bigger flat in Madrid.

I asked Nick to tell Kleber that we are interested. He in turn asked to be allowed to have a look at it with his nephew the next day.

I called Cristina, she is the administrator of Rodeo Grande. I asked her to show Kleber around tomorrow at 7:30am. She asked by horse or car. I said by car. We chatted about other things, but she didn't ask me why he wants to look around. I thought it was obvious. But I was not yet ready to tell her. When we rang off I felt I was betraying her, and the others.

But the sale might not go through. Not all of Rodeo is suitable for bananas. He might only want part of it. I might be left with some cattle after all.

Three days later Nick told me that Kleber and his two nephews would like to talk to me at 5pm in my office. I agreed.

It's getting on for my wine time. I ordered two bottles of Doña Paola wine and glasses.

I was nervous about the meeting. I am emotionally involved with Rodeo.

I have so many memories of days gone by. When my kids were small, they learnt to ride there. They invited school friends and we would mount up to twenty horses. My daughter Alexandra was baptized there.

Then there were the many years, when I was British Consul, Ceci and I held the Queen's Birthday party there. We would invite up to five hundred people. We requested that they dress in white and wear a hat.

We invited the British Ambassador, embassy personnel, the Guayaquil British community, government ministers, municipal dignitaries and the Guayaquil Consular Corp (about seventy countries have consuls).

We invited our group of friends, and some Agripac customers too.

That's how the numbers got to five hundred.

We had a band playing background music, and a disco for dancing.

Maria Dolores would supervise the food. We brought our own staff from Bandurria and hired extra waiters. We had thirty-five roast suckling pigs which were cooked over open fires on the lawn.

Ceci and I stood at the entrance to the garden and greeted each guest as they arrived, which could take two hours.

Then when all were present, the Ambassador would make a speech. After him I made mine. I tried to tie in a piece of history, before toasting first the Ecuadorian President and then the Queen.

It became one of the main parties of the Guayaquil year and invitations were sought after.

There were also my ten years as a 'bachelor'. I was married to Ceci but we had separate weekends. The children were at boarding school in England. She would go with her friends to the beach house and I would go to Rodeo with my two beagles. I would ride both Saturday and Sunday, and stay the night there. Amarilis cooked dinner for me and then went home. So I was alone with my dogs. I used to take a handgun with me. I reckoned that the dogs would hear any intruder and I could defend myself.

That was made a mockery on 16th December last year. I told Joseph about it. He said that if I had had a gun, I would be dead now.

More recently, with Kate we have made several Agripac calendars at Rodeo. She wore sexy outfits, rode horses, sat on the backs of bulls, held piglets and baby goats, milked cows and fed ostriches. So many photos. The team of photographer, hair stylist, make-up girl, the owner of the model agency and myself as technical adviser, would stay three days there. Each night we would drink and eat together. Happy memories.

My seven beagles are buried there. We made a small graveyard and each has a white painted headstone with its name and dates. They would remain. Probably the stones will be taken away, but their bones still lie under the lawn.

Perhaps someone will hear them howling at night.

The meeting went better than I had expected. For one thing there was no haggling over the price. I had told Nick I would sell at book value. Kleber had accepted that.

What surprised me was that it wasn't just the land he wanted, but the ranch as a going concern with cattle, horses, the house, and more importantly all fifteen workers led by Cristina.

He said that he had grown up on a ranch and had ridden as a boy. Now he wanted to recapture the pleasure of being a cattleman. We talked about security. He said he was only too aware of it and had his own security detail. But he didn't think he would spend the night there. He envisioned breakfasts on the balcony. We finished the two bottles of wine together, shook hands and I agreed to ask our lawyer, Alfredo, to draw up the Promise of Sale, while the legal papers were put in order.

He for his part said that he would advance the first cheque this week, another when we signed the Promise and the final payment when he got possession.

It all seemed so easy. I had sold the banana farm to him the same way.

Then I remembered the witch's prediction "There will be documents to sign. Lots of documents". She had seen that I would sell Rodeo Grande.

The first cheque duly arrived. Over the years Rodeo Grande has borrowed a lot of money from Agripac. It rarely made a profit to repay any of it. So most of the first cheque went to repay the debt. I will have to pay off the staff there for their years of service, which is the law here. After which Kleber will rehire them.

Even though the deed is done, I couldn't bring myself to talk to Cristina, and strangely I didn't tell Ceci either. I was in denial. I asked Fredy, who did Rodeo's accounts, to calculate the cost of paying off everyone. It was Fredy who persuaded me to bite the bullet and tell Cristina. She has been with me almost eighteen years. He said that rumours were rife about the sale. She had to hear it from me.

So I called her. First we talked about her son Mati, who is my godson. Then I had to broach the reason for the call. Had she heard rumours?

Yes, was I going to sell Rodeo? I said yes. There was silence on the line, then I heard her crying. With that I cried too. We couldn't talk. Then I heard her blow her nose.

"So what will happen to me?" I said that Kleber has offered to take her on, and all the others too.

"But I don't know him, what if I can't get along with him?"

He is a good man, I am sure you won't have a problem.

Then her feisty side showed.

"If I don't like the job I will leave".

We agreed that she should come to Guayaquil, bringing Mati and Cipriano on Saturday. We will have lunch together.

Nick had come into my office while I was talking to Cristina. He saw me crying and gave me a hug. Once I had rung off he sympathized with the trauma I am going through. We talked about Rodeo Grande and the many times we had ridden together there. I am glad we are getting closer, after some rough moments.

Ceci left in July to go to Amsterdam, meet up with our daughter Diana and fly on to Florence. They are going to an Andrea Bocelli concert. I received photos from them in Florence. They are staying at a boutique hotel near the Duomo. There is a street view from the hotel window and I could see the Louis Vuitton shop where Kate and I had bought a pretty pink pant suit.

One night they stayed in the fabulous Hotel San Michele in Fisole.

Kate and I stayed there too, in June 2022.

We had rented a car in Barcelona and driven from there to Gerona, Nice, Florence, Como and Milan. There we returned the car, and flew home to Madrid.

Kate had driven all the way. The rental car was a BMW X5. She drove very fast on the excellent highways through France and Italy. One amusing anecdote comes to mind. She overtook a Lamborghini, driven by a thickset swarthy man with a beard. We were doing a hundred and fifty kph. Clearly annoyed, he overtook us. She did it again, by now at a hundred and eighty kph. He hated being overtaken by a mere BMW, and worse still, driven by a girl. We got to a toll gate. He had a pass, we hadn't, so we had to stop and pay. He braked at the far side, revved his engine to get our attention, and put his arm out of the window with a finger in the air.

We laughed about it all the way to Nice.

We had stayed in great hotels in each place. But the best of the hotels, even better than the San Michele, was the Villa d'Este in Como. Standing on the edge of Lake Como, with a large and beautiful garden, it's pure magic. We stayed two nights and even swam in Lake Como, though it was freezing.

When the UK press published photos of us after the kidnap (millionaire playboy etc), Kate noticed one photo of us coming out of the lake. I am passing her a towel. But it wasn't taken by us. We have never seen it before. Who had photographed us, and then given it to the press eighteen months later? It's a mystery.

July 18th. Ceci and Diana are now in Tupgill. Steve, Diana's husband, has arrived from Los Angeles with their three boys, Oliver, Rocco and Dominic.

They will stay there for two weeks.

They had gone for a walk and as they passed the Coverham church graveyard they went into it to see the family graves. Dominic, always the joker, asked if Grandpa's grave was already reserved.

Well, yes Dom, it is. But there's no rush!

While at her boarding school, St Anne's in Windermere, Diana made firm friends with a group of girls. They have maintained this friendship through university and marriage and get together whenever they can, given that Diana lives in Los Angeles and the other girls in Britain. She nicknamed them The Ladies.

Now she planned to have a great reunion at Tupgill in July. Not only The Ladies, but all who she could contact from her year at school, plus husbands and children.

She sent me a photo today. There are about sixty of them, standing on the steps in Tupgill garden with Diana, Steve, their boys and Ceci.

She had pre-booked rooms at the Forbidden Corner with Leo back in March to make sure that we can accommodate them all for the three-day visit.

They have had picnics, walks, pub meals and have tried the new White Goose pizza house at the Forbidden Corner. We have only just inaugurated it, but it's already very popular. Luckily the weather is fine.

The grand finale last night was a disco in the Bell Barn. I got several videos of it.

I reflected on my own school days at Rossall. I have not kept in touch with anyone at all.

I made friends there of course, but we drifted apart when I went overseas. I have spent the greater part of my life out of Britain. I first left when I was twenty-one, and have only lived there for short periods ever since.

Leo has sent me a photo of my portrait, now framed. He has it in his office. I asked him not to hang it in Tupgill until I got there, as the family would probably use it for target practice.

But with the benefit of my new eyes, my face looks old and wrinkled.

In fact, I don't like the portrait at all. It isn’t flattering.

I guess if I live another ten years I might catch it up in wrinkles. So perhaps I have my equivalent of Oscar Wilde’s ‘The Portrait of Dorian Grey’, where only the portrait ages, not the man.

We met Laura Marcos some years ago. She has painted several portraits of Kate.

There is one of her sitting smiling at the viewer. Her hair hangs down, partially covering her breasts with a light brown background. She is wearing an emerald ring, which we bought in Colombia. It’s framed in green to match the ring.

Another is a pen and ink drawing of her sitting at the piano. It was originally nude, but she asked for it to be clothed. Laura simply made the dress transparent.

Another is of her on the pole, and this definitely is nude with her reflection in a mirror behind her.

A fourth one is Kate sitting on my knees. She is dressed in a long white dress and holding a bunch of roses.

the herd and rent pastures, sometimes a hundred kilometres away. It's traumatic.

Now at least I don't have to worry about that anymore.

I remember when I first bought Rodeo Grande in November 1977. I was so happy with my purchase. I had always wanted to be a farmer.

At Rossall School I would spend a lot of time in the library, reading the Farmers Weekly and making notes of how I will farm.

I told my father what I wanted to do. On the fifty acres at Tupgill I would farm intensive pigs and poultry. He replied no.

"When you are fifty you will still be doing the same thing and won't have a penny in the bank. Go and get a job".

I graduated from Harper Adams Agricultural College, and Writtle (Essex Institute of Agriculture) and then, not having a farm, I joined Imperial Chemical Industries Ltd.

At the time it was one of the biggest industries in Britain with headquarters at Millbank, London.

Today it doesn't exist. The agrochemical part is now called Syngenta.

They seconded me to Malaysia, then to Mexico and finally to Ecuador. Where I left ICI Ltd, and have remained for the last fifty-two years.

But we didn't go to Rodeo Grande on Friday. I talked to Joseph about it. He said no. It is not a matter of my being in immediate danger. He could send ten operatives with me. The danger is that the kidnappers will learn that I am back in the country. He reminded me that I had made promises to them. They might well threaten me again, or Cristina.

I couldn't live with that.

So we didn't go.

We told Cristina about it and she agreed with us.

Fredy will go alone taking the final payment cheques for each of them.

Today I went with Kate to see Raul, the dentist. He took an x-ray but the bone is still not thick enough to hold the implant. Come back in another month. So I am still gap toothed.

My chest has started to itch again, and there are one or two eruptions. We returned to see Dr Jose Maria. He confirmed his last diagnosis. The cancer is 90% cured. But there is still 10%. We have started the same treatment. Luckily we have caught it in time. This time the treatment is not painful.

Dra Martin, the Madrid dermatologist, did say that she had no history to go by. She was looking at it as a snapshot. Dr Jose Maria has attended me for some years.

But at least my eyes are good, and with the hearing aid I can hear!

We are house hunting too. Now that I have cash in hand I need to sort out our accommodation. I used to have five places to live. But Ceci now has our home in Guayaquil, Kate and I are selling the penthouse, and I have sold Rodeo Grande.

That just leaves a share in Tupgill, the family home, the flat in Madrid and the rented place we have in Guayaquil, which we don't like.

There are several areas of Guayaquil where houses are both expensive and safe. The two generally go together.

Kate contacted an estate agent and began to look at properties. She sent me photos and videos. Then we went to see them. We got the choice down to two. They are close together. One is a duplex apartment. It's very large, had lots of windows and would suit us well. But it wasn't finished. The owner had decided that the buyer could finish it as he or she wanted. That involved putting in lighting. Wires hung down from the ceiling and out of walls. There were no kitchen or bathroom fittings. It would take a month or two to finish and decorate. The extra cost, added to the asking price, took us over our budget.

There is a house we really like. The owners are moving to Dallas, Texas, only five years after building it. Once again it has large windows and lots of light. There is a large sitting/dining room two floors high, four bedrooms, kitchen, maid's room and two attached garages. It is fully air-conditioned. It stands on a quiet street shaded by mature trees. It has a small garden onto the street, and a bigger patio to the back which looks onto an artificial canal. There is a pergola on the patio equipped with a full kitchen. The owner said they never cooked indoors, always outside. There is no swimming pool, but there is space to put in a jacuzzi.

The enclosed area has a communal club with both a swimming pool and gym, just two hundred yards away from the house.

The garden would be ideal for Snoopy, so he can be outside most of the time. At the moment he just gets a short walk each day.

It was the smallest of the several houses we had looked at in the area. The others have five bedrooms, and lots of rooms to accommodate a large family. We don't need this for just the two of us.

The bigger the house the more expensive it is to cool (rather than heat) and clean.

Yaneth will transfer here with us. But she won't live in. She has a family at home and needs to get back there every day.

The owners of the house invited us to return the next evening to see how it looks at night. We did and indeed it is a fairyland with lights from adjacent houses reflected from the canal.

We are practically decided. We will put in a bid next week.

Friday, 26th July

Today is the opening of the Paris Olympic Games.

Kate and I sat in front of the TV for three hours watching it. It is a great show, but sadly the rain poured down the whole time. To be different from the usual parade of athletes, the

French have made a parade by flotilla on the Seine, six kilometres long. The bigger teams occupy a whole boat, the smaller ones shared. Some braved the rain, others huddled under umbrellas or wore transparent plastic raincoats.

The TV switched back and forth from the parade to entertainers. There was a group of drag queens who amused us, including one beautiful bearded lady.

There were acrobatics on floating islands on the river.

Both Celine Dion and Lady Gaga sang.

Finally the Olympic Torch was carried up the Seine by a woman on a galloping mechanical horse attached to a boat. She gave it to one athlete who transferred it to another, then one after the other they passed it on until finally the Olympic Fire was lit and went into the air on a giant balloon.

Tuesday 30th July

Suddenly things are moving quickly. Kleber had arranged the final payment of the ranch and wants to take possession next week. Alfredo agreed to that, even though the final papers were yet to be signed.

Our thoughts then turned to the ranch house.

Over the years Ceci has commented that I never even look at the house. I go to Rodeo, eat, drink, ride, and even sleep the night without noticing that the house needed attention.

And that is only too true.

Up to this point I had talked of taking my clothes, pictures and a few personal items out of the house and walking away from it.

But Kate had a different idea. As we couldn't go safely to Rodeo Grande, she asked Cristina to video the rooms.

She had originally said that she would like one piece of furniture. It is an attractive, mock antique, cupboard painted red and gold with angel-decorated panels. But when she saw the video that changed. She now wants a lot of furniture.

Suddenly, so did I. We are close to buying the new house in Guayaquil. We have very little furniture for it. It makes sense to bring the furniture from Rodeo. It will look good. A modern house rusticated with ranch furniture, my boots and saddle.

The furniture had all been bought second-hand forty-four years before. Not that we couldn't have afforded new furniture, but because it looked right for a ranch house. Some is Peruvian. Indeed most of it will now be antique. There are tables and chairs, cupboards, sideboards, a Welsh dresser, bedside tables, pictures, cowhides and lamps. But we won't take the beds. We have two from the penthouse. Anyway, we would never sleep again in the kidnap bed!

How crazy it would be to leave all this behind. The furniture contains memories of Rodeo Grande. I had told Kleber that I would be taking a few things from the house. Now in a panic I asked Alfredo if I had sold the house furnished or unfurnished. He replied that the furnishing was not in the inventory. So I haven't sold it.

I called Kleber and apologized saying that my wife (sic) wanted the furniture. He said that was perfectly OK. He really had not thought about it. He was concentrating on the land, not the house. Please remove anything you want.

There is the small problem of where to put it meanwhile. We didn't expect to get possession of the new house until the end of August. Agripac has plenty of warehouses, but they smelt of chemicals, and the furniture would soon pick up the smell.

A phone call in the afternoon resolved that problem. The seller of the house plans to move to the USA. He now called me and asked if we could speed up the sale, as his wife wants to leave before the end of August.

I called Alfredo. I had sent him the deeds of the house yesterday. How long would it take to complete the sale? He said a week if he rushed it.

I already had the cash to buy it so we agreed to try for a week.

Now that Kleber knows that I am taking the furniture there is no rush to get it out.

I had told him please feel free to use the house meanwhile, but eventually you will have to furnish it.

Cristina and Fredy will make an inventory so it is clear that it is mine.

Josef invited Kate and I to dinner last night. We went to a small restaurant that made the 'best pastrami in town'. The owner is Argentinian. While we were there a friend of the owner was giving lessons on dancing the tango. When it's done by experts it's a wonderful spectacle. Tonight was just beginners. But the music, recorded singing by Carlos Gardel (who died in 1935) got to us. Kate went on the floor with the instructor, even I was dragged on to it by a lady, who was really rather good at it. All I had to do was hold on to her and keep my feet out of the way of hers. There was polite applause afterwards, so I guess I made a sufficient fist of it.

I was grateful to Josef for asking us both. He and I have had many dinners together, on our own. It's the first time he has invited Kate. We are aware that this doesn't go down well with the distaff side of the family. Most men will avoid inviting her at their wife's insistence, out of solidarity with Ceci.

Last night Fredy returned from Rodeo Grande and came to our apartment. He brought with him several suitcases containing Kate's and my clothes, plus boots, photos, the school plaques and ornaments. But he brought me something much more valuable. He had gone there today to pay off the staff. After which he filmed the house room by room talking of all the good times we have enjoyed there.

Then he asked the staff to wait upstairs in the house and come down one by one. He stood at the bottom step with his camera and made a video. Cipriano was the first to come down. He stopped by Fredy, and after taking off his hat in respect, he talked to me in the video.

"Señor Colin, I want to thank you for employing me for the last twenty-nine years during which time I have paid for my children's education thanks to you. I will never forget your kindness. Goodbye, God bless you."

He was crying, and I cried too while watching it.

Then David came down and gave a similar message, then Español, Juan, Yoyo, Camacho, Maria, Daniel, and Miguel. So one by one all fifteen said their goodbyes. The last one was Cristina.

The video scanned the house and the lawn, before focussing on the team standing in front of the house. At a signal from Cristina they threw their hats in the air in my honour, and chanted

"Gracias Señor Colin".

I couldn't stop crying. This really brought it home to me. This was the final goodbye. Apart from Cristina, I would never see any of them again. It was rather like leaving school, but after many more years together.

Kate brought us a glass of wine. I really needed it. I thanked Fredy profusely for his thoughtfulness in making this video. I will always keep it to remind me.

We drank a lot of wine and ordered a McDonalds for Fredy and I.

Kate had soup left for her by Yaneth.

Once again I went to bed and left them talking.

I woke up at 5am, as normal, today and went to the bathroom. After showering I applied the many different creams and lotions that my aged body requires. Then I tiptoed through the bedroom, where Kate is asleep, went to the sitting room and I turned on the light. The first job is a quick inspection to see if

Snoopy has been a good boy or not. Today we are at peace. There is no poo or pee on the floor.

He is eighteen months old and is taking too long to get house trained. We had it all done, but when we went on holiday we left him at Rodeo Grande with the gardener Daniel, who has a dog, Toby. The two get on well together and play on the lawn all day. But he seems to have forgotten his manners.

If I find that he has sinned, I wait for him to emerge from the bedroom, yes indeed we are lax, he sleeps on the bed. Then I grab him, show him his sin and spank him with the newspaper. After which he bolts to his kennel on the balcony, and I close the door to leave him outside, until either Kate gets up or Yaneth arrives to take pity on him.

If he is a good boy then I open a sachet of dog food for him. If not, then no breakfast!

Then I make a cup of strong Yorkshire Tea (Taylors of Harrogate, 'Let's have a proper brew') and, depending on how hungry I am, either eat toast and honey, or put on the frying pan and make an omelet.

I have never been a cook, but after years of watching hotel breakfast bars make omelets, I thought I would try it at home.

My idea of an omelet is with bacon, onion, tomato and lots of chili as a filling.

I can't say they look perfect. Mine never flips over very well, but they taste good.

If I make a fried egg I inevitably break the yolk. As to opening an egg with one hand as hotel chefs do, forget it.

I read the newspaper quickly. I am pleased to see that Ecuador has won its first Olympic gold medal. Daniel Pintado won the twenty-kilometre walk.

Once again, Nicolas Maduro has stolen the Venezuelan election.

For the first time he at least made a show of it being free and fair, and invited international monitors into the country.

Old dictators can't give up and go home. When he suspected that he was going to lose, he quickly proclaimed himself the winner with 52% of the vote.

Well down from the normal 90% victory!

This time perhaps he won't get away with it. Not only the USA, but European countries and most of South America have not recognised him as president. Although the usual suspects Russia, China, Iran and North Korea have.

A message on my phone tells me that my escort has arrived. I drive fast to the office, closely followed by them. It's an art to follow another car, especially if I change lanes a lot, or take a traffic light late, when it's changing to red. But my guys are good. I enjoy driving fast through traffic. I think it keeps me alert. And I don't like being driven by someone else. I am very much a backseat driver continually pressing the floor of the car instead of the brakes. Worse, I suck air if I think we are too close to another car, to the annoyance of the driver. Kate hates that.

As we approach Agripac the uniformed guards in the street stop the opposing traffic with great flapping of arms and allow both cars to enter the car park gate.

I have got used to the face recognition security on the three doors before I get to my office. The air conditioner is already on and the office cleaners have left. It is cool and smells of floor polish. I smile as I look at my book collection arrayed on two walls covered in bookshelves at either end of the office. There are over six hundred books, with very few still to read.

The first thing I do is turn on the computer and get out my diary. I still have all my diaries going back to 1972. In the early years they were just lists of things to do. But more recently I put in a lot more detail about my day, who I see and how I feel.

When I wrote 'Behind the Forbidden Corner' in 1999, I used my dairies extensively as a source of history, as well as the correspondence with my secretary in England at the time, dear Elaine Lister.

The morning passes quickly and at exactly 12 pm I get up from the desk and go down the lift across the courtyard and to Bandurria for lunch. As always I give a kiss to Maria Dolores the manageress, who sits at her desk in the entrance to the building. We make some joke and then I walk to the service area and take atray. What is there today? There is always a soup and two options for the main course, fish or meat.

I choose mine and Jose, the waiter, carries the tray to my normal table.

I had just started the soup when my daughter Alex came in. We kissed and she got her food and joined me.

She asked what I had done over the weekend. The answer as always is "very little". As I can no longer go to Rodeo Grande on Saturdays I tend to go to the office. We sometimes go out for lunch to a restaurant, then go back home, have a siesta and watch TV.

We have watched several series of many episodes. There was Sex and the City which we ploughed through. Now it's Malcolm in the Middle.

Both were good for a while, but they go on so long that it gets boring.

I prefer to read a book.

I have just finished Einstein in Berlin by Thomas Levenson. Not only did I learn a bit about physics (not my best subject at school) such as light being bent by gravity, and what exactly is a Quantum, even its famous leap.

I also got the background on Germany from 1914, when Einstein arrived in Berlin from Switzerland, to when he left it in 1932 for the USA.

I had no idea of the privations caused by the British naval blockade in the First World War. We all know about the U Boats and what they did to the British merchant navy. But the British blockade was much more effective. Germany was at the point of starvation when the war ended.

Then came the years from 1918 until Hitler came to power in 1933. A complete collapse of the economy, hyperinflation, street riots and the rise of rightwing militarized groups, including the SA and SS who brought Hitler to power.

On Sundays also I go to the office in the mornings then get home for lunch. I can normally find some work to catch up on. Two days at home is not an option.

Alex's weekend was taken up with her three children, Sienna, and the twins Christian and Olivia. They have got to the age when they have parties and events. Christian plays football and has to be transported back and forth by Alex or Javi.

They have a beagle too, called Toby. I am angling for her to look after Snoopy when I go on holiday. She says no, but I think she is weakening.

The family is annoyed that I called him Snoopy. It was the name of our first beagle. He was given to us by Ceci's father when we got married in 1974.

Only Nick of my three children knew him. Sadly he died young at only five years old.

But he is part of family lore. Kate chose the name of the second Snoopy, not me.

But I like it anyway.

I still can't get Alex to call her Kate. We are getting away from 'that woman ' or other disrespectful terms, but she resists saying her name. She won't even say Snoopy, just your dog.

Javi is in Spain this week visiting his father who is not well. She tells me that he needs sheltered housing, but doesn't want to go to one. So it's a problem.

I joke that Kate is my nurse, so the family won't have to worry about me. She laughs at that.

I wonder how long it will be until anyone in the family will accept my situation.

We are gradually getting back together, but we ain't got there yet.

Another week has gone by, we are now into August.

Yesterday, Sunday, Kate and I had an invitation to a breakfast meeting with the sellers of the house. We met at a cafe where they serve Bolon and Tigrillo, two typical Ecuadorian dishes based on green plantains with cheese and pork scratchings.

They asked us to rejig the values of the house and the few pieces of furniture we are buying from them, to reduce capital gains tax. We agreed partially to it. We are getting close to signing the sale.

We took Snoopy with us, as he gets stressed if we leave him alone at home. One of our security guards was delegated to walk him, while we had breakfast. When we came out we saw him straining at the leash to get every interesting smell he could. Strange dog, he isn't easy to walk on a lead. He pulls like a train, but when he is onto a scent he won't budge.

We have a harness for him rather than a collar, but even so he pulls so hard that the strap around his chest makes him choke. We tried buying a bigger one, but he managed to get out of it. We will have to try again.

After breakfast it wasn't worth my going to the office, so we went home, opened beers and started to plan how we will furnish the new house.

Kate wants the Rodeo furniture to be varnished before we receive it. It's easier to do that at the empty ranch house than in our new one, because of the smell of the varnish. It’s all old and dark-coloured furniture. She said we cant mix it with light-coloured modern furniture. But we need a sofa, there is nothing very comfortable to sit on from the ranch.

We spent a long time grouping the pieces so the rooms don't have a mixture of old and new furniture. We were originally not going to take any beds from the ranch. But looking at the photos, she now wants two that have intricate carved bedsteads.

I asked her if we could change the mattress of our bed here. The one we have is an Italian one, very soft, with Memory Foam. I can't get comfortable unless I curl up in the fetal position. Lying straight makes my back ache. I need a firmer one. I was surprised that she agreed, as we bought the present one especially for her.

The mattress is only part of the problem. Kate tends to move a lot in the night and ends up spread eagled over the bed. What little space is left is taken by Snoopy, and Yours Truly hangs on to the edge of the bed trying to pull enough covers over him to keep from freezing. Actually we keep the air conditioner at 22 degrees centigrade, but even so you need a blanket over you.

We have the last of the ranch flowers on the table. They are Red Ginger. They grow well there. Since we stopped going to Rodeo Cristina sends us a bunch each Saturday along with a cheese, both to Ceci and ourselves. Now we won't get them anymore.

Fredy has made two trips to Rodeo bringing whatever fits into his car. The last load included the pewter mugs with our names on. Years ago I brought twenty-four of them from the UK. I gave one to each of the family and to Kate, Cristina, Fredy and Cipriano. There are still a few without names. These are what we used on Saturdays to drink beer at Rodeo.

We were running out of wine glasses too so Fredy kindly bought us a dozen more. We do seem to break a lot of them, when drunk and disorderly.

I was reading the life of Oscar Wilde by David Pritchard. Kate was watching Malcolm in the Middle. She finally got bored of it and came to talk to me.

I had no socks on and looking at my feet she pronounced that my toenails needed cutting.

She has done this several times this year. Prior to that I used to cut them myself, hunched over in the bathroom. But my idea of trim nails is not hers. She set to work, despite my grunts of pain when she dug too deeply under a nail. She cut them, filed them and finally painted them. Then satisfied with that, she took my hands and set to work on those nails too.

The pain was compensated for when she massaged my feet, that felt great.

As I told Alex, I have a nurse living with me.

Snoopy sleeps a great deal during the day. He has his favourite spot on the sofa which has to be vacuumed frequently, as he sheds a lot of hair.

But from time to time he becomes playful. This was one of them. He picked up his ball and came to offer it to us. But once you try to take it he pulls back, growling. When we finally get it from him and throw it he charges after it, bouncing on all four paws. Then the game starts again.

Kate was wearing shorts, and as he would stand on his hind legs when she held the ball, her legs got scratched. There's fourteen kilos of playful beagle behind those claws.

We are about to get a lot of memorabilia from Rodeo's furniture and pictures.

There is already a framed enlarged photo I really love hanging on the wall of the flat. It was taken by the photographer Pollo in August 2021, when we made the 2022 Agripac calendar at Rodeo. It shows Kate looking beautiful, mounted on her horse with me holding the bridle. She is wearing a black halter top, has a bare midriff and a black skirt, which shows off her legs but is draped over the rear of the horse. She has black calf-length boots and wears a pink gaucho's hat, which matches her pink saddle and bridle. The horse is a bay with a white blaze on his forehead.

It's taken outside the arched gateway to Rodeo's garden. Over us is a glorious flowering red acacia tree. My family coat of arms can be seen painted on a sculptured concrete base, on the right side of the arch.

Janina called me today. "How is life in paradise?".

I laughed "Well, we are not fighting".

She complained that we hadn't met up for some time. I said that was because we were sad about selling Rodeo Grande.

"What, you sold it?"

I hadn't told her, I hadn't told many people who were not directly involved. I guess I was still in denial. She was upset about it. We had been there together so many times, both she and her two daughters.

She asked when we were travelling again. I said that we had first to complete the sale of Rodeo and then buy the new house. Once again that was news to her.

We really have been out of circulation. So I described the house, and told her that we are bringing the Rodeo furnishings for it. I promised her that once we move in Kate will be keen to invite people again. For the moment she is in hermit mode.

I guess it's partly because she is not proud of the rented flat.

Kate goes to the gym most days. She sent me a message today that she had done a hundred minutes of cardio.

Now is the time to do the Agripac 2025 Calendar. It will be her eleventh one. Ever since we met in 2013, the company calendar has been hers. I get a lot of criticism from the family about this. Why does it have to be the same model year after year?

Answer, because I am sleeping with her.

More serious opposition comes from Alex. She is in charge of the corporate image and complains that the calendars are sexist. We have had one or two complaints over the years from feminist groups, especially when Kate asked me to put the calendar photos on billboards around the city.

The 2022 and 2023 calendars, to be fair, were a bit over the top, with Kate actually naked in one shot (though it was tastefully done).

In response to her complaints, we made the 2024 calendar very modest. Kate and another model, Nelvic, are prettily dressed and standing in flower, tomato and tobacco farms. One shot is in an Agripac shop and another in our factory. The sixth one is Kate dressed as a polo player mounted on a polo pony. All very modest.

When we began the series of sexy calendars in 2013, we modelled them on the world-famous Pirelli calendar. That is a collector's item. They really do them well taking the most beautiful models to exotic locations.

Then in recent years they too have bent the knee to Me Too.

I am happy to see in the newspaper that Pirelli was returning to its former sensual images, albeit with both male and female models. I sent the article to Alex.

Like Queen Victoria, she was not amused.

Kate announced that tomorrow we will meet in my office at 4pm to plan the new one. She has summoned Marcia, Gynna and Natalie. We will do the planning, then others will join us to produce it. I will have wine available to help the discussion.

She has just called me. Do I remember the tree she and Mati planted in Rodeo last year? She wants to transplant it to the garden of our new house.

"Honey, it's too big, it's a Roble (Oak). Within a few years we will have to cut it down as it will block the light from the windows.".

But she still wants to do it.

I remembered a line from the opera Lakme, spoken by Gerald's fellow officer Frederic 'It's always difficult to be the sensible one.'

I have known Gynna for many years. She owns a modelling agency, in fact I met Kate through her. We had not seen each other since the kidnap. Today she was quite emotional.

We decided on the calendar. It will be a series of six photos, each featuring a model surrounded by fruit. One will be lemons, another pineapples, another bananas etc.

Three photos of Kate, three of Nelvic. They will be dressed in the same colour as the fruit with large floppy hats. Snoopy will make a guest appearance in one photo.

We drank the wine, but I had a headache and couldn't get in the mood. So we finished at 5.30pm and went home.

I think I am getting the flu. There is a lot about.

I went to bed early last night, skipping dinner. Today I felt fine and made my famous omelet, before going to the office.

I have finished the biography of Oscar Wilde. I knew about his book The Portrait of Dorian Grey. But I had forgotten that he is also a playwright. Starting with 'Lady Windermere's Fan', he was also successful with 'A Woman of No Importance' and then the biggest hit of them all 'The Importance of Being Earnest', which is still playing in London today,120 years after his death.

One of his plays, Salome, was banned as obscene in England. But it was adapted by the Austrian composer Richard Strauss to make his opera Salome.

It's very sensual.

Salome is in love with John the Baptist. She demands she be let into his prison and tries to seduce him. When he refuses she swears vengeance.

She offers to dance naked for King Herod if he will grant her a wish.

Herod, who is mad about her, agrees.

She demands John's head on a plate.

When she gets it she kisses the severed head on the lips.

Herod, disgusted, says she has gone mad, and has her killed.

Then came his trial and imprisonment where he wrote the Ballad of Reading Gaol.

Finally his death aged forty six in Paris, impoverished but surrounded by his friends.

A flawed genius.

I can never be without a book to read. Even in the office I keep one to hand. When I can't advance on the work front, I open the book.

So today I ran my finger along the shelves to see what I hadn’t yet read.

I pulled out Canned Coffee and Kimonos by Tom Fitzmaurice.

It's his own story as a young man, teaching English in Japan from 2007 for four years.

I see it was published by i2i Publishers in Manchester in 2021.

I know the owner Lionel Ross. He published the two books I wrote, the first called Violeta, the second called Harry. Both of which I subsequently withdrew and destroyed. They were based on the history of Kate and I, written under a pseudonym.

We became friendly and he kindly sent me one of the eight books he has written, The Dalethorpe Chronicles, which I very much enjoyed.

My copy of Canned Coffee and Kimonos was given to us by Chinmay of Explorations. As is their custom, they arranged for a relevant book to be delivered, together with a bottle of champagne, to the first hotel room of each journey with them.

This time it was in the Aman Tokyo Hotel on 2nd April 2023.

We had planned to go on holiday to both Japan and China in April 2021. That plan was thwarted by Covid. Both countries were closed to tourists.

We tried to renew the plans in 2022. But it was still impossible.

Finally in 2023 Japan reopened for tourists, unlike China which had a zero Covid policy and closed down entirely for four years.

We brushed off the plans. We were able to save some of the pre-booked costs. Others had to be rebooked or a supplement paid. As we can't include China, we will go to Japan for ten days instead of the seven days previously planned.

Chinmay, who has been to Japan many times, prepared the package. We will fly to Tokyo from San Francisco and return via Los Angeles.

With Janina's help we booked flights from Guayaquil to San Francisco via Panama, and the Ritz Carlton Hotel there. We flew on the 28th March.

I have been to San Francisco many times, but it was the first time for Kate.What fun it is showing a place you know to a person you love.

The Ritz Carlton Hotel is a monumental building, which used to be a university. It stands high on a hill overlooking San Francisco Bay.

After breakfast on the first day we walked out of the hotel, and down steep streets.

We had not come prepared for cold weather. We had forgotten that San Francisco is a long way North in California.

As we walked it got colder with icy rain. I had a light jacket on, Kate only a blouse.

We needed to find a coat for her. There must be a Bloomingdale's close by.

Sadly in this neck of town there are no department stores, but as we walked into the next street, we found a smart shop selling coats.

We were greeted by a gay assistant. How could he help us? I told him that I had a frozen lady who badly needed a coat. He said that we had come to the right place. Had we anything in mind? Kate said she would like a leather one. He led us to that section on the next floor. There was a lot to choose from. We decided on a coat in brown leather lined with tartan-coloured wool. She tried it on and it fitted pérfectly. Just what she needed.

After that as we walked the streets the sun came out, and it got much warmer.

I could have saved buying the coat!

The following day we asked a hotel porter to arrange a tour for us for the whole day to go to Muir Woods.

At 11am Sam arrived. A friendly middle-aged man. He is retired from his career and now operates his own one man tourist company. He first took us to Lombard Street. It's a sinuous street winding down a steep hill. He explained that when San Francisco was founded there were only horses and carts. There was no way a horse could pull a load up the steep straight roads of today where the trams run.

Then we headed for the Golden Gate. Before getting there we crossed the land infilled from the sea for the 1915 Panama Pacific World's Fair. We circled around so that Sam could show us the impressive buildings still standing from the Fair. We had seen similar remaining structures from the Sevilla World Fair, in Spain. They are too nice to knock down after the fair ends.

We crossed the Golden Gate. We wanted to take a photo of it. But it's not easy. There is a photo spot on the far side where we stopped, but you cannot see the bridge from there. So we took photos of each other instead.

When we got to Muir Woods, Sam said that he would stay with his car in the car park. Take your time and we will meet back here.

Kate and I walked to the ticket booth. It was not crowded today, the schools were not yet on holiday. So we more or less had it to ourselves. What a wonderful experience it is to walk among the ancient giant redwoods, some up to six hundred years old. Kate, who had never seen them before, was fascinated. We followed a track on a circular route which took us about an hour. It finished, as they always do, by the souvenir shop. She had to buy something for each of her friends.

Sam told us that Muir Woods is one of the few small areas of redwoods left. It is protected as a national monument. They used to cover large areas of northern California, but logging in the nineteenth century to provide houses and forts for the gold rush, had almost made them extinct.

He took us next to Sausalito to a restaurant called Spinnaker, overlooking the bay with all its boats. We ate delicious scallops and then sole. The wine was a tasty Sauvignon Blanc from Cakebread Cellars in Napa.

Then Sam returned us to the hotel.

We had one more day before we flew to Japan. Once again we asked for a car. Today it was Michael (a friend of Sam) who took us.

We drove out of San Francisco, once more over the Golden Gate, to the Napa Valley. There we began to pass vineyards and noticed famous wine labels of Robert Mondavi and Stag's Leap. The winery we were to visit is Louis Martini.

We did the wine tasting accompanied by a young man called Eric. He is part Mexican and we talked in Spanish about his forthcoming marriage.

Each wine was accompanied by a small plate of food, so when we finished the tasting we didn't want lunch. There was no pressure to buy wine, and as we were due to fly to Tokyo tomorrow we didn't want to carry bottles with us.

That night we ate at an Indian restaurant near the hotel called Amber.

It was excellent. We love Indian food. Half the menu is vegetarian, so no problem for Kate.

Japan Airlines business class has a strange way of separating the seats. Compared to KLM or Iberia with their ergonomic designs it looks very primitive. These are square boxes made of plywood.

We took our seats. The rest of the equipment seemed usual.

When lunch was served there were two options, Japanese or Western. We decided that we would go for the Japanese option. We were getting into our stride for Japan.

When the food arrived I wasn't so sure. I picked at mine, but didn't like it. Kate was enthusiastic.

So I exchanged mine for cheese and biscuits. You can't go wrong there.

They kept serving wine (luckily Californian) and after that I slept for five hours, before waking up shortly before we landed. It is a ten-hour flight.

We had been instructed by Explorations that on arriving at Tokyo's Narita Airport we would face several checks for health (Covid), then immigration, then customs. To avoid talking in Japanese the necessary documents had been put on apps with Japanese characters. We would just have to scan them.

I got into a panic as I couldn't find the apps on my phone. So, to Kate's annoyance, I had to open my carry-on bag in the middle of a crowded concourse and try to find the apps on the laptop. I struggled with this, but couldn't locate them.

All the while a crowd of Japanese people pushed past us. They each showed their app to the scanner and passed through.

Kate had her phone open with her apps. But she waited for me.

Then, out of the blue, a friendly official seeing my distress came to help me. He took the physical papers in English (I always print everything, just in case) and led us through each control, translating from English to Japanese.

Being in Japan, I bowed and thanked him. No shaking hands here.

We are now in Japan.

The luggage was easy to find and as we left the customs area we were met by our guide. She took us to the hire car. She asked us if we had had any difficulty and when I told her, she apologized and said that guides are not allowed inside the immigration area.

The drive to the hotel took an hour and a half. California time was 1am, but here it is 6pm, rush hour. We were quite sleepy so didn't take in much of the journey. We arrived at the

Aman Tokyo Hotel. It is very new, and strangely, occupies the top six floors of a forty-floor skyscraper.

Our room was large and had the most wonderful view over the city. It is dark now, so all we can see is a mass of lights. But in daylight we can see all the towers of the downtown business area and a wooded park in the centre.

The room is decorated in a minimalist design of wood and stone. As well as the normal bathroom there is a giant stone tub situated by the window.

We found a bottle of champagne and the book, Canned Coffee and Kimonos, with a note from Chinmay wishing us a happy holiday.

I had been telling Kate since we planned the holiday that Japanese houses are built of paper. She believed me (do I ever lie?).

Now she was mystified as to how they managed to build forty stories high, just with paper!

Today is Monday 3rd April.

We woke at 4am because of jetlag. We just had to try the hot tub. It took a long time to fill as it was so big, but then we both got in and sat admiring Tokyo from above. A wonderful way to get the first impression of a city. Kate then took a cold shower, which she loves, I prefer a warm one.

We went down from our 36th-floor room to the restaurant on the 33rd. Breakfast had both Japanese and American menus. Kate had the first, me the second. Both were good. Then we went back to the room to put on comfortable tourist clothes and shoes.

As always I have brought my lace-up walking shoes. They are ten years old. We joke that they have walked six continents, the last being Antarctica. I put on my packable black fedora hat, which I had bought at Quito airport. It's great, you can pack it in a suitcase and it always recovers its shape. I don't risk the sun on my head.

Being April the temperature was very pleasant, and of course the cherry trees are flowering, that's why we chose this month to come here.

We met Mrs Takahashi at the hotel reception. She will be our guide for the next two days in Tokyo. A very pleasant diminutive lady. We bowed to each other and then went down the lift to the waiting car in front of the building. The driver was smartly dressed in a blue suit, cap and white gloves. We were to find this level of perfection whenever we took a hire car in Japan.

Today is our first day in Tokyo. We were excited.

First she took us to the Tsukiji street market selling food, clothes and whatever. We have seen many markets in many countries, but never one as clean as this. There was literally no rubbish on the floor.

We stopped at a kiosk selling oysters. Would we like to try one? Yes, of course. The vendor opened two and we slurped them down, they were very large and tasty.

While standing there an elderly Japanese lady spoke to me, craning her neck to look me in the face. I asked Mrs Takahashi what she had said. She replied that I was a very handsome man. I duly bowed and thanked my admirer, and felt better for it. Amazing what a compliment can do for your ego. It made Kate laugh.

As we progressed down the market we saw a stall selling dressing gowns that looked like kimonos. Kate tried one, it looked really authentic and was not too expensive, so we bought it.

Our next stop was the Meiji-jingu shrine. It's a Sintoist shrine situated in a large wooded park, dedicated to the Emperor Meiji and his wife Shoken, who are venerated as the founders of modern Japan.

Our driver parked the car outside and we walked through a typical Japanese gateway with two pillars and a crosspiece curved slightly upwards at each end. We continued down a wide avenue towards the shrine. At the side of the road was a stack of barrels, which seemed rather incongruous. Our guide explains that they are all brands of Saki. Each manufacturer wants to have his representative barrel here to ensure good luck with his brand.

We advanced to the shrine itself, in a red-lacquered Japanese building with a tiled roof curling up at the edges. Mrs Takahashi surprised us by kneeling down to pray. So we did the same, out of respect. Then when she finished she dipped her hand in water from the trough. We did the same, and then asked her why. She said that it was the custom, a symbolic washing away of sins.

We saw our first geishas. But they weren't real ones. Our guide explained that the girls had hired their kimonos, for a maximum of four hours. They came here to show them off and take photos of each other. They looked very pretty. We asked Mrs Takahasi if she ever wore one. She said yes, she had her own and put it on for formal occasions like weddings.

We saw a fence full of little wooden plaques with written characters on them. We asked her what they were. She said they were petitions to god.

We went to where there was a stall selling them and bought one. Kate wrote on it. I looked at what she had written, and agreed. We hung it on the fence. We hoped that despite not believing in Shinto, our prayer would be answered.

It had got to lunch time and Mrs Takahashi took us to a surprisingly small restaurant in a basement. The food was excellent and we had a Japanese beer each. We asked why it was so small and she said that the price of property is so high in central Tokyo, that restaurants have to operate from basements.

In the afternoon we visited the most beautiful garden that I have ever seen. Called the Shinjuku Gyoen National Garden. It's a paradise of flowering shrubs and trees and lawns with lakes and streams crossed by little Japanese bridges. Apparently three hundred years old, it was once the private garden of a prince. Today it's owned by the city. The cherry trees were in full flower, although they were beginning to drop their flowers which in itself was beautiful as they covered the ground beneath the trees in a pink mantel. The Azaleas and Camellias were in flower too.

We were in heaven. We wandered the paths, crossed bridges and took photos. Kate with the cherry blossom, Kate on the bridge, Kate by the pine tree. Then of us together, taken by our guide.

As we walked on we came across the sweetest little island in the lake, connected by a bridge. It has a stall selling green tea. We sat down and drank tea and ate little almond cakes, while we admired the view to the end of the garden and the city highrises beyond.

That was the end of our programme for today. We returned to the hotel.

Tuesday we set off again. We began with a visit to a Buddhist Temple. Different from the Shinto one, it was very high and had layered roofs. Once again the area around it was beautifully landscaped. Religion and gardens seem to go together in Japan.

Then we were taken to a saki tasting, in a cellar bar. We had one glass after another, accompanied by a small bite of something to eat. Apparently there is a subtle difference to each one. When asked to say which was our favourite we had trouble remembering which is which.

We emerged quite 'happy'.

After which Kate wanted to see the Ginza. I should have been warned beforehand so that I could lay off the saki.

We have a custom at Christmas in Ecuador when the wretched turkey, before being killed, is given alcohol. It's said to give the meat a special flavour.

Kate makes sure that I am the drunken turkey, before shopping.

We cruised along the Ginza admiring the top-end shops and the Swatch and Hermes buildings. Actually, Hermes is not attractive. It's covered in glass tiles and looks like an enormous toilet block.

My mind was somewhat fuddled by the saki so when I heard that Kate wanted to see Mickey Mouse I thought that the drink had got to her too. We were returning to Los Angeles after Japan. We could see him there in Disneyland.

But Mrs Takahashi smiled and gave instructions in Japanese to the driver.

We stopped at an imposing building and went inside. She talked to the receptionist who bowed to us, and showed us the lift to the next floor.

When we emerged we were greeted by a lady manager and invited to look around. Then it dawned on me. Not Mickey Mouse but Mikimoto, the best-known name in cultured pearls.

We wandered around looking at glass cases containing beautiful necklaces with strings of pearls. I had in mind a pearl choker. But they didn't have one. I have an opera DVD of Puccini's La Rondine (The Swallow). It stars the beautiful Spanish soprano Ainhoa Arteta. She wears a choker of four strands of pearls, and looks magnificent. It was set in the nineteen twenties, when pearl chokers were all the rage.

My mother wore a pearl necklace over a sweater and matching cardigan, what they called at the time twin sets and pearls. Indeed the late Queen often wore one.

Somehow pearls are not so fashionable now.

We sat at a desk with an assistant and looked at many different ones. By this time I had set a price limit for Kate. She pulled a face, as always what she likes is the most expensive. But we found one which we both liked, she for the pearls and me for the price. I correct that. I loved them too. They were perfectly matched and came with pretty pearl earrings.

I paid for it.

We had been given a glass of champagne, and little white flannels to wipe our hands.

I had read up about Japanese etiquette before we arrived in Japan. There are some no-nos. You can use the towels to wipe your hands, even to dab your face. But they must never be used for wiping your neck, or any other part of your body.

While waiting for the pearls to be wrapped, I felt an itch and scratched my head. I took my finger away and saw with horror there was blood on it. Without thinking I grabbed the little towel and put it to my head. It showed a patch of blood.

The shop staff looked at me in horror.

The gaijin has committed an unpardonable faux pas.

Kate was solicitous. I quickly passed her my handkerchief instead of the towel, and she dabbed at it.

The manager had recovered from the shock and asked if I was OK, did I need a doctor?

I thanked her, trying to make up for my sin, and said no. By this time the amount of blood on the handkerchief was minimal. I would not bleed to death.

Our beautiful pearls were put in a red box lined with white satin, then put into an oversized Mikimoto shopping bag.

The high-end shops do this, so that you become a walking advert for them.

Kate wanted to buy some presents for friends so we asked to be taken to a Pokemon shop. I am not into these things, but several of her friends are. She bought several toys, T-shirts and Hello Kitty socks. I had always thought that Hello Kitty was an American brand. Not so, it's Japanese.

There was a pet shop there so she bought a collar and lead for our new puppy, Snoopy.

`That was it for Tokyo.

We returned to the hotel, said goodbye and gave a tip to Mrs Takahashi.

We had been told that tipping is not generally done in Japan, but during our time in Japan we never had one refused. Perhaps that would mean losing face?

The next day we were going to Kanazawa. We had been instructed by Chinmay to sort our luggage and only take an overnight case with us on the train. Apparently bullet trains have very little luggage space. We will be two days in Kanazawa and then take another train to Kyoto. Our luggage will be taken by road delivery service directly to our hotel in Kyoto, which is the following stop on the tour.

We left the hotel at 11.30am and were driven to the station. It was very crowded. Luckily a lady guide took us to the right platform, and when the train drew in she showed us which was our carriage and seats.

The train seemed to take a long time to get out of Tokyo. There were endless houses and buildings for an hour after we left the station. Then we saw open fields, but they still had a lot of buildings around them. We saw snow-capped mountains and began to pass under them in tunnels until we emerged at the far coast, overlooking the Sea of Japan.

For a bullet train it seemed to stop remarkably often in the three hours it took.

We were met at Kanazawa Station by a driver who spoke no English. He waited for us on the platform with a card with our names. Then he mimed for us to follow him to the car.

It took an hour to drive through open fields to Yamashiro Onsen where we will stay in a ryokan.

We had been told that ryokans are inns traditionally placed by thermal waters, Onsen, where people go to health spas.

I had imagined, by Chinmay's description, that ours would be an ancient building in some isolated spot. But not so, the Beniya Mukayu ryokan is a modern hotel.

There were several other hotels close to it. I guess they all competed for the health-giving waters there.

We were greeted by girls in local dress who welcomed us and, after a brief tea ceremony, showed us to the room, one of only seventeen.

Ours was very spacious with divisions between the bathroom, dressing room, bedroom and sitting room. The dividing walls were indeed paper, and they had low sliding doors, which I had to duck under. So I am right, Kate!

There was a small balcony looking out into a tree-filled garden, with a wooden tub. It was full of hot water from the natural springs. We had to try this. A sign said that we should shower first before getting into the tub. We did, and slowly lowered ourselves into the hot water.

We appreciated it as the day was cold. We lounged in the tub using a wooden bucket to pour water over ourselves.

I had a skin rash on my chest, which I hoped the waters would heal.

We had been asked to put on the costumes we found in the room to go to dinner in the restaurant. We saw them neatly folded on the bed. We practised for a while and then got it right. There were sandals too. We saw that the white socks to go with these were split, so our toes could accommodate them. We looked at ourselves in the mirror. Wow, this was a big change. Now we looked Japanese.

To give ourselves courage we drank the bottle of sake from the minibar.

We self-consciously entered the dining room as Samurai and Geisha. Then we saw that everyone else looked exactly the same.

Once again there was a choice of Japanese or Western food. Kate had the Japanese, me the Western. The wine was French. We enjoyed a bottle of Chablis.

We began the next day, Thursday, with another dip in the tub. Today is windy, but it's a bit warmer than yesterday.

We met our guide Mrs Keiko Yamasaki at the hotel lobby at 10am.

She explained that she would do her best to show us Kanazawa in the one day we have available. Tomorrow we will take the train to Kyoto.

But we could only skim the surface, there is so much to see.

We drove the hour back to the city. The first stop was a covered market. As we walked down the aisle we saw a shop which hired kimonos. Kate wanted to buy one. Keiko said that they don't sell them, only rent. Would Kate like to rent one? No, she was adamant she wanted to buy it. We went in. Keiko talked to the shop assistant and we looked at several kimonos. They are made of silk and very beautiful. We were surprised how much cloth each was made of. They were displayed on double-width coat hangers and hung two meters to the ground. Kate was taken with a pink one with embroidered branches and leaves in blue and grey.

We asked to buy it, how much does it cost? Keiko asked the assistant. She looked nonplussed. She didn't know the price, she had never sold one. They only rented them. She called the owner of the shop. We waited and then he arrived. An elegant man in a black suit. He and Keiko talked. He asked which one she liked. Kate said the pink one. He instructed the assistant to look for a new one. He would not sell one that had been rented.

The price? He isn't sure. He will go to the office and do his calculations. He reappeared with a calculator in his hand and told Keiko a number of yen. We asked how much that was in dollars. It is almost three thousand dollars.

We agreed. Can she wear it now?

Yes, that is no problem. The manager talked to the assistant. She took Kate and Keiko into a dressing room while I took a seat outside the shop (there wasn't one inside) and waited for an hour.

The price includes the full monty. First they piled up her hair in geisha fashion. Then they dressed her in pyjamas. That was followed by a padded cloth board tied to her tummy. Then came two more layers of petticoats. The kimono itself is an art to put on. It is very wide and very long. The experts pleat the cloth, as though packing a very special parcel, with many careful folds, until it fits the lady. One size fits all. It's impossible to do by yourself.

If Kate ever wants to wear it again in Guayaquil or Madrid she will have to find a Japanese lady to help her. Even then not many Japanese know how to do it.

She was given split white socks, wooden sandals and finally a little white handbag.

They also included a small suitcase in which to pack the kimono and showed Kate how to fold it.

Hey Presto. Kate is a geisha.

When she emerged I was overcome with emotion, and shed a tear. She really did look beautiful. Though strangely the addition of the board on her tummy reduced her figure. The Japanese like their ladies to look like dolls.

We left the shop and drove to the Kenroku-en Gardens. Kate and I stood to one side as Keiko went to the ticket office. We looked at the crowd walking up the road to the gates. There were several ladies in kimonos. Keiko told us they were brides. They would take photos in the gardens.

Which is exactly what we did. The cherry trees were gorgeous. Kate stood in front of one and I took photos of her, the pink kimono against the pink flowers.

Then Keiko took some of us together.

We stood on a typical Japanese arched wooden bridge, as seen on Willow pattern dinner services. More photos were taken. It was a warm and sunny day. They are the best photos of a wonderful holiday in Japan.

We spent almost two hours in the gardens. Then we were hungry. Where would we go for lunch?

We went to a remarkable sushi bar. It is a do-it-yourself bar. We sat and drank beers. The waitress put little plates of fillings in front of us. Then we got a wooden box each. Inside were four tortillas. We followed Keiko's lead. Extracting one tortilla we placed the fillings in it, rolled it up and ate it.

We could select the fillings we liked. Good fun too.

After lunch we went to see the old city of Kanazawa. First, we went to the Geisha area. This was fascinating. It is exactly like the film The Last Geisha. The streets are narrow and the wooden houses have tiled roofs. We went into one house. The rooms are very small and divided by sliding walls. The ceilings are low. I had to bend my neck. Kate was still in her geisha costume. We took pictures of her kneeling on the floor.

I rather liked the idea of a submissive wife serving me on her knees.

Well you can always dream!

Keiko showed us a narrow lane between the houses. Each house has a small door leading on to it. This was the escape route for male guests to the house, if they had to make a quick getaway. We learnt that geishas are not prostitutes. They are instructed in the arts of pleasing men with music, dancing, serving food, conversation and playing games. A geisha may at some stage of her career become the partner of just one man. She continues to live in the house with other girls, supervised by Mama-san. But is available only for her client.

Just as in The Last Geisha, and the Chairman.

We went from there to see the Samurai district. Here we were shown a much larger house with an inside garden with a stream running through it. It is very peaceful.

Now it was time to return to our Ryokan.

When we arrived there we said goodbye to Keiko.

The hotel staff were impressed with Kate's kimono. Surprisingly, the diners in the restaurant were not. They all had their Japanese dressing gowns on, but Kate's kimono was outstanding.

We finished the day with a drink at the bar before going to our room.

I remember that, oddly, we talked about selling the apartment in Madrid and buying one in London. The idea was that Kate could perfect her English there. Anyway we know Madrid very well. It's time to sample the restaurants of London.

Friday 7th April. Good Friday

We checked out of the Ryokan and a car arrived to take us to Kaga Onsen station. Today there was just the driver. Though immaculately dressed, he couldn't speak English. When we got to the station I worried that we wouldn't be able to find the platform by ourselves.

But he parked the car and led us into the station helping us to pull our luggage. We were too early and the platform for our train was not yet announced. The driver pulled out a tablet with a translator on it.

"Train not here, would you like to eat something?"

We recently had breakfast, but it would fill in the time. We went to a station buffet and had a coffee and cake.

The driver kept looking at the train timetable on the wall.

Then he showed us his tablet "Do you want to go home?"

I indicated that I didn't understand. He put the question in Japanese again and showed us the translation "Do you want to go to the platform?".

The train took two and a quarter hours to get to Kyoto. There were houses all the way until we entered a long tunnel. When we emerged we saw an enormous lake. The rail line ran alongside it for half an hour until we arrived at Kyoto station.

We were met by another driver with our names on a board.

It took twenty minutes to get to the spectacular Ritz Carlton Hotel.

We emerged two hours later with a very pretty maxi skirt and a toreador top in blue and black check. Obviously, this can only be worn with new shoes and a handbag.

She has taken the monk's message to heart. Concentrate on everything you do!

We went back to the hotel at 5pm to change. After which we went to the hotel bar for a glass of champagne.

Explorations had arranged for us to have dinner with geishas. It was a rare and expensive treat. Even few Japanese have experienced it.

Yoshiko returned to pick us up at 6.30pm. We drove to the ancient geisha area of town, left the car and walked down the narrow street until we came across a house with a red lantern over the door. We knocked, it was opened, and we were led in by a maid. We had to leave our shoes by the door, and were given slippers. We followed her upstairs, through a low doorway, into a room. There was little furniture, just cushions which we sat on, and a low table.

The maid left us. We chatted in hushed tones.

The door opened and three ladies came in wearing kimonos. Two of them were young and had white-painted faces. One wore red lipstick, the other didn't. The third lady was a lot older. We stood and they bowed to us, we bowed to them.

Yoshiko talked to them. Then she explained to us. The one with the lipstick and yellow kimono is a geisha. She is twenty-one. The one in the white kimono, without lipstick is a Maiko. She is just sixteen, a trainee geisha. The older woman is their accompanying musician. She plays the shamisen, a three-stringed guitar with a characteristic twanging sound.

Maiko, as the junior, opened a bottle of saki and poured glasses for all of us. But not for herself. I had been told about this. I took the bottle from her and poured her glass. It's forbidden for her to pour her own glass.

Then they began their show. The geisha, to the sound of the shamisen and the elder woman's singing, danced very gracefully. It was lovely to watch her. We again thought of the film The Last Geisha.

Following that they served us food. They knelt by us and put pieces of food from the platter onto our plates and kept our glasses of saki full.

They asked us questions and we replied. Yoshiko translated both ways.

Then came game time. The geisha and maiko sat opposite each other on cushions. There was an inverted cup and a small ball on the floor between them. With great dexterity the geisha moved her hand lifting and putting down the cup. Sometimes you could see the ball, sometimes not. Then the maiko did it. The geisha won.

She asked me if I would like to do it. So I went and sat on the cushion.

No contest, she beat me quickly.

Kate did better but the geisha is an expert.

We laughed a lot.

They asked if we would like a photo with them. Kate and I stood in the center with the three ladies, while Yoshiko took photos.

Then they bowed to us and left the room.

We left too.

Easter Sunday.

We had a full program today, so we met Yoshiko at 8am. The first event was to visit a bamboo forest. We walked along paths with the bamboo towering above us. Then beyond the bamboo was yet another temple with a beautiful garden. On one side was a small ornate building.

Here we had a tea ceremony. We removed our shoes and went inside the small building. We sat in a circle around the tea lady. Making tea is a long process, involving washing the already clean cups.

But she finally poured us a tiny cup of tea each.

She asked us if we had been concentrating. Oh yes we said. Good then it's your turn to make tea. Luckily Kate went first. She really had been watching, while I was daydreaming. Now I paid more attention. When it was my turn I got it right.

We returned to the car and drove an hour through wooded hills to Nara, which had once been the capital of Japan.

It's a small city with a large park in the centre where a herd of sacred deer roam at will. There is no fence to the park, so the deer can wander into town. The stags have had their antlers cut off, to make them safe to the public. There are stalls selling deer food. We bought several packets and tried to feed them. But so many people feed them that they aren't interested at all.

Eventually, we found one who would accept food. Kate stroked it and we took photos together with it.

Then we went to see a huge temple containing a giant statue of Buddha. It is the Todaiji Temple. It's said to be the World's largest wooden building.

There was a long queue to get in. Yoshiko went to get the pre-booked tickets while Kate and I continued feeding deer.

The temple was very crowded, I guess because it was Sunday. Once in the temple compound we joined the queue to the temple itself. It was difficult to stop and get a photo of the vast Buddha, as the crowds pushed us on. It is thirty feet high and covered in gold leaf. Eventually, we managed it. Then we walked around the statue to the back of the temple where there were notice boards explaining the history of the temple which had burnt down and been rebuilt several times.

But there were too many people to be comfortable.

We soon left.

We drove back to Kyoto and said goodbye to Yoshiko.

Monday 10th April

Today we leave Japan.

We checked out of the Ritz Carlton Hotel and a car took us to Osaka Kansai airport.

From there we flew an hour to Tokyo Haneda airport.

The onward flight was Japan Airlines to Los Angeles.

Los Angeles.

We arrived at Tom Bradley airport, Los Angeles at midday US West Coast time.

There was the usual long queue at immigration, but eventually we got through and collected our luggage. Hauling all five pieces we left the terminal and looked for the taxi rank.

But there isn't one. For some strange reason taxis are not allowed to park at the terminal. You have to take a bus to where they are.

It was hot, we were tired (it was 4am Japanese time) and had too much luggage. The idea of waiting for a bus, then putting the luggage on board, then getting it all off again, did not appeal.

We stood helplessly looking for a white knight. And one came.

A Mexican asked us in Spanish if we needed a taxi. We said yes. He took two of the suitcases and set off at speed telling us to follow him. We did, and as he raced on, we worried that he might be a thief.

He led us to the multi-storey car park, across the road from the terminal. Finally, we got to his car. He explained that it was illegal to pick up customers at the terminal. The airport police did not allow it.

Now that we were out of sight he negotiated his price. Where are you going? The Four Seasons Beverly Hills Hotel.

$150.

OK. It was a ridiculous price, but we just wanted to get there and go to bed.

We set off. He said his name was Pedro. We introduced ourselves, Colin and Kate.

On the way to the hotel he got a phone call in Spanish.

"Hola Pedro, where are you? I am waiting for you at the terminal. My plane was early. I told you to get here in plenty of time".

To which he cheerfully lied that he was on his way to the airport. The traffic was bad.

He would get there as soon as he could.

He grinned at us.

So that was it. He was moonlighting. Instead of picking up his boss he was taking us to Beverly Hills Hotel and making $150 bucks on the side.

As we drove there I noticed the nodding donkeys of oil wells. They seemed to go on a long way. I asked Pedro. He said that Los Angeles sits right on top of a large oil field.

I had no idea it did.

When we arrived at the hotel the first thing we noticed was a statue of Marilyn Monroe right by the front door. It's the famous statue of her standing over a hot air grid, holding her skirt down. I forget which film it comes from.

Kate is a fan of Marilyn. We had to take photos of Marilyn with her, before we could check in.

Beverly Hills is a lovely hotel.

We were shown to our large suite. We had been travelling for nineteen hours. What we needed urgently was a shower. The bathroom was ample and we both were soon fresh again.

We were tired, but decided to see a bit more of the hotel before sleeping. We went down to the bar at 6pm and had cocktails, before going to the dining room. After ten days of Japanese food I wanted a steak. We drank a great deal of wine.

And then finally we did go to bed.

Despite sleeping early last night, we lingered in bed today. Finally getting up at 11am.

We wondered whether we had missed breakfast. Normally hotels have a cut off point between 10 and 11 am. After that no deal.

We asked the maitre'd in the dining room. Were we too late for breakfast? In that case what time do they serve lunch?

He smiled and said you can have whichever you want. My sort of hotel.

We chose breakfast. I wanted my favorite huevos rancheros.

On the way to the dining room, as we passed the hall porter's desk we asked if he could arrange a car and driver for today.

Now he sent a message that the car would be here at 12pm.

That was perfect.

Our driver is Ben. A young man of about thirty. He told us that he is an aspiring actor.

But as acting work is scarce he drives tourists.

I almost asked him if he knew my son-in-law, Steve, who lives in Los Angeles.

He is a few years older than Ben, he used to be a model and an actor.

He has appeared in promotional films, and one major film The Holiday, with Cameron Diaz and Kate Winslet.

But I decided not to. Just in case he said yes. A longshot, but if he did and called Steve to say that his father-in-law is here with a young girl.....no better not.

The family is not in tune with my new life.

So where would you like to go?

The first place for a girl new to Los Angeles has to be the Hollywood sign.

He drove us there. He knew of a good place to see it from. We wound uphill through smart housing until he pulled into a narrow road and parked the car. We walked with him for fifty yards, then looking up, there it was. We took lots of photos of each other and Ben took some of us together.

The very same photo which appeared in the UK press (Drug gang kidnaps Briton, 78) in December 2023.

As we drove back down the hill we came across a site where there were lots of tourists taking similar photos. But we had been closer to the famous sign.

Ben asked us what we wanted to see now. Kate explained that she is a fan of Marilyn Monroe. Could he take us on a Marilyn tour to the places she went and lived. He agreed. He too is a fan.

We will start with the Chinese Theatre in downtown LA to see the famous handprints and the venue of the Oscars. We got there. The traffic made it difficult to park, so Ben left us at the front of the theater and went to park in the next street. He gave us his number. Call me when you want to leave.

There are a lot of handprints. It took us a while to find Marilyn's. But we did. Kate knelt down and placed her hand in the print. It was the same size. There are brass stars inlaid in the pavement with the name of each star inside it.

A street trader asked her if she would like her own star. Yes, of course. He placed a gold coloured metal star on the pavement and put Kate's name in brass letters within it. Then took her photo.

The venue for the Oscars is close by. But on 360 days of the year it's nothing more than the entrance to a shopping mall. It's only for the night of the Oscars that it's decorated as the entrance to the theater. We went in and up the famous escalator. We had to wait until we got it to ourselves, as others wanted photos too. At the top is the real entrance to the theater. It was locked, we couldn't go in.

Next, Ben took us to Marilyn's house, where she lived when she was married to Joe di Maggio, the famous baseball player, in 1954.

We were surprised that it isn’t very large. He said that all the houses here had been the same size at that time. The neighbouring ones have been rebuilt once or twice since then and enlarged.

Would we like to see where Marilyn is buried?

Yes, of course.

It was not far away.

We soon arrived at Westwood Village Memorial Park and Mortuary. Ben knew exactly where her remains were. He led us to a wall of niches where each coffin had been inserted and then sealed up.

Marilyn Monroe 1926 -1962

We stood there for a moment in silence. A tribute to her.

Then Ben pointed to the one to the left hand side. We were amazed to see,

Hugh M Hefner 1926 -2017

The timing didn't seem right. That space had been left empty for fifty-five years, waiting for him? Ben explained. Marilyn had been the first of Hefner's Playmates in his famous Playboy magazine.

He had always been in love with her. Before he died he negotiated with the family of the neighbouring corpse, and for a mere two million dollars they ceded the space to him (grandad went elsewhere).

Our Marilyn tour then went past two hotels she frequented, the Beverly Hills Hotel and Chateau Marmont and finished at her last house, where she died.

Where to now?

To Santa Monica, said Kate.

Why?

Because that was where Jack told Rose (in the film Titanic) that she must see one day.

So there we went.

Arriving, it didn't look very attractive. We drove along the promenade until we came to a pier with a funfair on it. Kate wanted to go on the rides. We asked Ben to wait for us. We would only be half an hour.

We walked along the crowded pier. It was certainly popular. We passed a shop called Bubba Gump, selling all sorts of souvenirs.

Kate wanted to go on the Big Dipper. It was seriously big. Those on it now were screaming. So I opted out. She went on it alone.

Then, when she survived it, I went with her on the Big Wheel. This took us up about forty metres and there was a great view of the Santa Monica shoreline, until the mist came in from the sea. It got very cold. We weren't dressed warmly. Kate was shivering. She only had on a white blouse, the Chanel toreador jacket, and a bare midriff.

We just wanted to get down again.

And that was the problem. The wheel turned a bit and stopped as each carriage got to the landing platform where people got on or off. It took twenty minutes for us to get down.

I looked at my watch. We had been here over an hour.

We had told Ben half an hour. We called him. He said not to rush he would wait for us.

Kate wanted candy floss, so we bought that. We went to Bubba Gump's and bought all sorts of silly souvenirs for our friends.

Finally we walked back to the promenade.

We looked up and down the road. Where was he? I thought I recognised the car and we went to it. I opened the back door. The driver turned and looked at us wide eyed. It wasn't Ben. We apologized, and he laughed.

Then we saw Ben's car.

We got back to the hotel at 6.15 pm. We had been out six hours. How much?

It was twelve hundred dollars, plus a tip. But we thought that fair. We had seen a lot of Los Angeles and particularly the Marilyn trail.

We had dinner in the hotel and then watched a movie in the room. It was Pretty Woman, starring Julia Roberts and Richard Gere. We had both seen it before.

We were reminded of it as we drove downtown. Ben had pointed out the house where she lived in the film, with its fire escape, where she came down to avoid paying the rent and where Richard Gere went up with his bunch of flowers. We laughed at the lift boy at the hotel. He has an extraordinary face with which to express emotions.

Wednesday.

Our last day in Los Angeles. Tonight we fly back to Guayaquil at 2am.

We had paid for the extra night at the hotel, so that we could keep the room until we leave for the airport at 10.30pm.

Kate wanted to go to Chanel. She had once bought a white Chanel handbag and it had gotten stained when she wore her black gothic dress. She would ask them how to clean it.

As an excuse it was pretty weak. I knew my Kate. Once in Chanel I couldn't get her out again until she had bought stuff.

We asked the hall porter where Chanel is. He said it's on Rodeo Drive. That's where all the top-end shops are.

That was where Pretty Woman was taken to shop by the manager of the Beverly Wilshire Hotel.

He called a hotel limousine to take us there.

We passed Dior, Tiffany, Hermes, Louis Vuitton, Prada, Gucci, Cartier, Versace, Jimmy Choo, Valentino, Armani and finally we saw the Chanel shop .

We went in. A salesman (gay as always) came to assist us. He ran his practised eye over Kate and noted the Chanel handbag. Would we like a glass of champagne?

Yes,we would indeed.

She showed him the handbag with its stains. He tutted over it. You should never use a white handbag with black clothes. That we knew. How can we remove the stains?

He shook his head, there was no way to do it without ruining the bag.

Kate seemed to accept this explanation. She left me sitting with my glass and wandered off to look at the racks of clothes.

The assistant hovered around her. Whenever she selected an item he would rush over to help her find her size.

She finally selected a black skirt, pink cardigan and a pink handbag.

I had sat there for more than an hour. The glass had been refilled several times. Bored, I idly took my handkerchief and dipped it in champagne then rubbed the stain on the handbag. Wonder of wonders it cleaned it off. The salesman hasn't a clue how to do it. I had just discovered the way. But there again. Perhaps he was more interested in selling her another bag than cleaning this one?

We left Chanel and walked down Rodeo Drive. Quite by accident we saw we had come to the Beverly Wilshire Hotel.

This was too good to miss. We went in for lunch.

We asked the doorman if Pretty Woman was really filmed here, or was it a stage set? He said that only the exterior of the hotel was filmed. The interiors were done elsewhere.

He looked at Kate and said

"I see you have brought your own Pretty Woman, Sir"

I thanked him and we went in laughing.

Then I wondered what exactly he meant by that. In the film she is a prostitute!

Thursday 21 December 2023

The Daily Telegraph

Sport

Your 12-page section inside

How to avoid expensive pet bills this Christmas p.6

Features

The bizarre story of how a British consul ended up in the hands of Ecuadorian gangsters

Telegraph Front Page

Thursday 21 December 2023 The Daily Telegraph

Features

Clockwise from top left: Armstrong in The Forbidden Corner; with partner Katherine Paola Santos; and with police on his release; footage of Santos after she was freed appeared to show her wearing a bomb vest; the couple partying

The expat, the cartel and the kidnap plot

The details of Colin Armstrong's four-day ordeal could have come straight from the pages of a thriller, but it was all too real, as *Guy Kelly* reports

The story reads a little like a Graham Greene novel reimagined for the *Narcos* audience. The protagonist looks like John Waters playing Leslie Phillips playing Alan Whicker. The setting's exotic, the supporting cast extraordinary, the details bizarre. But for Colin Armstrong, the ordeal of the past four days must have felt all too real, and all too scary.

In the early hours of last Saturday, Armstrong, a 78-year-old businessman, former UK honorary consul and vigorous traveller from North Yorkshire, was reportedly kidnapped from a ranch he owned in the town of Baba, near the coastal city of Guayaquil, dragged to his own black BMW by more than 15 men wearing fake police uniforms, bundled into the vehicle and driven away to be held captive.

Armstrong's Colombian partner, Katherine Paola Santos, was allegedly also abducted by the men, who have been rumoured to work for a brutal drug cartel. The couple's car was later found abandoned by a roadside, as footage emerged online of a bloody trail at their ransacked home, known as Rancho Rodeo Grande.

"Following an apparent criminal act against a businessman in the early hours of this morning in Los Rios, specialist police units are carrying out operative and investigative work on the ground," local police tweeted over the weekend. The Foreign, Commonwealth and Development Office confirmed it too was supporting the Ecuadorian authorities, while a source inside Ecuador's security forces told *The Telegraph* that British intelligence services were also assisting, though not in an operational capacity.

Concern grew over the days that followed, and for understandable reasons. Incidents of kidnappings for ransom by criminal gangs in Ecuador have soared in recent years, especially in Guayaquil, a port city in the Los Rios province that exports cocaine to the US, Europe and Asia. Reports suggested Armstrong, who runs Agripac, a large agricultural supply company, may have crossed one such gang, Los Tiguerones, by refusing to pay protection money.

Photographs of Armstrong and Santos, who as a couple seem as improbable as they are enamoured of one another, spread across the internet. Armstrong's son, Nick, 47, flew to Ecuador to help the authorities. His daughter, Diana Armstrong-Bruce, an estate agent based in California, told MailOnline: "This is a critical time, we've been told not to say anything to anyone. We just want my father back."

Suddenly, Santos was freed, in a confusing release that reportedly involved her being deposited at the home of Nick Armstrong by taxi, and wearing a bomb vest. A video clip circulating online shows a bomb disposal officer freeing her. A source inside Ecuadorian intelligence then confirmed to *The Telegraph* that Santos was questioned by police about her alleged involvement in the kidnapping plot after a local former MP publicly implicated her in the crime.

And suddenly, Armstrong was also free. "On the road to Manabi, our units freed citizen Colin A. kidnapped a few days before in Los Rios," the local police chief, César Augusto Zapata Correa, tweeted early yesterday morning, before announcing that nine arrests had been made. "At the moment he is safe and healthy." He finished with the hashtag "Sin Tregua Al Delito" – meaning "No Trace to Crime". Since 2016, Ecuador's murder rate has risen by almost 500 per cent.

Telegraph Article

Police focus on drug gangs after kidnap of Briton, 78

Colin Armstrong, 78, was dragged from his ranch in Ecuador with his Colombian girlfriend, Katherine Paola Santos. The former honorary consul to Guayaquil, who owns the Tupgill Park estate in North Yorkshire, left, was found four days later

Mario Ledwith

For four nervous days the friends and relatives of Colin Armstrong, Britain's former honorary consul in Ecuador's largest city, waited for news of his kidnap.

The 78-year-old grandfather, who owns one of Ecuador's largest agro-chemicals companies, was brutally dragged from the ranch he calls home with his Colombian lover by criminals disguised as police officers.

British intelligence were said to be involved in the search, which ended in relief on Wednesday as he was found in good health on the road to the coastal Manabi region. Though his face was blurred in the rescue photograph released by police, his familiar grin could still be seen.

Speculation had flared, encouraged by a former MP in Ecuador, that Katherine Paola Santos, his Colombian girlfriend, could have been implicated in the crime, but police confirmed on Thursday that she was a victim.

She was found alive in a residential area of Guayaquil wearing a booby-trapped vest, although the explosives were later found to be fake.

After an interview with police, Armstrong was back in the arms of his family in Ecuador. A family friend said the rescue had come as a huge relief to his loved ones in Britain and Ecuador. "Colin has obviously been through a traumatic time and his rest and relaxation and family time is of the utmost importance," the friend said.

The saga began when a group of gunmen overwhelmed security guards at the perimeter of Armstrong's property, and dragged the couple into his BMW. A video showing blood in ransacked rooms emerged later.

Official attention turned to the drug cartels responsible for wreaking havoc in Guayaquil, Ecuador's largest city, in recent years. Ecuador's strategic location between the cocaine-producing hubs of Colombia and Peru has led gangs to play out an increasingly violent turf war for control of the city's port.

Since 2018, the homicide rate in Ecuador has more than quadrupled and gangs have been linked to a series of massacres.

Foreigners and the wealthy have been targeted for kidnap ransoms, and police confirmed that Armstrong's ordeal was an attempted extortion.

The terrifying experience was a far cry from his day-to-day life in the once peaceful country that he has called home for more than 50 years, where he lives as the quintessential English gentleman in Ecuador, and locals call him "Mr Colin".

Armstong spent his younger years in North Yorkshire as part of a horse-racing dynasty. His family home was the 500-acre Tupgill Park estate, in the *Yorkshire Dales, which was bought in 1904* by his grandfather, a jockey and horse trainer. His father, Captain Gerald Armstrong was also a renowned horse trainer and trained the champion jockey Willie Carson. Armstrong broke with tradition when, in 1968, he joined Imperial Chemical Industries (ICI) with the ambition of working overseas.

He landed aged 26 in Ecuador in 1972, after stints in Malaysia and Mexico, and was given the job of running a newly formed partner of ICI called Agripac.

Armstrong quickly settled into the Las Peñas neighbourhood of Guayaquil, eventually meeting his wife, Cecilia, who was from the city. They married in October 1974. He turned down a senior role in England with ICI, eventually taking over Agripac and transforming it into one of Ecuador's 30 biggest companies. His three children — Nick, Diana and Alexandra — were born in Ecuador.

They enjoyed trips back to Tupgill Park, which Armstrong started to turn into one of North Yorkshire's leading tourist attractions with 150,000 visitors a year, after inheriting the property *from his* father. In Ecuador, Armstro[ng] began representing British interests [in] his role as honorary consul to Guaya[q]uil, attending black-tie events wi[th] Cecilia. He retired from the volunta[ry] position in 2016 to be replaced by h[is] son, who led the British chamber [of] commerce in the city and joined th[e] family business. Armstrong was ap[-]pointed OBE and CMG by the Queen [in] 2011 for services to the monarchy.

In the months before his kidnappin[g], Armstrong appeared to have embrace[d] his new romance with Santos, wh[o] documented their travels around th[e] world on her social media pages. Th[e] pair posed together below the Holly[-]wood sign in Los Angeles, in front of th[e] Egyptian pyramids, on safari, sippin[g] drinks on boats and at a succession [of] parties.

Police subsequently raided 30 prop[-]erties in connection with the kidnap[-]ping, turning up six firearms, grenade[s,] ammunition and replica police cloth[-]ing. Eight Ecuadoreans were arreste[d] including three with a record of robber[y] and trafficking of illegal substances, a[s] well as a foreigner.

Fatal crush music club wants to reopen

Mario Ledwith

A woman remains in a critical condition a year after a crowd crush at the O2 Brixton Academy killed two people.

Relatives of the two who died after 1,000 fans forced entry to a sold-out afrobeats concert have joined the police's calls for people to come forward with information as a criminal investigation continues.

Following a campaign by local businesses and the music industry, Lambeth council determined that a list of stringent conditions must be met before the music venue can reopen.

Academy Music Group (AMG), the US company that has owned the south London venue for 20 years, said that it was still "working hard" to implement the 77 conditions. Requirements include strengthening doors and introducing new safety proceedures.

The Metropolitan Police had previously urged the closure of the venue, saying that it had no confidence in AMG. But the council's licensing sub-committee voted to allow the company to continue running the venue after a two-day review in September.

Gaby Hutchinson, 23, a security guard, and Rebecca Ikumelo, 33, a mother of two children, aged five and seven, died in the incident. A 22-year-old woman who was injured also remains in hospital in a serious condition.

The victims' relatives have criticised Asake, the Nigerian afrobeats singer who was performing at the venue.

Hutchinson's sister Kelsey, 26, from Billericay, Essex, said: "I think the main thing is the singer has such a big influence over his crowd." She said that the singer should urge concertgoers to come forward with any recorded video and information.

Last week, the police released images of 13 people it wants to speak to as part of its investigation.

Detective Chief Inspector Nigel Penney said that while 500 witness statements had been taken and 5,000 pieces of evidence seized "many unanswered questions" remained.

Mother appears in court charged with boy's murder

David Woode Crime Correspondent

A woman has appeared in court charged with the murder of her four-year-old son. Keziah Macharia, 41, was arrested after police were called to an "extremely distressing incident" at her flat in Hackney, east London, on Wednesday night. Kobi Macharia Dooly was found with several stab wounds, and died in hospital.

Macharia appeared at Thames magistrates' court in Bow yesterday, charged with Kobi's murder. She did not enter pleas and was remanded in custody. She is scheduled to appear a[t] the Old Bailey on Thursday.

Neighbours have paid tribute to th[e] "happy and energetic" boy. A hair[-]dresser, 36, who lives near by and aske[d] not to be named, said her neighbour[s] had "seemed like a loving family".

Detective Chief Superintendent James Conway, who leads policing i[n] the area, said: "This is an extremely dis[-]tressing incident, which will under[-]standably cause shock and disbelief."

He added that police were workin[g] with Hackney council to offer suppor[t] to the local community.

Times Article

Colin at Rodeo Grande

Colin & Kate outside the gates of Rodeo Grande

Tupgill House

With my Sisters

Rishi Sunak at Forbidden Corner with Leo and Ria, the manager of the Saddleroom

Everest seen from 6000 metres

Helicopter in Nepal

Equator Line near Quito

Igloos in Antarctica

Plane to South Pole

Signpost at Dixie's Camp

Sign pointing upwards says 'International Space Station 400 km upwards'

'Dixie's Camp 83 degrees South, 20 degrees East. (The most remote camp on Earth, Probably'

Sign to the left says 'South Pole 757 km'

Sign to the right says 'Whichaway 1458 km'

Lower sign to right says 'Wolf's Fang 1317 km'

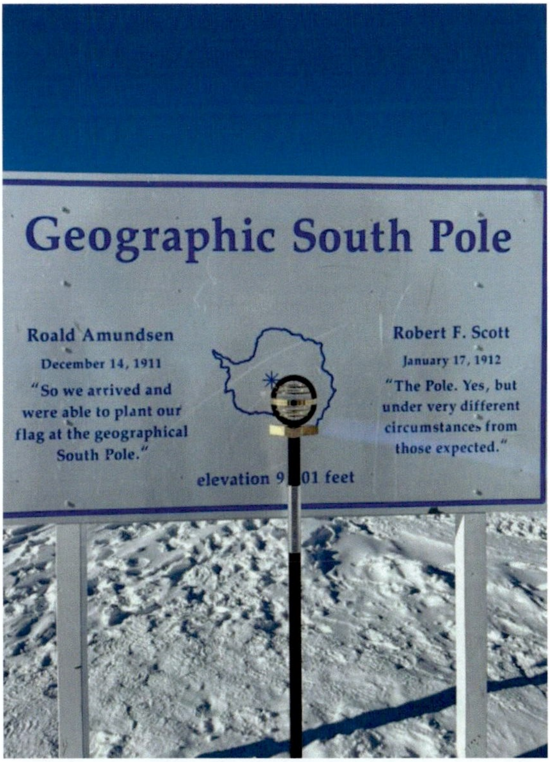
Geographic South Pole
Roald Amundsen
December 14, 1911
"So we arrived and were able to plant our flag at the geographical South Pole."
Robert F. Scott
January 17, 1912
"The Pole. Yes, but under very different circumstances from those expected."

South Pole

With Geishas in Japan

Kate in her Kimono

Taj Mahal, India in 2018

Guayaquil

We got back home to our penthouse at 2pm on Thursday 13th April 2023.

Two hours later Fredy arrived with Snoopy, who had stayed at Rodeo Grande while we were away.

As always, he ignored us at first.

Fredy stayed until 8pm. We shared several bottles of wine and told him about Japan.

Kate gave him his Pokemon items. He is a collector.

Then he left and, exhausted, we went to bed.

Tuesday 13th August 2024

Back to the present day.

I had a thought this morning.

I have been bewailing the fact that Agripac is going through a bad patch. Now I see that it's exactly what I need. I need a challenge to put the company right, before waving it goodbye.

Not that I am thinking of leaving anytime soon. But the decision may not be mine!

In fact, I think we are over the worst. There are one or two larks in the air, and that surely means Spring is coming.

Last night I drove home after a tiring day in the office. I shared a glass of wine with Kate. She was watching a program on TV about unsolved crimes. This chapter was about Jack the Ripper.

I watched it for a while until I got bored. Then I went to answer any late emails of the day, poured another glass of wine, and read my book.

She came to ask what I wanted for dinner? Yaneth had left something cooked.

All very peaceful and ordinary.

Then I suddenly remembered that Lien was in town with his son and his son's girlfriend. We were due to have dinner with them in a restaurant at 7pm.

How stupid of me to forget. It was now 6.30pm. I had despatched our guards until tomorrow morning. There was no way to get them back quickly, as they lived in another part of town.

Well, we will have to go without them.

No one except Lien knows that we are due to meet, the restaurant isn't even booked. It is Monday after all.

I shouted to Kate to get changed quickly. She protested that she hadn't done her hair, but she went to the bedroom.

I shaved, changed my clothes and by seven o'clock we were at the restaurant.

Shortly afterwards Lien arrived with son Hugh, and his very pretty Ukrainian girlfriend, Kristina.

It was a happy meal. We drank a lot and ate tapas, Spanish omelet and chipirones.

We didn't talk business. That would wait for Wednesday when Lien and I will meet with Nick.

Surprisingly, we managed to get home without mishap, despite being unguarded.

Today, August 14th, is a red letter day. We are going to sign the contract for the new house. We all met in my office at 3pm.

My lawyer Alfredo Ledesma with his secretary, the couple selling the house, their lawyer, the notary public and myself.

It only took half an hour. The notary read out the sales contract, we signed it, delivered a cheque for the deposit, and a bank guarantee, payable when the transfer is completed.

We shook hands and that was that.

We will get the keys the same day as they receive the balance of the purchase price, probably in two weeks.

We signed lots of documents. Once again the witch has been proved right.

I went home to Kate with the good news, and a bunch of yellow roses.

We drank a toast to our new house.

She had been in touch with Cristina, at Rodeo. Before sending us the furniture it needs attention. There were scratches on some pieces. They will be sanded down before the varnish is applied.

I will send her money to pay for the furniture restorer to do this.

We called our architect friend Juan Gabriel Ledesma (Alfredo's son) and asked his help with the new house. We want to make some changes, and build a jacuzzi in the garden.

Yes, he would be delighted to help us.

He had done a very good job when we bought the penthouse, seven years ago.

We have been planning another holiday. We want to go to Tupgill, to Madrid and Croatia. Perhaps three weeks in total. When shall we go?

We had first to complete both the sale of Rodeo and the house purchase. They are almost done. But now we want to take possession of the house and start the changes, to make it our home. We hope we will get the keys by the end of August.

Then there is also the Agripac calendar to do. That will take several days.

We had originally thought of going to Tupgill this month. But we can't as Ceci is still there. Diana and her family have returned to Los Angeles. But Ceci has invited friends from London to stay. She sends me lots of photos. The weather is beautiful so they walk in the countryside, drive to local villages and eat at pubs. Today they are in Edinburgh to see the Festival.

I think they leave Tupgill in another week, to go to London, Stratford on Avon and Bath. Finally they are all going to Santorini. After which she gets back here in early September.

I am happy that she is enjoying herself. Her friends are my friends too. But, as always with a separation, they have to decide, it's one or the other.

I have a painting in my office, painted many years ago when we lived at Ferngill. It shows Ceci and myself standing, with the lake in the background. The artist captured the children, each with his or her hobby. Nick aged fifteen has his shotgun, Diana at twelve is riding her horse, and Alex at ten, has her bike.

It was a good time. Ceci and I were happy together then. We are still on good terms. It's just that we can't do things together, while I am with Kate.

Today is Alex's 43rd birthday. The family chat has been active. We have all wished her Happy Birthday. I am going to have dinner with her tonight. Sadly I can't take Kate with me. We haven't got to that point yet. Perhaps we never will. But Kate understands. She won't try to separate me from my children.

Three days later, we have begun the calendar process. Gynna will get the outfits and we will do the shots in her studio. It's cheaper to do it inside as opposed to venues around Ecuador. Anyway I am not allowed to travel at the moment.

We have done some wonderful calendars over the years.

We have shot photos in Rodeo Grande for several years. We have gone to farms both on the Coast and the Sierra, and the Botanic Gardens of Guayaquil.

But the best photos were shot in the Galapagos Islands in 2020.

The Galapagos Islands belong to Ecuador. Although they are a thousand kilometres off the coast.

Charles Darwin spent some time there when he was doing a circuit of the world in HMS Beagle, and came up with his Theory of Evolution, which he published in 1859.

It was the evolution of finches, among other creatures, that confirmed his theory that animals adapt (evolve) to their environment.

Today the Galapagos Islands are Ecuador's claim to fame. Most tourists who visit Ecuador include a trip there.

It's a wonderful experience. Despite thousands of tourists, the animals and birds remain unafraid of humans. The National Park is well managed. Tours are guided by experts. The rule is that you can leave nothing behind, and take nothing away.

I have been there many times over the years both with Ceci, with the family and twice with Kate.

Once, in my capacity as Honorary British Consul, Ceci and I had the honour of meeting Prince Charles and Camila, Duchess of Cornwall, when they made a visit.

On another occasion I helped David Attenborough, when he went to Galapagos to make a film.

On the 6th September 2020 we went there for five days to produce theAgripac 2021 calendar. Covid was at its peak, tourism had almost vanished. We would have the islands to ourselves. It was an opportunity not to be missed.

We flew there, all eight of us, wearing the obligatory masks. The local airline announced that because of Covid there would be no service on board during the two-hour flight. The seats were double spaced.

We arrived at Baltra airport, the small island just off Santa Cruz. There we had to pass by ferry the short distance to Santa Cruz Island, and take a taxi to the town of Puerto Ayora, where we were booked to stay at the Hotel Sol y Mar.

We were the only guests in the hotel. Tourist boats were at anchor in the harbour. Galapagos was empty. Only residents were there.

By the time we got there it was too late to take photos today. We had dinner and a lot of drinks at the hotel. We were excited at the prospect of a really exceptional calendar. Tomorrow we will begin. We need six photos.

After breakfast, Kate was made up by Marcia, and her hair done by Denis. This took two hours. After which we took a boat from the pier in the harbour to Las Grietas.

This is where the sea has cut through rocks to form a deep, clear pool of water surrounded by sheer cliffs. It's a popular tourist spot. There is a sign telling tourists not to dive from the top of the cliffs into the pool as it is dangerous.

But I have seen them do it.

Today we had it to ourselves.

Kate was wearing a pink bathing suit. There were no animals involved, she just lay on rocks and looked beautiful.

Despite sounding easy, it took three hours to get the photos that Pollo wanted. He is a meticulous photographer. He won't be rushed.

Meanwhile, we idly watched and enjoyed the sunshine. At this time of year it can get quite cold in the wind, and the sea is cold too.

One in the bag.

On to the second shot.

Before we left the shelter of the rocks Kate changed costume for a green swimsuit. Natalie, Gynna's assistant, was in charge of the suitcase with the changes of clothes. Once again Marcia and Denis prepared her, while Gynna and Natalie used tan-coloured cream to cover the white bikini marks. Kate doesn't normally wear full suits.

Then we got back into the boat and went to the Playa de los Perros.

There is a jetty there and three sea lions were sunning themselves on it. A male and two females.

We took the boat up to the jetty. They were now only a few metres from us. Kate jumped from the boat to the jetty. We pushed off and took photos, leaving her alone there, so we didn't spook the sea lions into diving into the sea.

The male was annoyed at her proximity. He barked at her and showed his teeth.

She bravely posed with her back to them, while we all held our breath. If he attacked her we couldn't get her off in time.

We beseeched Pollo to be quick. But, as always, he takes his own sweet time.

Finally, we got Kate back on board.

Two shots in the can.

We beached the boat further along the shore and walked across the peninsula to the other side, which was full of iguanas. Kate changed into a red crossover swimsuit. She lay on the sand amongst the black sea iguanas. They carried on sunning themselves, ignoring her.

She moved position several times. And we got great photos

Number three.

The time was getting on for 6pm, and the daylight was going.

We headed back to the hotel.

It had been a successful day, three photos on the first day, with two more days available.

There was a celebratory dinner at the hotel. There are very few restaurants open.

The next day Fredy, who was organizing the trip, had arranged a boat to take us out to sea.

We were going to a small island which was famous for Albatros, those huge seabirds who can fly hundreds of miles out to sea. They are often the sailors' first sign that land is near.

Once Kate was made up and coiffed we left in a small boat. We were going out to sea. The boat seemed a bit small for this, but it had comfortable seats and a roof to protect us from the sun. We set off. But we didn't get very far.

The boat captain got a message from the harbour master to say that he was not licensed to take us out to sea. We would have to change boats. He took us into the harbour.

When we saw which boat it was, we were horrified.

It was an open fishing boat, with only one seat at the stern, which we had to share with the captain, and no shade at all. It had an outboard engine.

But it was either that, or we didn't get to go.

We dubiously clambered on board. We, the seniors, Gynna, Kate and I shared the captain's seat. The others had to sit in the bottom of the boat, or perch on the struts that crossed it.

We set off. The sea was calm until we left the harbour. But once away from the protection of the hills the wind got up. So did the waves. The boat was now jumping from wave to wave, and crashing down, which jarred us each time. The sun burnt down, though the wind was cold.

We had only baseball caps to protect our heads. Most of them wore a T-shirt. Luckily I had a long-sleeved one. I can't take the sun.

The sea got rougher. The captain said we should go back to the harbour.

But we refused. This was a photo we really wanted. How far was the island?

He said fifteen minutes away.

Well we could put up with discomfort for that long.

We ploughed on. The waves got higher, and higher. The boat started to roll.

We had begun the voyage chatting. Now we were all quiet. Faces were looking distinctly green.

First, Natalie vomited over the side. The wind brought the smell of the vomit, it was nauseous. Several others began to vomit. Only the three of us sitting on the seat at the back were OK. I had been in this situation before and told the others to focus on the horizon.That way you avoid sea sickness. At least we were sitting down, and could see the horizon. Those who were now lying at the bottom of the boat had no chance.

In their misery they got alarmed that the boat might sink. Who can swim, who can't? Someone recommended we hold onto the boat, even if it was upside down it wouldn't sink as it was made of wood.

Marcia asked plaintively, "Who will look after my cats?"

It was a lot longer than fifteen minutes when we finally saw the island in the distance.

We all looked forward to getting off the boat.

Hopefully on the way home the sea would be calmer.

The captain was staring at the shore and the waves breaking on to it

"We can't land in that surf. We'll have to go back."

Oh no !

We have been on the boat for an hour and a half. Now we face another hour and a half to get back to the harbour.

What's worse, the sea seems to be getting rougher.

There were groans all around as he turned the boat towards home.

Curiously, I didn't feel too bad. We had brought sandwiches for lunch.

I ate one, and opened a can of beer. The others looked at me in disgust. Yuck!

We finally got back to the harbour, looking like bedraggled refugees.

We were all relieved to leave that damned boat and get to the hotel for lunch.

Or at least those who could eat!

We were frustrated.

Yesterday everything had seemed so easy. Now we had used a day and a half for only three photos.

We needed to catch up this afternoon.

We took a taxi to Garrapata Beach.

Kate was dressed in a red polka dot bikini. Here were pelicans. As with all birds and animals on Galapagos, they are very tame. We didn't touch them, but when Kate walked slowly up to them they didn't move. Pollo got a bunch of photos. We would select the best one later.

The last photo of the day involved both Fredy and Kate.

Fredy had asked me some time ago if he could be a model. He is a young man with a good physique. OK, for a change we will have one photo with both Kate and Fredy.

But on one condition, Fredy had to go to the gym with Kate and get some abs.

They started going to the gym together a month before the shots. But Kate reported that Fredy wouldn't work as long or hard as she did.

When it came to the photo, he didn't have any abs to show for it. However Marcia came to the rescue and painted them on him. It looks great on the photo.

Kate was in a blue one-piece bathing suit showing a lot of her boobs, Fredy wore brief trunks. We had borrowed a small yellow kayak. They stood in the sea by the rocky shore where the waves were strong. They had to hold the boat between them as though they were launching it into the sea.

Pollo took a lot of photos. The two models complained that they were standing on sharp rocks which were cutting their feet.

Never mind, keep smiling!

That was it for the second day. We had recovered our schedule. We now had five shots.

One more to go tomorrow.

The final photo was in the Chato Tortoise Reserve. The islands are named for the giant tortoises, called galapagos.

There are many wild galapagos on the islands, but the reserve protects them to increase the chance of their breeding. A tortoise can live to a hundred years old. Some of the old ones were big enough to ride on, though of course that is prohibited.

The problem in obtaining the photo was that they wouldn't collaborate. They didn't run away, or even walk away. When we got close to them they simply went into their shells. They withdrew their heads, which rather spoiled the photo.

We moved well back. Kate would creep up behind them, but not too close. Pollo used a long-distance lens. We had to wait ages for the head to emerge again.

But eventually the tortoise thought that we had gone and looked out. We got our photo. Kate wore a gold coloured bikini. By photoshop Pollo put them closer together.

Before we left the reserve a park officer came to tell us that we had better clear the photos with the park authority before leaving Galapagos. He said that a magazine had been fined a million dollars for publishing illegal photos.

That worried us. We went back to the hotel while Fredy went to the park's office, with Pollo and his cameras.

They returned crestfallen. The photos with animals were illegal. No person should be closer than five metres to the animals. Our photos would give the public the wrong idea.

The photo of the sea lions had to be discarded. The others would be allowed, if Pollo moved the animals back from Kate. He would have to send proofs to the parks officers to get their OK.

The threat of a million dollars fine was more than enough reason to collaborate.

Without the sea lions we are one photo short. We are leaving tomorrow. What to do?

We sat on the hotel patio drinking beer. Then I thought of the obvious solution. Wendy.

She is a sea lion who comes to the hotel each day out of the sea, and to the alarm of the bathers, and to the amusement of the other guests, swims in the hotel pool.

Kate had one costume left, a silver bathing suit.

She put it on, was made up and coiffed. Then we waited for Wendy.

What if she didn't come today? But she did.

Keeping the regulation five meters away we got our photo.

The team had a surprise in store for me. I had not said anything, but Kate had told them.

They had found a restaurant that was open and suggested we go there.

When we arrived, there was a large table for eight prepared for us. There were two bottles of champagne being chilled, a cake and a sign on the wall at the back:

'Happy Birthday Colin'.

I am seventy-five today.

That was four years ago. I will be seventy-nine soon. The only redeeming feature of becoming seventy-nine, is that I didn't die at seventy-eight.

Well I didn't, but my alter ego Harry died at seventy-seven.

Let me explain. I have mentioned earlier that I have written four books about Kate and I, two got published, two didn't.

I was Harry. Why that name? I had just read The Snows of Kilimanjaro by Ernest Hemingway. Harry came from that. It's a short story of a man and his wife on safari. Harry has had an accident, his leg is gangrened, he is dying. They can't get help because their truck is broken down. This is the 1930s, way before mobile phones.

He recalls incidents in his life.

And Kate is Violetta, from the Verdi opera La Traviata. My very favourite opera.

I had first seen it in the Scala in Milan. It was a corporate invitation from ICI Ltd in 1980.

It was only my second time at the opera. The first was Verdi's Rigoletto in the Bolshoi theater in Moscow in 1969. I was travelling back from Kuala Lumpur to the UK at the time, and flew on Aeroflot with the offer of three days in Moscow, absolutely free.

However, it was December!

Kate and I saw La Traviata together last year at the Royal Opera House in London, just after arriving from New York on the liner Queen Mary II.

I splashed out on a box in the theater. Paying for the four seats, so we could have it to ourselves. I always cry at the end of Traviata. It's better if I am not on public display.

So let's get back to Harry. He existed in the books doing exactly what I did, from August 2013 until June 2022. Then sadly I had to kill him, so that the story could move on to post-Harry, and eventually two more generations.

I chose a car crash. He was on the way to Rodeo Grande. He was alone, Violetta was not with him that Saturday. She has to live on.

He had a heart attack while driving and hit a banana truck, head-on at speed.

'Who would have thought the old man to have so much blood in him'? (Lady Macbeth).

We measure our lives in birthdays. Where was I when I turned 50,60, 70 etc? In fact I know them all. Remember, I have kept a diary since I was twenty-six years old.

Last year I spent my birthday with Kate in The One and Only Gorilla's Nest Hotel in Rwanda. As the name suggests we had come to see the Gorillas.

We saw them yesterday.

They were not far from the hotel. But it involved a walk up a steep hillside. We had guides and porters to carry our rucksacks, but even so it was strenuous. At least for me. Kate is very fit, so no problem for her.

When we got close to them we were asked to put on facemasks. Covid was on its way out, but the authorities could not take risks. Gorillas and humans are closely related. We could pass Covid to them, and they have no defence against it. By careful management the gorilla population of Rwanda has increased in the last years to about a thousand, but they are still endangered.

We were instructed not to get too close to them, and if approached stand still, show no fear, don't move back. We came upon them very suddenly. We were a party of just eight tourists. The guide leading us signaled for silence then pointed at the side of the path. There, only five metres away from us, was a female gorilla squatting on her haunches pulling leaves off a tree and eating them. We were fascinated and took lots of photos. Perhaps this would be the only one we saw? Far from it. From there on it was one after another. We saw the dominant Silverback male, and a female with two cubs which rolled over each other as they played.

They were not afraid of us at all.

We had flown from Amsterdam to Nairobi last week and from there by plane to Cottars 1920 Camp on the Masai Mara. We had three days safari, sleeping in a palatial tent. They even prepared a bath for us in an inflatable tank in front of the tent. They filled it with hot water and left us to enjoy it.

To save time returning to Nairobi, we took a private plane from Mara to Kigali, the capital of Rwanda. Then by hire car to the Gorilla's Nest Hotel.

It was organized, as always, by Explorations.

Rwanda impressed us. Following a civil war and genocide between the tribes of Hutus and Tutsis, the country now lives in peace. Ruled by its longtime president Paul Kagame. Today there is no tension between tribes. We saw an impressive number of new schools, cooperatives, markets and small holdings. Tourism, especially to see the gorillas, plays a big part in the economy.

All of which would have been threatened if the crazy idea by the British Conservative government in 2020 had taken shape. I refer to the plan to send illegal immigrants to holding camps in Rwanda. We are talking of hundreds of thousands of people. Where and how they would have been housed, protected, controlled and policed beggars belief.

But thankfully now, in August 2024, the Labour Party is in power in Britain. The idea has been ditched.

I need to say nothing about Brexit. The same government was responsible.

We have enjoyed so many holidays organized by Explorations. We have thousands of photos to help us remember. There are photos of Kate wearing a sari by the Taj Mahal, of us on a Nile boat, riding horses by the pyramids, riding elephants in Thailand, in a helicopter towards the summit of Mount Everest, riding horses in Jodhpur, watching tigers at Pench in India, of a leopard sitting close by the jeep in Kenya, Kate dressed in a Marilyn Monroe wig on the QM II, and of course of her dancing in her bikini in the Antarctic.

Chinmay Vasavada has always been our contact in Explorations. The company was founded by Nicky Shepherd many years ago, she now has other partners.

We had never met them. So after we arrived at Southampton on 14th July 2023, on the Queen Mary II, we arranged to have dinner together.

Their offices are at Poulton in Gloucestershire. They booked us into the Manor House Hotel, Lower Slaughter. Nicky picked us up from there at 7pm and we met Chinmay at the Feathered Nest restaurant for a wonderful and amusing dinner.

In fact we did more that day. Kate had always wanted to see Stonehenge. I had only once seen it as a boy.

Chinmay organized a car and guide to collect us from Southampton docks. We first drove to Salisbury and saw the magnificent cathedral. Then we drove on to Stonehenge.

It began to rain heavily when we arrived. David, our guide, an ex-military man, had his waterproofs ready. We had only light jackets. We ran from the car to the visitor's shop. They sold plastic ponchos. I bought one but Kate refused. She said it looks silly. So we saw Stonehenge and she got soaked. Then we went to the visitor centre and saw how Stonehenge was built and what it looked like when complete.

We had an invitation from Lein to meet him and Rita at the Beckford Arms near their home. When we got there Kate went to the ladies and changed her clothes. The lunch was good. It is the first time that Rita has met Kate. They got on well together.

The following day the same car took us to London, where we were booked into the Connaught Hotel. And it was from the Connaught that we took a taxi to the Royal Opera House, Covent Garden, to see La Traviata.

Yesterday, Saturday 17th August 2024

We went out to lunch in the Spanish restaurant Tasca del Norte, in Guayaquil. We were in a reflective mood. One glass of wine followed another.

Kate asked me,

“What would you like to do for your birthday Honey?”

“It would be nice to get the calendar group together for dinner.”

“When can we go on holiday to Madrid and Croatia?”
“We need to finish the house purchase and take possession, or at least get the architect started on changes. So say at the end of September. Why don't we go to Tupgill for Halloween? The Forbidden Corner is doing a Ghost Trail, that would be fun.”

She was quick to say that her birthday coincides with Halloween, on 29th October.

“If we go to Tupgill I want to invite my mother and my sister Luisa.“

“OK, let’s do it. Your Mother has never been to England.”

The plan began to fall into place. She wanted to return to see Dra Martinez de Carneros, her eyes were worrying her. She thought she had astigmatism.

We will go first to Madrid and get a diagnosis. If she needs an operation we can either do it before or after Croatia. Then at the end of the month we will go to Tupgill, and back to Guayaquil in early November, to move into the house.

Our apartment is rented until February. We will have to pay for the year anyway, so no need to move out before the house is ready.

Kate's birthday has recently become quite an event.

In 2021 we went to Rodeo Grande with our group of friends.

Kate and Janina (and I admit to a glass or two) had drunk two bottles of champagne in the car before we got there. Then, before the others of our group arrived, Kate said she wanted to ride her horse. But it was nearly 6pm. I protested, but she got her way (it's my birthday, I'll ride if I want to).

Cristina sent the cowboys to bring the horses to the garden.

It was still light as we left, we saw the most beautiful sunset, but we got back to the house an hour and a half later in the dark. It's the first time that I can remember riding in the dark. It's not easy. We crossed fields where there were fallen branches off the trees. In daylight we would guide the horse around them. In the dark the horse had to fend for itself, we couldn't see a thing. They seemed to have night vision and followed one another. We got home without mishap.

The rest of the group got there about 9pm and the party went on to the early hours. Before I went to bed at midnight, I saw the girls on the lawn with loud music imitating the famous walk at the opening of each series of Las Munecas de la Mafia (Mafia dolls). This is a Colombian TV series bordering on paedophilia.

Some pretty teenage girls come out of school in their uniforms and get into SUVs with muscular men. Then they are seen in a swimming pool party, wearing tiny bikinis. Finally they are delivered home in the same cars, dressed in new outfits and carrying shopping bags. The rest is left up to the imagination. The actresses I suppose must be of legal age. They just don't look it.

In 2022 Kate, Janina and I went to Punta Cana in the Dominican Republic. The Hotel Margaritaville is an all-inclusive resort with many bars and restaurants. They put a plastic band on your wrist. All food and drinks are included in the price. Though in practise they have a menu and a la carte. If you want the second option it's extra. The same with wines. But that was fine, we ate and drank well.

We went into the hotel's giant pool. They have a machine that makes foam. So much foam until you can't see anyone in the pool at all. Then there was a crack of thunder, we got a tropical downpour. It was surprisingly cold rain. We raced back to the rooms.

On Kate's 29th birthday we had dinner and saw a show in the hotel and then (to my alarm) they wanted to go to a disco called Coco Bongo.

Discos are not my scene. They begin after midnight, when I am normally asleep.

We took a taxi from the hotel.

Coco Bongo is a vast hall, perhaps it holds a thousand people. The seating is in tiers up the walls. Being Saturday it was packed. We got what they described as the best box seats. But in reality there was a narrow shelf in front of the seats to put your drinks on. It was so crowded that we could hardly sit down anyway, if we wanted to see the show.

We ordered a bottle of champagne, and then another. The music was deafening, the dance floor full to bursting. There was an aerial pole dancer way above the stage.

On the stage itself there was a mock talent show. This was hosted by a dwarf with the white painted face of a clown, dressed in a suit of blue and white stripes, like pyjamas.

There were several pretty girls on the stage.

I turned to Kate, but she wasn't there. I asked Janina if she had seen her. She laughed and pointed to the stage. There was Kate, who had joined the other girls.

The waiter had asked her if she would participate in the show. She had not told me in case I said no.

What would she have to do?

I soon found out.

The dwarf, who I had nicknamed Chuki, was fooling about doing a mock striptease as though showing the girls what to do. The crowd roared as typical stripper music played.

Chuki removed his jacket, his tie, and his shirt as he writhed to the music.

He was wearing a brassiere. To the roar of the crowd he flipped it down, then indicated for the girls to show their boobs.

There were deafening catcalls and whistling from the men.

The girls looked at each other to see who would go first. There was a lot of giggling.

One by one the braver ones pulled down their dresses and flashed their boobs.

The more timid girls didn't.

Then Chuki led them off the stage. The show was over.

And Kate, did she or didn't she? What happens in Coco Bongo, stays in Coco Bongo!

I had not brought a costume for the Halloween party on the 31st. There was a competition at the hotel with prizes of bottles of champagne for the best outfits.

Both Kate and Janina dressed as putas (prostitutes) with black leather corsets and mini skirts, black fishnet stockings with suspender belts, and very high black heels.

There was another couple there dressed as an American policeman and policewoman.

I asked them to arrest the girls. That caused hilarity among the other contestants and the audience. We have great photos of them being handcuffed as they struggled to get away.

And we won a bottle of champagne.

Just one more birthday I must recount, and that's because, according to the British press at the time of our kidnap, it was an orgy.

It wasn't.

It was Kate's 30th birthday. She wanted to do something special. We went to Montego Bay, Jamaica, and stayed in Sandals Hotel for four days, taking nine people with us. Of those nine, there were her mother, brother and sister, then our good friends Janina, Fredy, Omar, Andrea, Orlando and Paola.

Kate insisted we hire a yacht for the 29th.

That is where the photos were taken, which mysteriously got to the press.

True that the girls were dressed in bikinis (but they didn’t take them off).

True that we were all drunk.

True too that we were smoking pot (you can't move in Jamaica without being offered ganja). There was loud music, that's why we anchored 500 metres offshore.

But that was as far as it went. Remember her mother was present.

It was a fun day of sea and sun. Some of us swam in the lovely warm sea.

There was one more photo published from our hotel in Montego Bay, of myself in uniform.

Erroneously it was described as a pilot's uniform, at the fancy dress party. In fact, it was a mock naval uniform. I had had it made years before by a military tailor in Guayaquil.

At the time we did a skit for the Agripac convention. It was HMS Pinafore and of course I was the Captain (and a right good captain too). My right good crew were girls who danced in miniskirts!

At today’s event I won first prize.

Back to the present. Today is Tuesday 20th August 2024.

Yesterday I went back to see Dr Jose Maria. Kate had noticed a small lump on my face. Three years ago I had had a similar one, and did nothing about it, until it was the size of a quail's egg.

Then I had a two-hour operation to cut it out, roots and all. That was a different doctor, who sadly has died. Today I am told that it might or might not be malignant. There are in fact two of them. So a biopsy was taken of each.

While there he checked my chest, and declared that it is 98% healed (slowly improving).

I was shirtless lying on the doctor's operating table. Kate pointed out some warts. He said they were not harmful, but did we want them removing. She quickly said yes.

She clearly doesn't love me warts and all!

My visit extended to an hour: two biopsies, four extractions and then liquid nitrogen on some spots on my head. I was walking wounded when I came out.

The doctor joked that with all my problems when I die I can go straight to heaven, I needn't pass hell. I have already been there.

But the day improved. First came the news that the house purchase is concluded. We can have the keys at once. Though the sellers asked for a couple of days to remove their stuff. They invited us to their/our house tomorrow so they could show us how everything works, and we suspect to try to sell us more items that they still haven't managed to get rid of.

Jaime, the Quito manager, is in town. I invited him to have a drink with us at 7pm. Several bottles of wine and a Domino Pizza later he left! We talked about the new house. We will invite him to see it once we are installed.

It was a fun evening.

We have only made plans up until Kate's birthday. What are we going to do for Christmas and the New Year? We have never spent Christmas together, and only one New Year.

At some point we want to go to Australia and see my sister Catherine, my niece Emile and her children Dan and Sofie.

I think we can fly from Ecuador to Santiago, Chile. From there to Sydney. Rather than repeating Los Angeles.

Kate has never been to Chile (one more country for her collection).

Emilie's family lives on the Gold Coast near Brisbane. So we can see both cities and perhaps drive between them.

Then there is the Sydney Opera House. I saw it when I went with Ceci and the kids thirty years ago, one of the great Armstrong Family Holidays. But only from the outside. Hopefully there will be an opera playing while we are there. Or the other way around. We can see the opera program, and plan accordingly.

Last night I went home to Kate, as normal after finishing in the office.

She had her piano teacher there. I was greeted at the door with the sound of music.

I kissed her on the lips, and the lady teacher on the cheek. Then not to interrupt I got myself a glass of Doña Paola and sat on the balcony. Snoopy came and joined me there.

Kate is getting on well with the piano. I sat and listened to Lady in Red, then the theme from the film Titanic and the dance of the Sugar Plum Fairies, from Nutcracker.

The balcony looks out over a communal garden for the apartment block, with a large lawn, a swimming pool and a jacuzzi at the end. Beyond that is the river. It's about a kilometre wide at this point. It's tidal, so the current flows both ways, taking the water hyacinth with it.

The sun is sinking beyond it, giving a lovely red light to the river.

We will soon be leaving the apartment. We have actually grown to like it more after being here for six months.

There is a problem with the garden. The lawn is prohibited for dogs. Emilie, Yaneth's niece, walks Snoopy around the streets and in the small park of the urbanization. But she doesn't come every day. Kate is often out all day at her various exercises and I get home looking forward to a glass of wine, rather than dog walking. So Snoopy doesn't get out every day.

Even so we are improving on his manners. He rarely misses breakfast now.

But it can't compare to our new house. There too we have seen the sun go down over the canal at the front, when we went there this week to learn how the house works, and drink a glass of champagne.

There is a small garden with a lawn. At least Snoopy can lie outside and sun himself.

If he uses the lawn as a loo. Well that's OK. We can pooper scoop from time to time.

We will get the keys tomorrow. The couple selling it still have some items they have to sell. Would we like to buy any of them?

There are four paintings on the two-storey-high wall in the sitting room, and one more outside the door of the master bedroom. They are by the Ecuadorian artist Ramirez. They are not really my cup of tea. They are surrealistic. But on the other hand they are brightly coloured, and more importantly cover the wall. We have nothing else to put there.

They also offered us a tan coloured sofa. We have already bought the two matching armchairs, but Kate didn't want the sofa. She wanted a bigger one, but also argued that it was too light a colour to go with the dark-coloured furniture from Rodeo.

"How many times do I have to tell you, we can't mix old and new furniture".

But having already bought the armchairs her argument seemed flawed.

She was on the phone to the doctor who was selling the house. He gave us a price for the paintings, the sofa and threw in a carpet free.

She offered half the price. He said, laughing, that she was negotiating as though in the souk of Istanbul. Eventually we agreed on a price, and bought the sofa too!

What encouraged us to buy them was that I had asked Kate to invite friends for my birthday to the new house.

Cristina is working towards getting the Rodeo furniture, at least for the sitting room, repaired and sent to us before the 9th September, as she is invited too.

There is nothing like a deadline for getting things done.

The good doctor was right about the souk in Istanbul. We went there in November 2017.

We stayed at the wonderful Ciragan Palace Hotel on the Bosphorus, and one day we went to the souk.

Kate wanted a belly dancer outfit. We found a shop selling them. They are very flimsy transparent things. She chose a red one. The shop owner asked if she would like to try it on. Yes, she would. He showed her a tiny cubicle where she could change.

I suppose most girls would put on the outfit over their underwear.

Kate didn't think it looked right. When she emerged to show it to me it was totally transparent, she showed her all!

By this time other stall owners had come to have a gawp, as I imagine they did every time a girl put one on. There was great excitement, I thought there was going to be a riot, until feeling embarrassed, she went back to the cubicle and changed out of it.

Now we came to the time to pay. I imagined that they would cost about fifty dollars. They were cheaply made. The shopkeeper asked for a thousand dollars.

We said no, we would leave it. He came down to seven hundred. No!

Then with a great show about his losing money on the deal, he said four hundred.

In the end we paid three hundred.

It wasn't worth the hassle to argue further, as his friends sided with him.

But Kate did look great in it when she gave me a private show!

We saw a lot of Istanbul with an excellent guide, Hakan.

We visited the Blue Mosque. Before going in we made a call at a small shop and bought a long coat for Kate to hide her legs, and a headscarf. There was a service in progress, but we were allowed in anyway. After that we went to the Topkapi Palace and were impressed with the huge area reserved for the hareem (the good old days?). In the palace museum we saw the famous Topkapi Dagger with its huge emerald. It is famous for the film of the same name. A group of English crooks decide to steal it.

Then we went to the underground Roman water cistern. There was a photographer there who dressed us up in Turkish outfits and sold us photos.

After that we went to the best of all, Hagia Sophia.

That wonderful church, cum mosque, cum Wonder of the World. Built by the Roman emperor Justiniano between 532 to 537 AD. I wandered around craning my neck to see the amazing arches and dome. It's incredible that the Romans could build such a thing, and that it has stood for 1,500 years. Kate wasn't impressed with it, and finding a cat there played with it, to the annoyance of Hakan who, as all Turks, holds it in very high esteem.

We booked a night cruise on the Bosphorus. This was rather disappointing. We were in a saloon. The windows were misted up and we couldn't see anything of the city. It seems to be for families. We were practically the only couple. There was a lot of food served, but they were all sweet dishes, which we didn't much like. There was Turkish dancing. I couldn't fathom it and gave up. But a rotund waiter kindly partnered Kate, and showed her the steps. Then came a show by Whirling Dervishes, which was very good.

A young, and handsome, photographer came around, took our photos and asked Kate if she would like to go up on deck for more photos. We went together. He had only asked her, but no way!

It was quite cold on deck. We were the only ones there. I hung about and watched while the photographer asked Kate to pose standing, leaning on the rails and lying on the deck.

She was wearing a short blue and black dress with a zip down the front.

After a while he asked her "Excuse me miss, can you make it a bit more sexy please ?"

I thought she would pull the zip down a little to show more boob.

To my horror she unzipped the dress entirely, took it off, and gave it to me to hold. She was left wearing matching black satin and lace underwear and black riding boots.

The photographer was delighted. My protests were overruled by both of them.

"I am a model, and I have shown more than this to the camera before now".

There were a lot more photos, before she put the dress back on again.

We went to his office and bought a selection of her photos in cardboard frames. He asked for her Instagram, which she happily gave him.

For months afterwards she showed me messages from him asking her to return to Istanbul, alone of course.

"You will not sleep all night, my angel".

Friday 23rd August 2024

I had to ring the dermatologist's assistant at 9am to see if they had the results of the biopsies. I rather hoped they hadn't. But they did. We have an appointment at 1pm.

Kate slept until midday.

We had asked the guards to come at 1pm so that we could go out for lunch.

But we wanted to see our new house again before then.

I am always practical. I told Kate that I am taking a toilet roll with us. I can't remember if Monica had left any there, so just in case.

She agreed and then took the idea forward. Let's take towels too and soap. She got out a suitcase and began to throw all sorts of things into it. Silver picture frames, perfumed candles and whatnot. I added three bottles of Doña Paola, two corkscrews and a box of six wine glasses.

We set off with Snoopy.

This was the symbolic taking possession of the house.

Snoopy was pleased to be there and explored the garden. Our guards looked at the house entrance and gave us advice on what extra security we will need. Josef is coming on Tuesday afternoon to look at it too. The front door is glass but has an ornate metal rack on the inside. That is OK, but there are other areas to improve.

Having put out the toilet rolls, towels, candles and picture frames we opened a bottle of wine.

We sat on the new sofa and began once again planning furnishing.

Kate mischievously suggested we should baptize the house. I pointed out that we don't have any beds, and the sofa, as the only other option, is visible through the glass door to our guards by the car outside.

So not today Josephine!

But at least the idea helped us decide on our bed. We had thought of buying a new mattress and the box to support it, then bring our rustic bedhead from Rodeo. Now the plan changed. "Let's bring our bed from the duplex and buy a new, firmer mattress for it."

We agreed. She will talk to the removal company and get them to bring it next week.

Though it does come to bits, they are very long. It won't go into the lift. It will have to be carried down the stairs, all fifteen floors!

The sitting room is double height. The marble staircase goes from the sitting room up to a balcony, which leads to three bedrooms. One we will convert into Kate's dressing room, together with her pole. The other two will be guest rooms. One we will furnish with rustic furniture from Rodeo, the other will be modern. We will bring the guest bed from the penthouse for there. The master bedroom is downstairs.

We have made a start at taking possession of the house. Tomorrow we will bring more things. Soon we will have the problem of,

"Where is the corkscrew? It's in the other house".

Juan Gabriel, the architect, is coming on Monday to help make the pieces of furniture we want to hold the large TV screen in the sitting room, as well as having shelves for my opera DVDs. I want them displayed so I can run my finger along the shelf and select one.

In the flat they are in drawers.

We had thought of making a bar below the stairs. Now we think the piano will go there.

Kate looked at the space available and declared that it is big enough for a baby grand piano. She will ask her piano teacher if she knows of one for sale second hand. Otherwise we will have to splash out on a new one. So much for pulling up our roots in Ecuador, we are growing new ones!

We will make a space for the wine fridge and bar in the kitchen.

Kate wants to change some pieces in the bathrooms as well as the kitchen.

Here we have another potential conflict of interest.

She says that the workmen need to finish and leave before we move in. I want to move in immediately. She has brought one suitcase full of personal stuff today. If she continues bringing things, then I will get my wicked way.

Once there are items to steal we will have to be living there, or Yaneth will have to come to watch them.

I dream of returning from the office to our beautiful house. My glass of wine will taste so much better there than at the flat.

I am already working on my birthday plans. There are still two weeks to go. We have to get enough furniture from Rodeo to make the sitting room look furnished. Cristina is working towards it.

While we were chatting her mother called.

She congratulated us on the new house.

I sent her my regards and said she must come and visit us. I get on very well with Margarita, she even takes my side against Kate, from time to time!

After she had rung, we talked about Christmas. We have enough space for her family to stay here. Why don't we spend Christmas here, then Kate and I go to Australia for the New Year?

So our plans go forward. But perhaps New Year is not the best time to visit Australia if we want to go to the Sydney Opera House.

I can check.

At 5pm we were hungry and left the house to go to a restaurant, and then we went back to the flat for a siesta.

I woke at 7pm.

We watched Game of Thrones. But today's episodes were very bleak.

There is the massacre at the Frey wedding where Rob Stark, his wife and mother are all killed. It is organized by the Lannisters.

Theon Greyjoy is castrated by Bolton's bastard son, and Jon Snow (you know nothing) is with the wildlings on the south side of the wall.

Daenerys however is going from strength to strength, building her army and taking cities with the help of the Unsullied and her dragons.

Sunday.

Once again we moved items from the apartment to the house. But today's items are small pieces of furniture, which our security guards helped us to carry to and from the cars.

There was a small difficulty with the urbanization security. Yesterday they had allowed our guards to pass without problem. Today was different. They noticed that their pickup had furniture. That breaks the rules. No commercial operations are allowed at the weekend, which includes moving furniture. This is to protect residents from noise.

We argued with them. It was more difficult because there had been no official communication to them from the administration that we had bought the house.

But in the end they allowed us to pass.

We unpacked the things that we had brought and placed them in the sitting room. They seemed dwarfed by the large room. We only occupied a space bounded by the sofa and armchairs, about a quarter of the room.

We never had a full dinner service. We either ate out or ordered in food at home. Both the penthouse and the apartment in Madrid are small. So no dinner parties. Six plates were sufficient.

Now we might just do them.

We need to look for dinner service, silver cutlery and glassware.

We are like newlyweds, but of course there have been no wedding presents, which normally provide these things.

Kate had started to go to Pilates class a month ago. She told me that there was a group of mature ladies, they were very friendly and chatted to her.

I said that I'm sure they are friends of Ceci, in which case they will know who she is.

But no one had snubbed her, even if they did know.

Today she called me.

"I have a surprise for you. But before I tell you what it is you have to agree to it". Several things crossed my mind. She had talked of getting another dog to keep Snoopy company. But no, it wasn't that.

"I have arranged for you to have Pilates classes for an hour, three times a week. It will be a private class just for you. Will you go?"

The 'private' made a difference. I have my pride, and to flake after fifteen minutes, only to see octogenarian women fill the whole hour would be humiliating.

So I agreed.

This afternoon we will go to the mall and buy the necessary kit.

She has long said that I must do exercise to keep my mind and body alert. She is quite right. The office keeps my mind active. But I sit down all day. I don't even ride a horse any more. I walk quite a lot when in Madrid or for a longer distance, in Yorkshire. But I do nothing in Guayaquil.

I wonder if my enthusiasm will survive the first few classes.

Years ago she persuaded me to buy a sports kit for the gym. But I only went once.

Today 26th August is my father, Gerald's, birthday. If he had been alive he would be 125 years old. He was born right at the end of the nineteenth century, in 1899, at the height of the British Empire.

When father's sister, my aunt Do, died in 1992, I cleared Tupgill House prior to renovations. It took me a long time to do it, as I continually found things of interest. One was a 1910 school atlas with Gerald Armstrong written inside it. It had a map of the world with the Russian, French, Dutch, Portuguese, German and British Empires marked in different colours.

The British one was in pink. The text proudly claimed that it occupied a quarter of the Earth's landmass.

How are the mighty fallen!

Two world wars and the end of the colonial period later, Britain was very much reduced.

There was also an article from a newspaper, the Daily Mail, with a map of Europe dated 1914. It was a cartoon titled 'Hark, hark the Dogs will bark'.

The European powers were represented by dogs. The Germans and Austrians were a pair of dachshunds. The French was a poodle, the British of course was a bulldog.

This was the year the First World War started.

The jingoistic text was that the dachshunds had better behave themselves or they will get mauled by the bulldog and poodle. If the dachshunds were stupid enough to turn to the east then they would be flattened by the Russian steamroller. There was a cartoon of the Czar of Russia driving it.

How very differently it all turned out to be. The dachshunds almost destroyed the bulldog and poodle. Meanwhile the Russian steamroller imploded with the revolution, but only after being severely mauled by the dachshunds.

After work today I went with Kate to Marathon Sports in a shopping mall.

She took charge. She told the sales girl that she wanted a kit for her husband. We selected two pairs of XL pants, two sweatshirts with sleeves and then looked at trainers. There was a big selection. But when I said I was size 45, that reduced it to only two. We bought the black ones with a red stripe. They fitted and look quite good.

I am all ready for the trial run.

She organized that for tomorrow, Tuesday, at 3pm. But we have a problem. Josef is coming to look at the new house to advise on security.

OK, she agreed that would be difficult, so Wednesday at 3pm? No again. It's our 11th anniversary. We are going out to lunch at my club. It would be a rush to get finished by 3pm.

By this time she suspects I am putting off the evil moment. OK then Thursday 3pm. She dared me to object. I had run out of excuses. OK.

By the time we got to our new home Juan Gabriel and Sebastian, the two architect brothers, were there. We looked first at the site of the jacuzzi in the garden and decided how big it would be and where it will go. Then we looked at the sitting room and described the piece of furniture to hold the TV and my DVDs.

We talked about the Rodeo furniture to come. Where will we put it?

We showed photos. They asked if they could go to Rodeo Grande and see it for themselves. Yes, we would arrange that with Cristina.

Kate took them from room to room, asking for small changes to be made. Her dressing room took a bit more time to work out. After that I lost interest and opened a bottle of wine in the kitchen.

We all left at 7pm. I wanted to get back to Snoopy. He doesn't like to be alone in the apartment and can savage the place. When we got there we found that Yaneth had shut him out on the balcony. He was an unhappy beagle. A few days later we got a request from the administration not to leave him on the balcony as he barked for hours.

I have finally collected the file of documents that the administration demands to register us as house owners. Kate took it to their office. She collected the tag for the guards' car. I have to go personally and get mine today.

Then we are fully fledged residents.

All went well and I was taken in the car, together with the tag, to the entrance so that the electronic reader could see the tag. From now on there should be no delay in getting in.

We gave the administration credit card details for the monthly payments. They thanked us and said that August's amount is due. I had thought we would get away with this month as we had only just bought the house, but no.

By the time we got to our house Joseph had already arrived with a security expert. They looked at all the vulnerable points in the house and made suggestions. As I suspected it's going to cost a lot more than I thought. Also there is the time factor. They said about a month, if so then we can't sleep there until October, when we are due to go on holiday. So maybe it will be November.

There won't be many months left on the present flat rent contract, which expires at the end of February.

But, as Kate told me, if we are going to sleep there, we need to know that we are safe.

We are still vulnerable to the same gang who took us in December.

If it were to happen again I doubt I would survive.

When they left we poured a glass of wine and sat on the patio looking at the lights on the houses across the water. The evening is cool and there are no mosquitos, though they will come in the hot, rainy season.

Kate made her first order for groceries, to see if the delivery boys are allowed in. They are, and the order arrived.

We are now waiting for Dr Juan Jose who promised to bring us the final keys and controls for the house. He came at 6.30pm.

I poured him a glass of wine and we chatted. He asked if he might make a video of the house as a souvenir. Of course he can. Then he became nostalgic. He told us of building the house and living there with their two daughters, who are now married.

After an hour I wondered how long he would stay and began to hint that we had to go.

Kate nudged me with her elbow to shut up.

She had noticed that he was crying.

Then I felt bad.

He was clearly very upset about selling the house. Just as I had been about selling Rodeo Grande. How insensitive of me not to notice the symptoms.

Kate stood up and gave him a hug. He calmed down, but stayed another hour reminiscing.

The contract is completed, the house has changed hands. He is going to live in the United States. We may never meet again.

He has been a gentleman in all the proceedings, which is not always the case in Ecuador.

Of course, as we drove back to the apartment Kate gave me a lecture on sensitivity!

We took Snoopy with us when we went to the new house today, to avoid him being left on his own.

Yaneth had said earlier that he looked sad. We saw why. As we walked him in the park by the new house he twice made poo. It was not the kind that we could pick up with the plastic bag. It was serious diarrhoea.

Poor fellow. We know what caused it. Two days ago we gave him a piece of salmon that had been in the fridge for several days. Kate didn't want it. He wolfed it down.

From now on we will stick to his regular dog food, produced by Agripac. Plus perhaps a piece of cheese from time to time.

Both the architects and security people are going to take a month to get the work done.

But we already planned to bring the furniture. That from the penthouse is due this week, and the first load from Rodeo next week. We have someone interested in buying the penthouse. If we are going to remove furniture then we need to do it before we make the sale, as it was advertised as furnished. We will have to adjust the price accordingly.

The new owner of Rodeo Grande has allowed us to restore the furniture there before sending it to us. But I guess at some point he will want to use the house. So we can't wait too long.

Which all adds up to a messy waiting period when the furniture is in the house but not set out.

I had lived in Rodeo for forty-seven years without having this problem!

Then there is my birthday coming up. It's only two weeks away now. Do we have a party there or not? We don't want to hold it in the flat, it's too small. I keep asking Kate if we should invite such a person. She refuses to plan until she sees what the house furnishing looks like. Catch twenty-two.

Last night she declared that I always invite people and then fall asleep at the table, and go to bed leaving her to entertain the guests. Good point. I often do.

So in a bad temper I declared that I wouldn't have a birthday party after all. I would hide away that day, (or go into the garden and eat worms).

My latest idea is to invite our soprano friend Viviana and ask her to sing to us.

She did it once before. My son Nick organized it.

It was at my last Queen's Birthday Party in 2016, before Nick took over as Honorary British Consul. By this time it was held annually in the garden of the beach house.

As usual I stood up, made a speech to the four hundred guests, and raised my glass to Her Majesty the Queen.

Then while there was a moment of quiet Viviana began to sing Andrea Bocelli's song Time to say Goodbye. It made me cry. I have been Consul for thirty-five years. It's now time to say goodbye. I stood there in front of everyone blubbing like an idiot!

I felt very foolish, but I will certainly never forget it.

Wednesday 28th August

Today is the eleventh anniversary of the day we met.

It was at a casting for models for the Agripac calendar in August 2013. Gynna, who owns the model agency, will line up twelve girls for my selection.

Kate was in Ibague, Colombia the day before, visiting her mother.

Gynna called her and told her that she must come back to Guayaquil. She has a good chance of winning.

The journey was an odyssey. She couldn't afford a plane ticket. She took a bus from Ibague to Ipiales on the Ecuadorian border. There was a transport strike. The bus left her several miles away. She hitched a lift on a motorbike, holding her suitcase. The strikers punctured the tyres of the bike. From there she had to walk to the border and get a bus to Guayaquil. A journey of thirty-five hours.

She had only arrived this morning, showered, changed and gone to Gynna's office.

The girls paraded in bikinis. They were all tall, slim pretty girls. Kate's bikini was an orange one, I will never forget that. Where Kate stood out was that she smiled, the only girl to do so when we interviewed the finalists. We asked each one if they were prepared to work at the ranch, could they ride a horse, were they afraid of animals, did mosquitos bother them?

To all of these she replied correctly.

Today we are supposed to go to the Union Club at 1pm. She called me to say she had just got out of the hairdresser's. She will pick me up from the office at 1.30pm.

It's been a long time since we have been to the club together. Ceci is well known there, as for more than forty-five years we have gone there as a couple.

Once before, on Kate's birthday in October 2020, I invited her and two friends for lunch there. It was an occasion for making up, as we had a serious separation at the time. She had only just returned from Madrid the day before.

I had been very nervous about who saw us together at the Club.

Now, it doesn't matter. Kate and I are officially a couple. The gossip of Guayaquil will have spread word of my separation from Ceci. It's old news.

We got to the club at 2pm. Kate had put on new cream-coloured pants and a black tight-fitting sweater and black heels, she wore red lipstick. She looked very smart.

I put on a tie and blazer.

We asked the waiter to take a photo. It looks really nice. She sent it to our friends.

I was welcomed by the car park attendant, the lift operator, the maitre'd and the barman.

I have been a member for fifty two years, since the first month that I was in Ecuador.

Back then the terms of a secondment from ICI Ltd included membership of one club. I chose the Union Club, it was by far the most expensive, but it raised no eyebrows at the company. They invested in me and have been repaid many times over.

The club, founded in 1869, stands proudly at the end of the malecon, and has wonderful views over the river Guayas. It's the top venue for weddings and social events.

Outside the club there is a patio leading to a church. On occasions a wedding would be held in that church and the guests then walked to the club for the reception.

There is another structure close by. It's an enormous wrought iron and glass building. Formerly it was a vegetable market. Now it's used for exhibitions of art and trade fairs. The name of the maker and the date is shown on one gable. Its Gustave Eiffel, 1910.

The very same man of Tower fame.

The Union Club, as with the Royal Opera House in London, once stood by a vegetable market. Today neither does.

After fifty-two years in the present location, the club is about to move venue. Lovely as the view is, it's situated downtown. That is fine for lunches, but with the current insecurity the members don't patronize it much at night. The club committee has sold the building to the municipality and is constructing much larger premises on the Samborondon Road, closer to our new house.

There has always been a waiting list for membership. It's restricted by the size of the premises. I hear that in the new, much larger building, the club has accepted eight hundred new members. No doubt their entrance fees will go a long way to financing the building.

I didn't know any of the members in the Terrace dining room today. There was a table of four men in suits who recognised me and said hello, one man who stared at me but didn't acknowledge my hand wave, and a party of six ladies of a certain age, who were seated some distance away.

We had a couple of cocktails in the bar, while we selected from the menu, and then went into the dining room. The waiters called me Sr Armstrong, and addressed Kate as niña (little girl) which made her laugh.

We began with a plate of oysters, prawn and crab (I avoided the oysters). Then we had the lobster, Kate's was grilled and mine thermidor. We chose a bottle of Paz Señorans from Galicia. This wine has memories for us. Before we had the apartment in Madrid we stayed many times in the Ritz Hotel. The lady sommelier in the Goya restaurant recommended it as the perfect accompaniment for oysters.

One bottle led to a second one.

We left the club at 4:30pm. Pedro, our guard, had to drive us home, we were to say the least, happy.

Kate loved the pink, white and blue roses I had ordered for her. Yes blue. It's done by standing white roses in water with a blue dye. They look lovely.

Then we went to bed for a siesta.

When we woke at 7pm Kate told me about her dream. She referred to it as an Astral journey.

She dreamt that she had left her body and was looking down at her own sleeping form. She said it scared her, even in her sleep.

I have never had that experience.

We got up in our pyjamas, poured the inevitable wine (hair of the dog), and talked about my birthday. She has now come around to my way of thinking. She has arranged for the movers to collect the penthouse furniture, including four pieces in the flat, and take them to the new house tomorrow. So very soon this rented place will not be liveable, and de facto we will move to the new house, without waiting for architects and security folk to complete their tasks. Victory!

The Rodeo furniture will come next week. With that the house will be more or less liveable.

She has invited thirty friends to come for the birthday party. She asked me to talk to Maria Dolores of Bandurria (the office canteen) to provide the food and waiters. In fact, we are back on form, with no further mention of my falling asleep at the table.

At lunchtime today I talked to Maria Dolores. But she already knew all about it. Kate had called her. She told me not to worry about the party she would do everything. She would send tables, tablecloths, plates, glasses, cutlery, a cook, waiters and of course the food.

I had asked for the famous bean stew. She said that she in turn had asked Amarilis from Rodeo Grande to make it for me and send it with Cristina.

She will prepare it one last time, after forty-seven years.

I thanked her and invited her to come to the party, which she accepted. As long as her daughter could come too, she depended on her for transport. Of course she can.

Today is my haircut day. I am going back to the Union Club, where they have a barber's shop. We listen to opera while Carlos cuts my hair. I asked him how long we have known each other. He replied twenty-two years, and before that his father cut my hair (there was more of it to cut in those days).

Josef has called to give me contact details for the security company which will install both stronger doors and windows for the vulnerable places of the house.

Juan Gabriel has sent me a quote for the architectural drawings.

We still have the dilemma of to move or not to move, before the changes are complete. They will take at least a month, but already there is little of our furniture left in the flat, only that belonging to the landlady. Last night we discovered that the phone chargers had all gone to the new house, in a drawer of a small table! It has begun.

Friday, 6th September

I have been a member of another, rather less elite club, the Phoenix Club, since I arrived in Ecuador. This one I paid for myself. It wasn't expensive.

It was founded by a group of British expats in 1949, when there were a lot more of them in Ecuador. In those days the British in Guayaquil worked for shipping, electricity, telegraph, oil, banking and insurance companies.

Now the day of the expat is over. Multinational companies employ either Ecuadorian nationals or those from Latin America. They speak the language a lot better than we expats ever did, but perhaps being young, we had more enthusiasm for the job. We wanted to make our names with the companies which had sent us. We are only here temporarily. Then our careers will continue back in England.

I have been president of the Phoenix several times over the years. We used to have Mondays as club night. But since I met Kate I haven't gone much. It's a gentleman's club. Only at the annual Christmas party are ladies invited.

Son-in-law Javi suggested we go for lunch this Friday, they are serving fish and chips.

I haven't been for a year . He said he would ask Carlos, the administrator, to round up the old gang. I agreed. It will be fun to see everyone again.

It was fun. There were twelve members present. Of my generation, Nelson was the oldest at eighty five. He is an architect. We worked many years together before he retired.

Holger, my German friend, is approaching eighty. He worked in a shipping agency.

Les, ten years younger than I, is still working for FIFA.

Victor Hugo used to work for Agripac, then set up his own company.

Julio, now lives in Madrid and is still working for an exporter of sea food.

Of the younger members, Matt was at Newcastle University with my daughter Alex. He came to see her in Ecuador and stayed, working for Agripac as purchasing director.

There are two brothers Martin and Albert, sons of my best friend Stanley, who sadly died some years ago. Martin works with me too.

We drank beer out of our personalized pewter tankards, ate peanuts and told stories (oft-repeated) of the old days. There was a lot of banter and laughter.

When lunch was served we sat at a long table with the current president, Esteban, at the head. He said a few words of welcome to the old lags, and hoped the club would see us more often. We promised to do that. I look forward to the next time. Not too soon, perhaps in two or three months.

It was now 3pm. I only had time to go back to the office, collect what I needed for the weekend and leave again.

Kate told me to come to our new house at 4pm where we would meet with Janina and Jorge Cepeda, who had just arrived in Guayaquil for the weekend.

I had already begun the weekend at the Phoenix Club. What they refer to here as San Viernes (St Friday), when the good and the great knock off work at midday and start the weekend with a long lunch.

I got to the house and Kate was waiting for me with Snoopy. After a few minutes there was a phone call from the guards at the entrance announcing our guests.

Yes, they can pass.

Janina has already seen the house, but Jorge has not. Kate showed him around. Then we sat on the terrace and drank a bottle of wine, while we planned Kate's birthday party at Tupgill. We will combine it with the Ghost Trail at the Forbidden Corner for Halloween. Jorge promised that he will come too.

At 6pm Kate ordered us to move. She had reserved our favourite Italian restaurant La Riviera, in Urdesa. We all got into my car including Snoopy, followed by the security detail.

The traffic is bad at that time of day. It took us forty minutes to get to the restaurant. I am getting stressed by this time. I have a favourite spot for parking. The attendant waved me in. Kate said no, she had reserved a space in front of the restaurant. We argued about it.

But I parked where she wanted me to.

She went into the restaurant with the others while I manoeuvered back and forth until I was parked by the curb. Then rather annoyed, I followed them. The waiter showed me to a private room at the back.

Kate, Janina and Jorge were looking at me expectantly. When I said nothing Kate pointed to the display of pink and green roses and balloons with the inscription Happy Birthday Colin.

What an idiot I am. I hadn't twigged it at all. I should have suspected something with the insistence that we get there on time. The special parking place. It had all been arranged.

Now I hugged her. "Thank_you My Love".

It is an early birthday party as Jorge won't be here on the 9th.

A bottle of wine was brought in and a board of cheeses with ham and mortadella.

Waiters began rearranging the tables. I wondered who else was going to join us. But it was not to make space for more people. They cleared an area in front of our tables. We heard a violin playing.

The door opened and the violinist came in. He had a microphone strapped to his violin connected to a music system which gave the backing. He played cheerful Neapolitan music while we clapped in time.

Then he finished and left us.

There was a pause while the main course was served.

We heard a lovely voice singing. I stood up and said to Kate "Oh No. You are going to make me cry!" She squeezed my hand.

Viviana entered singing Oh mio babbino caro.

And I did cry. It was so beautiful.

When she finished I hugged her.

She next sang an aria from Carmen. Afterwards I teased her that Carmen is a mezzo soprano, Viviana is soprano coloratura. She said she had only sung it for me. She would never dare sing it in public.

Then I introduced her to our friends and she joined us at the table.

A strange incident came to mind. Just before he left for London I happened to be in Quito with Kate. We were in our first days together. We would go to a hotel and, to save face, book two rooms, even though we only used one. I even went to the trouble of ruffling the sheets on the unused bed.

This time we stayed in a small, boutique hotel close to the airport. We were in the bar together when the Ambassador came in. He recognised me and waved his hand, but I pretended not to see him. He knew Ceci, and I was with Kate.

I have often thought how stupid I was. After all he is a diplomat!

Yesterday after work I drove to the new house. Kate was already there. It was a hive of activity. The first truckload of furniture had arrived from Rodeo Grande. Kate was busy pushing pieces around, to try different positions. Luckily it slides easily on the marble floor. She was working hard and I could see sweat marks under her arms, and both on the front and back of her tee shirt.

Now came the moment of truth. Would she, or would she not like it, after our discussions as to mixing old and new furniture? Yes, she did like it...., Phew!

To me it seemed a good mix too.

I looked at the dining table. I had expected it to be shiny but it was matt, as was all the rest. For the other pieces it didn't matter. But I wanted a shiny table top to reflect the light from the chandelier above it.

I called Cristina, but she told me I had asked for matt varnish. I asked her to send my saddle and bridle, she is making a wooden stand for them. I will make a small shrine with them, my hat, boots and whip, in memory of nearly fifty years in the saddle.

There was one more piece to complete the transformation of our new house into Rodeo Grande. I asked her to remove the sign, made of tiles, at the front door, and send it to us. It reads Rodeo Grande 1980. The year I built the house.

Kate said we could cover the table with glass. But I don't like glass on a table. This table had been shiny before. I would get it varnished again or polished.

I looked around the house. Most of the Rodeo furniture is in the sitting/dining room, but some is in the bedrooms.

We have one more truckload to come, but already the house is looking somewhat full. Have we overdone it?

Well, let's see what looks best, we can always give some pieces away.

There were workmen in the house, not only from the furniture removals company, but also the security firm. They are measuring up for the changes we had discussed with Josef.

All systems go.

I asked the man in charge when he would give us a price. He said this week.

How long will it take to make and install? Two weeks.

So we can move in after that.

This morning Snoopy had a relapse. There was a poo on the sitting room floor. We thought that we had him trained. It's been a long time since the last one.

He was still asleep on the bed with Kate. I hadn't the heart to drag him into the living room and show him his mistake. I cleaned it up. The rule is no breakfast for him. I made my tea, read the newspaper. Then he arrived. He crept in with his tail between his legs and sidled up to me. I put my hand down and he licked it. He knew he was in trouble.

Before I left for the office I filled his breakfast plate. That's what friends are for. Anyway I am sure he was very sorry for what he had done.

In the office I told Jorge about the matt finish on the table. He went to the house with Jose, who works as a waiter in Bandurria. They checked that the barbeque is working for Monday's party, and that there is gas for it. On their return Jose said that he can fix the table with a shiny varnish. It will be ready for the party.

Tonight we received the last truck of furniture from Rodeo. There was more than we had anticipated. Rodeo Grande is a larger house than this new one. We took out all the modern pieces, brought from the penthouse, and sent them upstairs to the bedrooms. That allowed the rustic furniture to go downstairs. There are twenty boxes of plates, vases, lamps, pictures and other decorations. The movers unpacked everything, and Kate put the decorations back on the shelves, much as they had always been.

We stood back and took photos of it.

We have moved Rodeo Grande to Guayaquil. Rus in urbe.

Of course now there is no space for the new piece of furniture we planned to make to hold the TV.

Well, we will have to think again.

Yesterday, Wednesday, I had my second Pilates class. Kate came with me. This time she decided to do her own exercise rather than just watch me. On the contrary I watched her, until told to concentrate by the coach. Kate is something of an expert.

As to myself. The exercises were much the same as last time, but a little harder. I am starting to get the hang of it. There were no aches or pains afterwards, but I felt a bit dizzy as I got back on my feet. Take it slowly. In fact last night I felt rather good, I felt stronger than I have of late. There might just be something in exercise after all.

Kate dosed me with her protein anabolic whey, from a firm called Kevin Levrone. Apparently it's the most famous brand in the industry. Afterwards I was allowed a McDonalds.

I found a fruit in the fridge that I had never seen before. I asked her what it is. It's called Borojo. Apparently it is full of vitamins, and good for you. But the smell is offputting, rather like Durian. They are both supposed to be aphrodisiacs too!

We are planning to go to Miami next week. I asked Janina to reserve the tickets and hotel.

It's to do with a family trust in the States. We need to be there to sign the documents on Tuesday 17th September. We will go next Saturday 14th and come back on Wednesday 18th. So we have a few days' holiday. Janina has kindly offered to dog-sit while we are away. She will move with her two daughters into our apartment. I think the swimming pool is the attraction.

Fredy is back from his European holiday with Omar. It was their honeymoon. They got married last November on the beach at Playas, as the sun set over the sea. Kate and I were the witnesses. It was a great party which went on until dawn.

Gay marriages have only recently become legal in Ecuador.

Fredy kindly brought me some skin creams from Madrid, which I can't get here. He asked about the new house. I invited him to come and see it after work at 5pm.

Kate came to the office to collect me, bringing Snoopy with her.

When I told her that Fredy was coming to see the house, she complained that she had not been consulted, that she didn't want to see anyone tonight, apart from the architects who were due to visit the house.

She said that I do this all the time. I invite people home. She is tired, she hasn't had time to get ready to receive people and her hair is a mess.

I reasoned with her that Fredy is such an intimate friend that she doesn't have to prepare to see him.

We drove to the house in silence.

Shortly after we got there Fredy arrived.

Wonder of wonders she excitedly showed him the house, as I tagged along behind. He has brought some Dutch cheeses for us. After the house tour I opened a bottle of wine and cut the cheese into bite-sized pieces.

The architects are running late. They will be here at 6.30pm.

By the time they arrived we were already animated. We gave them a glass of wine and shared the cheese. At some point they looked at where the piano will go, and other matters, but it was mainly a social evening. When they left at 9pm we carried on.

We asked our guards to go and buy food from a nearby restaurant both for us and themselves. It was just as well.

Kate woke me, I was asleep on the sofa, at 1am. She and Fredy were clearing up the glasses prior to leaving.

We drove home to the apartment and straight to bed. Before the guards left I said they could come tomorrow at 9am, rather than 7am. They would have a short night by the time they got home.

So much for not wanting to see anyone. We have had our first party in our new home.

My third Pilates class. Gradually the coach is increasing the pressure of the springs. But I can still manage it. I am beginning to feel some small advantage from the exercise. The opera music helps me to ignore aching muscles.

Today's hour left me out of breath. I had to sit and have a glass of water before leaving. Kate paid for eight sessions, so I am committed that far.

She made us laugh by telling how she went to her other Pilates class yesterday. She planned an hour but stayed for the second hour. A lady of the incoming class said that she was using her reformer. Please go to another one. Kate pointed out that there were two more free, but the lady wanted hers. That was the one she always had. Kate allowed her to have it as she was an older person. She remarked that women are territorial.

As we left she told me that she needed a pair of pink panties for the calendar photos tomorrow. She didn't have any at home. Please take me to a shop in the mall.

We got there but the lingerie shop she wanted wasn't there any more.

We went into a large store nearby.

She went to the sector selling underwear. One pair of panties turned into six, plus the brassieres to go with them. I hung about, being somewhat sensitive to looks from other lady customers, a man in the knicker section!

Looking around I spied a chair outside the changing rooms. I told Kate, and went to sit down. At least I can do my emails. She eventually came to the changing room with an assistant and an armful of clothes.

One by one she tried them on. There is a white linen three-piece suit we both liked. Then a blue denim dress that buttoned from hem to collar, again we both like it. So on and so forth. After an hour and a half we left with a bunch of bags!

We only came in for a pair of knickers! But she is a happy girl.

Saturday 7th September

Today is calendar day. We will go to Gynna's studio. All the shots will be indoors, to save expense. But before we get there she needs some props. We go to the most wonderful shop in Guayaquil for fancy dress called Pelucas and Postizos (wigs and falsies).

She bought several wigs, contact lenses and other bits and pieces. I wandered over to the section where there were sexy outfits, for a different sort of party. I rather liked the police woman, and the lady sailor. But I was told no.

She was greeted by her tattoo artist. He said that it was so good to see her. He had prayed for her during the kidnap. I knew him too, we shook hands. I have delivered and collected her from here many times.

Our escort walked behind us in the shop. I wondered what opinion they have of me now!

We got to Gynna's studio at 11am, only to find that there was no light. There is a major power cut in Guayaquil. She had called an electrician and he is connecting a generator.

We said hello to the team. Gynna, Natalie, Marcia, Denis and Pollo.

Fredy arrived with Janina. The whole gang was assembled.

I know the form. To get Kate ready with makeup and hair takes two hours. I told them that I would go to Agripac, which is close by, and work in my office until they are ready.

Fredy went to buy champagne, an essential item for the photos. Denis set to work on her hair, while Marcia put on her makeup.

Exactly two hours later I was summoned back to the studio.

The props are already set up. There is a stall with coconuts piled up on it, with a large photo of the sea in the background. There is also a table with thirty baskets of strawberries in front of a set showing a strawberry field.

One more table has a pile of red pitahaya fruit. Behind which was a photo showing a pitahaya plantation.

Kate is heavily made up for the camera. She is wearing a white dress and heels. The first shot is of the coconuts. She poses in front of the stall, holding a coconut with a straw close to her mouth, as though drinking the water. Pollo has his camera on a tripod. It's connected to a laptop on a table. He asked me to sit on a stool, look at the screen, and comment on the photos. Lights are focussed on Kate. Gynna leant over my shoulder. We alternated with yes, yes, no, yes etc as to whether we liked each shot. After some fifty photos were taken we reckoned we had plenty to choose from.

Kate stood down. There was time for a glass of champagne, then her makeup and hair were altered and she changed into a white dress with printed orange flowers, and wore a large red hat, for the strawberry shot.

This was followed by a green dress for the pitahaya photo. Then we were finished for the day.

Before we left, the fruit was divided among the team. We got two large trays of strawberries and a big box of pitahaya. Far too much for us to eat, we would have to give most of it away. Though Yaneth did make some delicious strawberry jam.

Pitahaya is well known as a laxative, the jam would be far too dangerous!

The coconuts had all been devoured during the day. First we drank the water, then split them open to eat the delicious white flesh.

This brought back memories of my kidnap, when I lived on coconuts for four days.

Sunday.

Today there is another model, a tall slim girl called Nelvic. She was a finalist in the Miss Guayaquil contest last year.

She will do the remaining three photos for the calendar, involving oranges, watermelons and pineapples. There is a seventh photo too, just in case we need it. This one has the two models with their dogs.

Kate took Snoopy to the studio and Nelvic took her bulldog.

We kissed goodbye as I was invited to my daughter Alex's house to have a birthday lunch with my family. We are doing it today, as tomorrow I have a party for our friends in the new house. Never the twain shall meet.

Ceci has arrived back from her long stay in Tupgill, Edinburgh, London, Stratford on Avon, Oxford and Santorini.

Nick and his children, Sofia, Willie and Vicky are here. Almu is in Madrid.

Alex, Javi and their children, Sienna, Olivia and Christian are here too.

It was a lovely lunch. It's good to be together as a family. Sadly this doesn't happen very often now.

The smaller grandchildren made me a birthday card, drawn in crayon, on four large pieces of paper stuck together "We love you, Granddad".

The others gave me wine. An easy choice.

Alex has a beagle too, called Toby. True to form while we were taking photos he put his front paws on the coffee table and wolfed most of the ham, salami and cheese. He got whacked by Alex, but probably thought it worthwhile!

Our cook, Magda, has worked for the family for more than forty years. We used to take her with us to England as a nanny when the children were young. There she learned the art of making Yorkshire puddings and gravy.

Today as a special treat for myself she produced roast chicken, mash, Yorkshires and gravy.

Luxury.

I left Alex's house at 5pm, when Kate returned with my car and minders. Then we went to our flat. Once again she has brought fruit from the day's photos, this time watermelon, oranges and avocados. Our kitchen looks like a greengrocer's shop.

She told me about her day. She said that yesterday's pitahaya certainly worked. They took it in turns to use the one bathroom in the studio.

They managed to get the photo with the dogs after trouble with Snoopy. He got very protective of her when Nelvic's bulldog came too close. There was almost a dogfight.

We will have a meeting next week to select the best photos to use for the calendar.

Pollo had a present for her.

He gave her a book made of enlarged photos of her birthday party in Jamaica last October. Most of the photos were of the party on the yacht. There is one of all twelve of us standing or sitting on the deck. We are all wearing white. I am sitting cross-legged wearing my Panama hat. Fredy and Omar are standing behind me. The ladies, Margarita, Luisa, Nichol, Paola, Andrea, Janina and Kate are in white bikinis. There are two other men, Orlando and Kate's brother Jose.

I think I look rather like Huge Hefner (minus the dressing gown) surrounded by my playmates.

This of course is the famous orgy photo!

I will get a copy made for me. Not sure where I can put it. The office is a bit risky.

Monday 9th September

Today is my birthday. I have to look my best. I applied Just for Men to my hair. It lasts about ten days before I have to repeat it.

I remember a poem from my youth by TS Eliot which finished with the line:

'I measured out my life in coffee spoons'.

In my case it's in Just for Men. I have used it for over twenty-five years. It was originally recommended by Ceci. But as the years passed she asked me not to use it anymore and let my hair return to white. But no, I won't do that. I am addicted to my younger self.

Hair colourant is commonly used in Ecuador. In Agripac I have noticed that several of my managers use it (or another brand). There is even one who I think uses a toupee, but as I have never seen him without it, I can't be sure.

Vanity of vanities, saith the preacher; all is vanity.

Thinking about my 79th birthday.

My godfather Jimmy Clark, who lived to 92, remarked on the death of his sister at 80.

He said that she fell at the first fence. A horse steeplechase phrase.

I trust I will get over that fence too.

There is a comic actor who coined the phrase:

You are only as old as the woman you feel!

Birthdays tend to be times of reflection. There was not a lot to do in the office today, except to acknowledge birthday congratulations by email and WhatsApp.

I let my mind roam.

Where did it roam? To Tupgill.

I have always associated with the house. It transcends more than one generation of the family. I am the third of that name to own it, and I hope not the last.

The house was bought by Bob Armstrong in 1904. He was a racehorse trainer at Eamont Bridge, in Cumbria (it was Westmoreland at the time).

He bought Tupgill with its stables, hay barns, staff quarters and fifty acres of land as an investment. The family didn't move in until 1920. That was when it got a makeover. Eleanor, my grandmother, was not happy with the house as it then was. She added bow windows, a new dining room and a conservatory.

After that there was virtually nothing done to it until eighty-four years later, 2004, when it was in a sad state. The roof leaked, the windows sills were rotten and the electrics were positively dangerous. I practically had to rebuild it from the foundations. In fact, I had to put in foundations, there weren't any. It had been built right on the earth in a shallow trench.

Of course my grandparents had long gone by that time. I inherited the house from my maiden aunt Do in 1992. She had lived there for seventy-two years, with her parents until they died, and then by herself.

As it was continuity, rather than a new purchaser, she accepted the house as it stood.

In those days everyone had a maiden aunt. She was the product of the First World War, when a million British men died. So the same number of women never found a husband.

On taking over the house and surrounding land, I began to plant trees, both for the pleasure they give and to block the view of neighbouring properties, some of which I subsequently bought.

I continued planting for twenty years. Today it's a very wooded estate. There is a wide variety of species with sycamore, oak, ash, mountain ash, birch, elm (American elm, as Dutch elm disease has done for the English variety) scots pine, Douglas fir, thorns and the ubiquitous Leylandii of suburban fame. It's a fast grower and quickly covers eyesores.

My pride and joy are the Wellingtonias, giant redwoods (as in Muir Woods, San Francisco) .

There are thirty of these scattered throughout the woodlands. Today they are only just showing above the treeline. One day they will tower over the other trees, and become my memorial.

At 4.30pm I left the office and went home to the flat. Kate has decreed that the dress for the party is white shirt and black pants (or skirt). She is already dressed in her white blouse, pleated black mini skirt, black stockings and high heels. She had laid out my attire.

The guests are invited for 7pm to our new house.

We got there in good time, after leaving a guest list at the gate to the community.

We found that the Bandurria crew had already put out six tables with white table cloths on the patio overlooking the canal. It all looks so lovely with the lights in the garden reflected from the water, and others showing from the windows of the house. I had ordered a large display of orchids and these had pride of place.

The waiters are preparing for the feast, in their smart white jackets, polishing glasses and getting buckets of ice from the freezer.

The chef is busy at the barbeque in the gazebo. There is a wonderful smell of cooking meat.

Inside the sitting room the newly varnished furniture shines in the light of the magnificent chandelier above the table. There are still pictures to hang and decorating to do, but for an impromptu party it looks wonderful.

The guests began to arrive. We stood by the front door and welcomed each of them with a hug or a kiss.

We are a group of thirty-five.

They have mostly followed the dress code. What I didn't know (but should have guessed from Pelucas) there is a sea of purple wigs. That made it fun.

The girls and Fredy (in drag) made up an impromptu dance team. They put on loud music and began their act with a synchronized dance, the macarena, while the rest of us clapped.

There was a short break while glasses were refilled and then a mariachi band appeared. They paraded through the house and onto the patio, playing as they went.

Two of them removed their remarkably heavy sombreros and put them on Janina and I. It is a double birthday party.

They began with Las Mañanitas, the typical birthday song in Mexico. Then they played and sang a selection of songs for us, and finished with the macho anthem, El Rey, just for me.

It's the most popular of all mariachi songs and goes like this:

Whether or not I have money,
I always do as I please. My word is law.
I don't have a throne or queen,
Nobody understands me.
But I will always be the King.
(It rhymes in Spanish)

The food was served. Amarilis and Maria have come from Rodeo to make the menestra bean stew for me, for the last time. They both wear purple wigs, to rather frightening effect. The beans are accompanied by fillet steaks, pork chops and chicken. There is a bucket of white rice too.

Who doesn't enjoy it? The waiters refilled plates until bellies heaved.

Fredy had brought two birthday cakes. One for Janina and one for me.

Janina's is decorated with a plane and signposts for destinations in Europe and the USA. As she is a travel agent.

My cake has a Colin-like figure wearing a sombrero, with a Snoopy-like beagle sitting next to him.

Only Janina's cake was eaten at the party. So I still have mine to eat with Kate bit by bit, it's delicious. We will keep the icing-sugar figures.

A great deal of wine and champagne was poured during the party. Curiously I didn't get too drunk. As host, I kept putting down my glass to welcome someone, and it got taken away.

Viviana is here with her husband Carlos. We all moved inside the house, for her to sing because of the acoustics. We sat on the marble staircase, which made a grandstand, while she sang below us. She began by singing Oh mio babbino caro, then a piece from Romeo and Juliet, and Summer Time from Gershwin's Porgy and Bess.

I held up well. I didn't cry until she sang the last song, Andrea Bocelli's Time to Say Goodbye. Then I did cry. She had sung it at my last consular event in 2016, after thirty-five years service.

Now she sang it for me to say goodbye to Rodeo Grande, after forty-seven years.

Thursday 19th October

We returned from Miami last night. It's a four-hour flight by American Airlines, not my favourite airline. The seats in business class hardly recline, the food is not great, but they serve wine in tumblers. So after two of these I slept through most of the journey.

Kate watched the Barbie film, only redeemed by the beautiful Margot Robbie.

I had bought the Economist at the airport and read it, until falling asleep.

We had left Guayaquil last Saturday. As always, we bought Panama hats at the duty free. Kate looks lovely in a hat, as do most ladies. As for me, I might say I look more distinguished. At least it disguises my thinning hair. I can buy hats at the artisan market near my office, at a fraction of the airport price, but had forgotten to bring one with me. Hats tend to make a one-way journey. You either wear them, or carry them. But you can't pack them in a suitcase, as I can with my collapsable fedora. In mother's day ladies had hatboxes to travel with.

I have a collection of Panama hats in Tupgill and Madrid.

We had achieved what we wanted to do in Miami. Diana flew there from Los Angeles and I met her for dinner on Monday. It's lovely to see her. We ate at the excellent Cipriani restaurant. We have a lot to talk about, I had not seen her for ages. She had been to Tupgill in July, but of course I wasn't there then.

I left her at her hotel. We will meet tomorrow.

She used to live in Miami, so knows the street where we will meet.

We went to the lawyer's office on Tuesday, together with Alfredo, and signed the necessary trust documents. We had time for lunch, then we took a taxi to the airport. Diana caught a flight back to Los Angeles.

The rest of the time I was with Kate.

We stayed in Mr C Hotel in Coconut Grove. I understand that the C is for the Cipriani group, which owns a chain of restaurants, including the one I ate in with Di.

It's a small boutique hotel with an excellent restaurant on the fifth floor. We ate there the first evening, and I had breakfast there each day, while Kate slept in. In the daytime there is a wonderful view of the sea and moored yachts close by, beyond the mangrove trees.

The restaurant opens at 7am. One morning I was there just before then. The sky was red with the rising sun. This had me puzzled, as daylight in Ecuador is from 6am to 6pm, and that is a long way South. Until I remembered that the US has daylight saving time. It is really 6am here.

It was such a beautiful morning, and then half an hour later there was a downpour. That sequence extended to every day we were there.

I had stayed at this hotel once before with Ceci and my daughters in May 2021. Coconut Grove is a pretty area of small restaurants and bars, and importantly has a bookshop around the corner from the hotel, called Books and Books.

The last time I was here I discovered 'A Gentleman in Moscow' by Amor Towles.

It's probably the book that I have most enjoyed, of the thousands that I have read over the years.

It recounts the story of an aristocrat, Count Rostov, who after the Communist Revolution is sentenced to death by the regime. But the tribunal was shown an extenuating poem that he had supposedly written years before, in praise of communism.

His sentence is commuted to permanent exile in the grand Hotel Metropol in Moscow.

The book has some wonderful scenes. Early in his stay at the hotel he sees a beautiful, willowy, actress in the hotel lobby. She had been given two Borzos (wolfhounds), which she can't control. The hounds spot the one-eyed hotel cat and give chase around the lobby. The Count likens the pursuit to the Battle of Borodino, in 1812, with Napoleon pursuing the Russian commander, the one-eyed Marshal Kutuzov. But the Marshal (and the cat) knows the terrain better. When the hounds get too close to catching it he, as master of hounds, whistles them and they come to heel.

The willowy actress is annoyed that she had to rely on his help. But that leads on to romance.

By coincidence (or not) Count Rostov features in Leon Tolstoy's War and Peace, and in the opera of the same name by Prokofiev.

As an aside, I once had lunch at the impressive Metropol Hotel during my three-day layover in Moscow, when I flew by Aeroflot from Singapore to London in December 1969.

That was the first time I had ever seen an opera. Aeroflot provided tickets to the Bolshoi Theatre as part of the package deal. It was Rigoleto, by Verdi.

Books and Books has a large selection of them. But unlike WH Smith, or Hatchards in London, they are not indexed by authors. There are many rows of shelves from the ground upwards to about three metres high, so without the use of a ladder, you are limited to viewing the first six shelves. They are vaguely labelled as Fiction, History, Art, Biography etc.

It means that you have to run your eyes along each shelf, competing with others, until you find something that interests you. Then if you don't know the author, you take the book out, open the flyleaf and read the summary.

I had already laboriously selected five books when I found The Lincoln Highway by Amor Towles. His third book, following A Gentleman in Moscow and Rules of Civility, which I have read too.

I bought a total of nine books by different authors. It's difficult to get English language books in Ecuador.

I continue writing 'Kidnap '. I am up to eighty thousand words. It's important not to make a book too long, my last two books got to 150,000 words each. I think that was why they put people off, that and the fact that I couldn't promote them, as I wrote under a pen name.

I got back in touch with Lionel Ross last week, who owns the publisher i2i, in Manchester.

He hadn't heard about the kidnap, but sympathized with me. He said he would be delighted to publish this book. But hoped that it would be given a fair chance to sell, and not be pulled after six months as the last two had been. Also that I would be available for a book launch, if he can arrange one. Of course I will be, at Hatchards perhaps?

I asked him about the title 'Kidnap'. Did he think I would have trouble with the executors of Robert Louis Stevenson? He said no. It was published in 1886, anyway the title is 'Kidnapped'

He is now eighty-nine years old and still working. An example to us all.

Then, when Kate got up, we went next door to a ladies clothes shop called Love Shack Fancy.

It's a zany sort of place. The clothes seem to be for little girls of all ages. There are a lot in pink and white semi-transparent gauze with frills.

But she loved it. We came out with two large carrier bags full.

That evening I wanted to eat at the hotel again. But Kate put her foot down. She had come to see Miami. To remain in the hotel, was not seeing it.

We ask the concierge to call a taxi. And that is how we met the Venezuelan, Pedro. We chatted as he drove us to the Mandarin Oriental Hotel. He told us that he had been mayor of a small town in Venezuela. During the Chavez government he had been forced into exile, and lost his property. Now he drives a taxi.

We ate at a Peruvian restaurant on a terrace of the hotel, overlooking the sea. From then on Pedro became our driver. He drove us back to the hotel on Sunday.

On Monday he drove us to a shopping area where we bought a handbag.

Towards eight pm he drove us to the Cipriani restaurant downtown, where I was due to meet Diana.

Then he took Kate to a bar.

After dinner with Di, I took her to her hotel. Then back to mine. It's midnight.

I looked in our room, but Kate wasn't there. I went to the bar, but it is closed. I asked in reception if there is a bar close by that is still open. They told me of one behind the hotel.

I went to it. There were two men and two girls there. No Kate.

I was worried by this time and called Pedro. He said that he had taken her to a bar. They are now on their way back to the hotel.

She came to the door of our room supported by two people from reception at 1am, very drunk. She said that she was upset that Diana didn't want her to stay for dinner. She had drunk far too much with a group of Colombians.

That is a difficult one. None of my family wants to meet her. I have tried my best to convince them, but to little effect. So far.

After the trust signing on Tuesday, once Diana had returned to Los Angeles, Kate and I had dinner at the wonderful Il Gabbiano restaurant on South Biscayne Boulevard.

Finally on Wednesday before we went to the airport, Pedro took us to Little Havana, the street of Cuban restaurants. We asked him to join us to thank him for looking after us. Then of course I had to pay his taxi bill, which had gotten remarkably high.

Thursday 19th September

I am back in my office. Despite answering lots of emails on my phone while in Miami, there is a number that I needed to look at on the big screen, such as balance sheets. So today I am busy.

At 2.30pm Kate came to collect me for the next Pilates class. This is the seventh. I am just beginning to feel benefit from them. I feel that I am walking more upright. The leg and foot exercises avoid my tripping, I pick my feet up more. Now we are moving on to arm and chest exercises, that is where my muscles are seriously depleted. Watch out Superman!

Also I am pleased to see that I have put on a kilo of weight.

My weight as a younger man had been 78 kilos (172 lbs). A month ago it had gotten down to 70 kgs, now it's 71. All to the good.

I get my haircut every three weeks. I need to go today, so that I can get in one more just before we leave for Madrid on the 8th October. Strangely, I can never seem to find a good hairdresser on my travels.

Today's opera is a video featuring Luciano Pavarotti, Placido Domingo and Jose Carreras (the Three Tenors). Then, by coincidence, Andre Bocelli and Sarah Brightman singing Time to Say Goodbye.

I was almost reduced to blubbing in the barber's chair!

By association I thought of Andrew Lloyd Webber, who was once married to Sarah Brightman. That led on to the musical The Woman in White, which I saw in London many years ago. Count Fosco is the bad guy, but he has the best songs.

He is an Italian who has the lines "Put on a Bella Figura, a Good Show. One more encore, leave the audience wanting more".

Now I am getting gloomy.

It's the tradition at funerals in Ecuador for there to be music. Normally there is Ave Maria or other religious pieces, but not always. I have sometimes heard the favourite music of the deceased.

So perhaps when it comes to my turn (or shortly before) I will ask Viviana to sing Time to Say Goodbye at my funeral. That way, those present will surely cry, for the music itself if not for me!

I will put on a Bella Figura to the very end.

We have got into the habit of ordering both food and supermarket items to be delivered to our flat. It's undoubtedly easier, but lacks the fun of looking at the shelves for impulsive buys.

Saturday, after Pilates, we went to Supermaxi together. But not alone. Jose and Pedro, our security detail, followed us in. This makes shopping easier. Kate and I select items and they pushed the trolleys. We divided what we bought between the flat and the new house. For the flat there was cheese, ham, eggs, smoked pork chops, two tins of beans, Corona beer, champagne, bread etc.

For the new house it's cleaning materials, plant pots, towels and gardening implements.

We will soon start to position food in the fridge there and take clothes to change into. But not yet. We have contracted the security items we need, but they won't be installed for two months, not the two weeks originally offered.

That limits us. While builders are there anything we leave will get covered in dust.

There is a large amount of wine left over from the party, so we can, and do, have a glass each time we go there.

I used to be reticent about shopping with Kate, before I was living openly with her. I didn't want gossip to get back to Ceci. We would walk down the mall separately, just in case we are seen by those who know Ceci and I.

Now of course it doesn't matter. Just as well. Oscar came up and said hello. We are both members of the Phoenix Club. I introduced him to Kate. He has not been to the Club in years. He told me to let him know when I am next going. I asked for his number so that the next time we have an old lags meeting I can call him.

Our two trolleys were holding up the queue at the cash desk. There again there was a couple behind us who knew me, I have no idea of their names. I shook hands with them and apologized for holding them up. They were all smiles for both Kate and I, and said no bother.

So, if they knew me from my past life they now have no problem with Kate.

We are just back from Miami and we are planning to leave Ecuador again. Janina has arranged the flights. We will leave Guayaquil on the 8th October for Madrid, and return the same way on 4th November. We are flying with Air Europa this time.

When we went to Miami, Janina kindly dog-sat in our flat. The next stay will be for almost four weeks. What can we do with Snoopy? I have abandoned hope that Alex will have him. It's not the dog, we are back to principles. She wants nothing to do with Kate.

The problem is now solved. Emilie, Yaneth's niece, comes to work with her on the days when she is not at university. She always walks Snoopy in the nearby park. It seems they have bonded. She has offered to dog sit. She and Yaneth will work this out, so that Yaneth is there when Emilie is at her classes and Emilie will sleep there. A perfect solution. Snoopy is cared for, and Emilie makes some extra money.

Snoopy is not happy to be left by himself and barks. We have had complaints from the neighbours.

Janina will spend a couple of days with us in Madrid and then go by Ave to Barcelona to see her cousin, who is sadly ill with cancer.

Then Margarita arrives from Colombia. She is going on holiday with her other daughter, Luisa, to Italy for five days.

Kate and I will return to the eye clinic so she can have tests. If she doesn't need an operation, or if it can be done quickly, we will go to Croatia for a few days.

After which we have tickets to London on the 26th October with Janina, Margarita and Luisa too.

We will spend two nights at the Landmark Hotel in London. Kate and I have stayed there before and liked it with its huge atrium in the centre and palm trees. It's a five-star hotel, though not of the Ritz standard. We are five people, economies must be made.

But it's certainly not slumming!

On the 28th we will meet up with Jorge Cepeda at King's Cross, take the train to Yorkshire, and stay at Tupgill.

Together we will celebrate Kate's birthday on the 29th October and then the Halloween party at the Forbidden Corner, with added Ghost Trail.

I have just finished one of the books that Kate bought for me in Hatchards, Marcos Aurelius, by Frank McLynn. It has taken me a while to read and absorb it. I got somewhat bogged down in philosophy, he was a Stoic.

But there is a great deal about the Germanic wars, both on the Rhine and Danube. Its a period of Roman history I was not familiar with. It's the time the Romans conquered the Sarmatians, a tribe of fierce horse warriors. They incorporated 5,000 of the defeated warriors into the Roman army in 170 AD and posted them to Britain, where they were stationed at Hadrian's Wall to resist incursion from the Picts.

It has been said that they might be the origin of the King Arthur legend of armoured knights.

The Armstrongs, and other border clans share DNA with them. The love of horses passes through generations.

Of course that period in history was made famous by the film Gladiator. Marcus Aurelius dies and his despicable son Commodus inherits the Empire. Poor Maximo (Russell Crowe) suffers the consequences.

I am always amazed that we have so much detail about the Roman period. We can read the letters written in Marcos Aurelius' time. We know who were his tutors, where he travelled, what he achieved and who he put to death.

All this because of the level of civilization they reached.

But from the time of the fall of the Roman Empire we enter the Dark Ages and know practically nothing, except what the few literate Christian priests recorded.

It has been said that Britain lost a thousand years of development between the year 400 AC when the Romans left, and 1400 AC when we had just about recovered the level of civilization the Romans had.

One can only wonder how much more advanced the World would be today if the civilization of the Roman Empire had survived the invasions of the barbarians.

Today, September 20th, the newspapers ran a headline that President Daniel Noboa has announced that he will send a bill to the Assembly (congress) to overturn the ban on foreign troops being based in Ecuador. What to me is splendid news was quickly set upon by the other candidates for the Presidency in next February's elections. There are arguments that a lot has changed since 2009. Technology has moved on. Now we don't need a physical presence. And the familiar grumbles about sovereignty, national dignity etc etc.

The US Embassy has stated that they have no plans to base troops in Ecuador. But that might be a ruse. Peru has a group of US military who have a year's contract to train both the police and army.

To my mind Ecuador cannot win the drug battle without US help. The armed forces are only one aspect. The US has the biggest drug enforcement team in the world, called the DEA. They are active in Colombia. Are they armed forces? They are certainly armed.

Together with extradition of criminals to the USA, the DEA could hammer the drug cartels and make a huge difference to Ecuador's safety.

The US navy has been collaborating with Ecuador for some years. They patrol outside the national maritime limit to detect both planes and boats carrying cocaine.

Additionally they have offered to give Ecuador two coastal patrol boats to work within the maritime limits.

Perhaps we really are working towards a safer and better country. One can only hope so.

I have spent more than fifty years here and I love Ecuador.

There was a late-night party in the downstairs flat last night. I think they have just moved in. It has a wider balcony than the ones above it, so we overlook them.

But with the air conditioner on in the bedroom we had no trouble sleeping.

It's not a particularly noisy area. There was a wedding party nearby which went on until 2am a couple of weeks ago.

Apart from those there are continual children's birthday parties in the garden of our block, or neighbouring ones. But they are in the afternoon. The only irritation is the lady animators whose amplified voices sound like Minnie Mouse.

An idea crossed our minds that we might buy our flat when we sell the duplex. We now know it well and no faults have shown up. It would be a source of income.

How our views have shifted. At first we hated it, now we are comfortable with it. And even thinking of buying it.

It was for sale when we first rented it. But at the time we hoped we would not stay here long.

A lot of water has passed under the bridge since March.

Sister Catherine has asked me to help her with return tickets from Australia. She and Emilie are coming back, but not to England. They are going to live near Cork in Ireland to be close to Emilie's father. It seems their emigration is not a success. They found the property market too hot. There was nothing they liked that they could afford. Also, both of Emilie's children, Sophie and Daniel, said they wanted to live and work in Europe for a year or two.

So why stay in Brisbane?

Jane is happy about this. She misses her sister. Cork is a great deal closer than Brisbane.

So much for our plan to go and visit them in December this year. We may still go to Australia but now there is no rush. I suppose I am relieved in a way. We will return from our holiday in November. From then on I prefer to stay in Ecuador, and in the office, through the main planting season which runs from December to March.

I see signs of a recovery in the market. Customers seem keener to sort out their overdue accounts, so that they can buy again.

I hammer this into the sales force each week as the figures come in. If you don't collect before December, then you won't be able to sell to them again.

We really need a good end to the year to recover from our downturn.

My promise to the family is that I will stay long enough to see Agripac regain its health and strength.

Actually I might well stay a lot longer, if I am spared.

Towards that end, I persevere with Pilates. I have done eight hours so far. I feel better for it. Yesterday’s session was a bit harder. When the hour was up my legs were trembling. Kate had to help me stand up. But from then on I was OK.

I am afraid I must report that Snoopy had a relapse this morning. I found poo on the sitting room floor. He knows the rules, if this happens then he gets no breakfast.

He followed me out of the bedroom but didn't even come to the kitchen to look at his bowl. He went and laid on the sofa. I growled at him as I picked up his droppings. He opened an eye in acknowledgement.

He is becoming manipulative. Yesterday Kate left him in the flat while she went to do her nails. A neighbour called to say that he was howling. She had to return, collect him and take him to the salon with her. Then he was happy.

The problem is that Yaneth doesn't get to the flat until eleven o’clock. Kate goes out to the gym, Pilates, or whatever, at 9am. He knows we are coming back, but makes a show.

Living with a dog, especially a beagle, ain't easy.

But he makes up for it. We love him.

Last night I prepared a can of local beans to eat with sausages. Kate advised against it. She said that tinned beans can't be healthy. Nonsense I replied, thinking of the many cans of Heinz baked beans that I have enjoyed. She shrugged and left it at that.

I should have been warned. On opening the can all the liquid was at the top. The beans themselves seemed to be a congealed mass at the bottom of the can. I poured the juice into a saucepan and then scraped the beans out with a fork. I only prepared half the can. The rest I put back in the fridge.

I woke up at 3am this morning with violent tummy pains. I was blown up with gas, like a zeppelin that is about to take off.

I took an Alka Seltzer, my perennial standby, and returned to bed. An hour later I was sitting on the loo. The pain is still there. This time I took paracetamol. Half an hour and another loo trip. It got to 5am, my getting up time. I went to the kitchen and made a cup of tea…..and then went back to the loo. A ditty ran through my head, paraphrasing HMS Pinafore,

"Stay close to the loo, and never go to sea, and you too could be the ruler of the Queen's navy". The actual words are "your desk", not the loo.

I see that Kate had binned what was left in the can.

Things seemed to calm down. It's time to drive to the office, my escort is waiting for me.

Well, it's only a fifteen-minute trip. I can stand that. Then I have my office loo waiting for me.

Exactly. But with the frequent power cuts when I got to my office door the camera wouldn't recognize me. I couldn't get in. I called security. Along came a guard with a mastercard to open the door. That didn't work either. I called Carlos from Systems department. He is still on his way to the office.

I sat outside my office, holding my guts, praying that they wouldn't take long to open it.

Then Jorge turned up and solved the problem. He had a key to the adjoining conference room and opened the door. Then I could access my office, and ran to the loo!

Perhaps I should have heeded Kate's warning.

I have two interviews to do. Two senior managers are in a serious dispute and one threatens to resign. As we northerners say, Trouble at Mill.

And indeed it is the mill. It's our factory which produces feed for cattle, pigs, chickens, pets and shrimp. This last one is causing the problem.

Ecuador has grown swiftly in the last few years to become the largest exporter of shrimp in the world. Sadly, now there is world overproduction. The Chinese, who are great consumers, are in a recession.

Prices for shrimp have slumped, and many producers have gone out of business. This has caused big problems for us and the other feedmills. The remaining customers have become more and more demanding, which in turn raises our costs.

Hans, our Dutch friend and advisor, has finished his seven-year stint with us. We have replaced him with a local advisor. But since he came in everything seems to have gone wrong. Now we are in the blame game. The sales manager versus the factory manager.

One handed in his notice yesterday. I called him to ask him to reconsider. Today he will come to my office and we can talk. The other will come in tomorrow.

This is my elder statesman moment. Now then my boy (I can give both of them thirty-five years).

I hope it works. I don't want to lose either of them, they are both twenty-year employees.

Kate has a lunch date today. It's with the lady who she calls her best friend in Ecuador. They met even before I knew Kate. Olga is a Ukrainian lady, a few years older than her. She came to Ecuador long before the war with Russia. She met and married an Ecuadorian musician who was studying in Kiev. They have a son, David. But the marriage didn't survive.

Olga is tall, slim, blonde and very attractive with her slavic features.

She took up modelling, and that is how the girls met.

Unfortunately she is going out with a man who we don't much like. But we put up with him to maintain our friendship.

Their relationship is very tempestuous. I can remember at least five occasions when she said she had left him for good. The last time we drove across town to her place to collect her with half a dozen suitcases. She said that she will come and stay at our penthouse for a few days. But she always goes back to him. I think that she is a submissive.

Then, about a year ago, she broke contact with Kate. It was impossible to call her. We blame her man for poisoning the friendship.

Last week she called and suggested they meet for lunch today.

Kate is very nervous about it. My advice is not to demand any explanation. Just continue as you left off a year ago.

Fingers crossed that it goes well.

And it did go well. Olga arrived half an hour late, but from then on it was a love fest. I saw Kate at 5pm. I half expected to see Olga too, so that we could show her the new house. But Kate said no. Little by little. Olga has invited us and Janina for dinner in her boyfriend's house next Saturday.

Kate and I met at the new house today because Juan Gabriel and Sebastian are coming. They have made computer renders of how the new furniture will look. These are interactive so we can experiment with ideas.

The TV furniture is too tall. We wanted three metres, which is the height of the French doors into the patio. They had planned 3.5 meters. But it was quickly changed. As with most architects they like to play with designs to make them harmonious. But in this case I want space for a large TV screen, then around it shelves for my 500 DVDs and or books. I despair of getting new opera (or any other) DVDs. It seems they have been discontinued. The world has gone back seventy years to vinyl discs, just like the ones my mother had.

Sadly DVDs wear out. When that happens I will have to throw them away. So the shelves should be of a size to accommodate books as well. I measured the bookshelves in my office. They are 28 cm high. That's really too high for DVDs, but better that way than having to change the furniture in the future.

We looked at changing the colour of the doors in the sitting room to brown to match the ranch furniture. That looked good. Then we looked at brown wooden handrails for the stairs, instead of glass, yes that works. They showed us what wooden panelling would look like to cover the wall on the dining room side. That way the two doors to the kitchen blend into the panels.

They have gone overboard on the jacuzzi. From a two by three-metre pool it has doubled in size with another sunken hole for sitting in (why?) and a water feature around the whole thing. It would take up half the patio. I turned this down, but Kate liked the sitting hole. We will have to discuss this one. They also drew a second pergola over an outside bar. That isn't necessary. We already have a good-sized pergola.

I am afraid the project is getting out of hand. We doubled the cost of our penthouse with improvements. Now trying to sell it we will lose about a third of the value. People want to decorate the house to their own taste. The last owner's taste doesn't count.

It will happen here when she tries to sell the house one day.

As we were planning the house the lights went off. This is happening more and more frequently in Ecuador. It's blamed on the lack of rain in the Sierra and Amazon where all the hydroelectric dams are. Several houses close to us have generators. There was a humming of diesel engines as they all came on. We will have to get one. It's becoming too frequent to ignore. Not only do the lights, airconditioner and TV go off, but the freezer defreezes.

At the moment the temperature is not too hot at night, and we can sleep without an air conditioner. But from December to March, no way.

The flat we are in has a generator for the building, as does the penthouse building. But individual houses are on their own. Both Nick and Alex have installed them, now Ceci wants one too.

As for Agripac. The office block has two huge generators which switch on immediately when there is a power cut.

But the factories don't. The biggest, the feed mill, has problems just now. There are threatened power cuts of up to twelve hours a day in October. We are looking at buying a generator for its four-megawatt needs. But it will take several months to arrive from China, and it costs the top side of one and a half million dollars. Meanwhile we have to prioritize. There is fierce competition between the three sales managers who sell animal feed. We can't produce everything in the limited time available, so something has to be sacrificed.

That is what brought the fight to a head between the factory manager and one of the sales managers. I saw one yesterday, and talked him out of resigning. The other I will see today.

To paraphrase another Gilbert and Sullivan play, The Pirates of Penzance,

"A President's lot is not a happy one". It is really a policeman's lot.

My little songbird, Viviana Rodriguez, came to see me at the office yesterday. We have made modifications to our in-house theater. We have built new kitchens for Bandurria, they now do two hundred and fifty lunches a day. That allowed me to remove the staff bathrooms and changing rooms to the left side of the stage. We knocked through and now the stage runs the whole length of the building. Well, what the audience can see remains the same. But at last we have a place for the piano, or orchestra when we have one, to the side of the stage. A horizontal orchestra pit. It will allow space for scenery to be placed too.

Upstairs, above the new kitchens, there is a large room which we have made into a dressing and rehearsal room, which includes their large wardrobe. We have costumes from a dozen operas. A lot of pieces get reused. For instance there are soldiers in many operas, and opera can be transposed in time.

This rearrangement will allow the artists more space and free up the area where they used to change for more audience seating.

Our next venture is Rigoletto, by Verdi. We plan this for the 14th November, once I am back from holiday.

The second manager came to see me on Friday afternoon. He began with a litany of complaints. I listened and then reasoned with him. It's a difficult year. We are all under pressure to achieve our objectives, especially as they are tied to bonuses. But we must respect others in the same position. High tension management doesn't work.

We talked about the company history and his twenty-seven years with us. He explained that part of his anxiety at the moment involves his own security. This led on to my kidnap experience. He is sympathetic. The meeting finished and we are onside again.

Kate and I have interviewed a young man, Celso, to work in the new house. We have Yaneth to cook and clean. She will move there when we do, but the house has a garden, a jacuzzi and a lot of windows to clean. So we need a man.

He will work different hours from Yaneth, from 7am to 3pm. That allows us to be out in the mornings and he will look after Snoopy. Yaneth leaves at 5pm, when one of us is generally back. We have a demanding dog.

I told Joseph about Celso. He advised me to arrange a polygraph test, to be sure that he has no contact with the underworld. I asked Celso if he would help to do this, and he agreed.

We already know Celso's family, as his brother works in Bandurria.

This led me to think about the crime situation in Ecuador. As in war, the aggressor has every advantage to start with. Think of Germany in the Second World War. But then the Allies fought back, especially when Russia and the US joined in. Gradually the balance changed as Germany was worn down, leading to its defeat.

In this case it's the forces of law and order that have to fight back. The USA has a vested interest in stopping cocaine reaching its shores. This needs the Ecuadorian government's cooperation. Perhaps we are getting there.

The government has raised taxes this year with the express intention of beefing up the police and armed forces against organized crime. The police force will be increased from 60,000 to 80,000 officers.

Then there is the private sector.

Joseph's security company employs over a thousand people. There are many private security companies. I have no idea of the total manpower (it tends to be men), but at a guess there must be 30 to 40 thousand well-paid, trained and disciplined armed guards. Most companies use them to guard offices and factories. Hotels, shopping malls, ports, airports and walled housing enclosures have guards. There is also a custody service for protecting trucks from the port to the factories, and from there to the shops. We use this too. We have had many trucks hijacked.

Surely it must be getting more difficult to kidnap the more important targets as they, like myself, drive armoured vehicles and have a security detail. It seems to be true. There are more kidnaps but lower value ones. Agripac has had a field technician taken, but released after payment by the family for a relatively small amount. I read today of a taxi driver taken too. The market is losing value.

Not everyone sees it like this. There are plenty of doomsayers who insist that security is getting worse. But then I am an optimist.

I have lived in Guayaquil for fifty years and associate with the city. When I arrived here in 1972 it was largely a wooden town, of half a million people. Today the wooden houses have vanished to be replaced by concrete houses and highrises. It's now home to three and a half million souls. By comparison Birmingham, the second British city after London, has two and a half million people.

When I arrived, the place for the middle class to live was a recently developed area called Urdesa. Ceci and I lived there, and so did most of our friends.

Then in 1985 the President of Ecuador, León Febres Cordero, built the ring road around Guayaquil. That opened to development an area between the rivers Daule and Babahoyo called Samborondon. Today it is the growth area of the city.

Along a strip of thirty kilometres (which includes the canton of Daule) there are scores of walled enclosures, high rises, shopping malls, restaurants, schools hospitals, clubs (including the new Union Club), the racecourse and the city's biggest cemetery.

It is home to half a million people.

There is another area of development on the road that runs from Guayaquil towards the beach towns of Salinas and Playas.

For me the exciting thing is that building has not stopped. There are dozens of building sites. Security in Samborondon, while not perfect, is better here than downtown Guayaquil.

Joseph, Kate and I go out to dinner from time to time. He suggested we return to the Tango restaurant. But I had a better idea. I had seen in today's newspaper that the Oktoberfest is on at the Hilton Hotel for two weeks.

I love it. I have been every year, for many years.

So we decided on this. I talked to Kate and we invited Janina, Fredy and Omar to join us.

We all met at the Hilton at 7.30pm. We can't leave Snoopy at home, he would howl, so he came with us. But he is not allowed into the hotel. Jose, one of our guards, will walk him around outside, while they wait for us. Guards need a lot of patience, they spend most of the day waiting for us.

As we went into the hall two members of the German oompah band, dressed in lederhosen and hats, said hello to us. The same band has been coming for years,and they knew Kate and I.

The hall is in the basement of the hotel. It is decorated as a Bavarian bierkeller with adverts for Erdinger beer. There is a bandstand in one corner and tables of eight laid out. We were only six, but we got the table to ourselves. The waiters and waitresses were dressed in Bavarian dress. We ordered blond Erdinger beers to start the night.

The band struck up. They would play a piece and then raise their bier steins in a toast, to which the audience joined in "eins, zwei, drei, Prost". This happened a great deal, so we drank a lot. The waiters kept our mugs topped up.

One of the typical pieces of music they play sounds exactly the same as the Cockney song Roll out the Barrel. But then why not? Both the German and British armies sang Lilly Marlene in the Second World War. It was originally sung in German by Marlene Dietrich.

When we got hungry we went to the buffet and ate pork knuckle with sauerkraut. There was a chicken alternative for those who don't eat pork.

The band has the same acts as always. In one, a man dresses in a costume resembling a cow. He lays out hand bells on a table then plays a tune on them as though they were cowbells, used in the mountains to locate cows.

In another act, he dresses as a rooster and sings a song with audience participation. This involves clapping hands, bending knees and jumping up and down. Which really got the audience excited.

To finish, as it got towards eleven o'clock, they played dance music and we got up and danced.

A great evening.

I was all for calling it a day. But Kate invited everyone back to our flat for an 'after '.

We drank several bottles of wine there.

Four of us, Kate, Fredy, Omar and I were involved in the kidnap. We talked about it, at first seriously, but then when we got on to Janina's witch, with laughter.

It's now over nine months since it happened.

There is a magazine in Ecuador called Vistazo. I normally don't read it, but in September each year they publish the list of the top thousand companies by sales. I got it last Friday.

I was pleased (relieved) to see that Agripac maintained its position as number 35 in 2023, despite sales falling ten per cent. But then most companies didn't grow much, and a lot lost sales. It was a difficult year.

I go through the list carefully looking at our customers and competitors. It will take me time to analyze it. There are articles too about a selection of companies which I find interesting.

Yesterday Nick ran the Berlin marathon. He sent us photos and his time, three hours fifty-two seconds, an average of 5.36 minutes per kilometre. He is pleased with his time. He is a veteran marathon runner having done Madrid, Chicago, New York and London marathons. He aims to do Tokyo next year. He has also run a bunch of half marathons.

He has always been more of a sportsman than his father. I played rugby at school and university, but with more enthusiasm than skill, in the third fifteen. He was in the Sedbergh first fifteen rugby team (no mean achievement at a serious rugby school). He played for Nottingham University and finally for a club in Madrid. Now his sport is running.

Alex is in Spain this week. She went for a medical checkup in Madrid. But has taken advantage of being there. She invited seven ex-school friends, from St Anne's School in Windermere, to meet her in Palma, Mallorca.

Not up to Diana's gathering of practically all her St Anne's class. But it's good that she still has so many friends from that time.

She sent us photos of the lineup, inevitably with a glass in their hands.

Kate called me to say that I must get home by four-thirty pm to look after Snoopy as she is going to a Telas class (aerial silk) near my grandchildren's school. I had to wait for the lady who was bringing my euros for the coming Madrid trip. Then I drove home, followed by the guards.

As soon as I got there she left.

I made a cup of tea and settled down to read my latest book The Wide, Wide Sea by Hampton Sides. It's the story of Captain James Cook's third and last voyage which began in 1776. His instructions from the Admiralty were to sail to Polynesia and return a Polynesian man, called Mai, to his home. He was returned together with a bunch of farm animals, guns and tools donated by King George III. Mai had been taken to England two years previously and had caused a sensation as the Noble Savage. The King thought that returning him with many gifts would sway the Polynesian population to favour England over the claims of France to overlordship.

Once this had been done Cook was to proceed to the North West coast of America and search for the passage across to Newfoundland, and hence back to England.

I got well on with the book before Kate returned. She had enjoyed her class, but said that all the other girls (no boys) were ten years old. They asked her name and whether she was an instructor, she said no, she was a student like them. I asked if she was well ahead of them. But she said no. At their age they are super flexible and very light. They can shin up the tela easily, which costs her more with her weight.

Laughing, she said that she was sure the girls were in Alex's daughter, Sienna's, school class. She wondered how long it would take for their mothers to work out who she is.

She was hungry. What did I want to eat? I threw caution to the wind and said McDonalds, which I am rarely allowed to have. Surprisingly she said she would have one too. I did a double take. She hasn't eaten meat in years. But tonight she will.

While waiting for them to be delivered we went to watch another episode of Game of Thrones. Years ago I had read all the books. But I don't remember this part.

I believe that the film makers have taken the story a lot further than the author George RR Martin wanted to go. I suspect he is right.

Jon Snow, now Lord Commander of the Watch, is set upon and killed by his colleagues, rather as Cesar was murdered. One after another stabs him while saying that he has betrayed them by letting the Wildings through the tunnel in the wall of ice.

I was sad to see Jon Snow leave the series. But of course he didn't. The Red Witch revived him. He then proceeded to hang the five main perpetrators, took off his black cloak and declared that his watch had ended.

Now I surmise that he will return to Winterfell, sort out the reprehensible Boltons, and get what's left of the Stark family back together.

I am going to have to talk seriously to Snoopy. We allow him on the bed, and he settles initially at the bottom between our feet. But I get up several times in the night (old man's problem). Each time I return to bed I find that Snoopy has taken my place on the pillow. Kate as usual is sprawled over the bed. Which one to move ? They both growl at me if disturbed. But his growl is the lesser.

My favourite cousin John replied to me today. I had written my six-monthly email to him, telling him my news. He used to own, and run, a large agricultural estate in Yorkshire, an hour from Tupgill. But when it was clear that their only daughter, Louise, was going to live in London, he and his wife Anne sold up in the North and bought a house near London, to be closer to her.

He made a wonderful comparison. He had to sell a thousand acres in Yorkshire in order to buy a smallish house near London.

I had twelve cousins, but four have left this world. As John said years ago, the last of the uncles and aunts have gone. Now it's our generation that's in the firing line.

Only two cousins are Armstrong. The others are Wilsons, mother's family name.

My grandfather William Wilson had seven children. He owned the family business which was a hat factory, Joe Wilson and Sons, in Manchester, UK.

John sent me an old photo recently of the factory. I was taken there as a lad of twelve and given two trilby hats which I wore for years. It's a most impressive redbrick building, five stories high with rows of identical windows and a huge chimney stack .

The factory did very well while both men and women wore hats. Look at photos of an early twentieth-century gang of men building roads or railways. They all are wearing bowler hats.

Today the only men who wear trilby hats are the horse racing fraternity. Bowler hats used to be common in the City of London. But have almost disappeared.

My mother's was the third generation of Wilsons to run the factory. They were sporting folk who rode to hounds. The factory was increasingly run by the foremen. Men of undoubted experience but little foresight. When demand diminished they didn't diversify into other lines. The business collapsed in the nineteen fifties.

I wear fur-felt fedora hats. There is a well-established hat shop in St James Street in London called Locke.

When I first bought a hat there in 1982 I asked an elderly assistant if he remembered Wilson hats. He did.

Yesterday I went to see our Balanfarina factory with Nick, Javi and Gustavo, the managing director of Agripac. We arrived at 8am and found the workers leaving. The power cut is from 8am to 8pm. We lose the whole day's production, and just work nights. This is seriously worrying. We can’t supply all our customers. We walked around the darkened plant. We have decided to buy the big generator needed to run it in power cuts. But it won't be here until early next year.

We looked at a huge pile of sacks waiting to be reprocessed. We have been trying to reach new, exacting standards of excellence. But have missed by a few percentage points. Customers, knowing that there is spare capacity in the industry are becoming more and more demanding. But now the boot is on the other foot. There's a shortage of shrimp feed with the power cuts. I told the sales manager to offer the same product they rejected to each customer. Let's see if they feel the same today, or if they are glad to get any feed at all.

I had a dentist appointment at 11am, so went home to collect Kate, after the factory visit, and then to see Raul the dentist. It's been six months since I had my tooth removed. Raul is waiting for the jawbone to thicken to encase the screw he inserted. He made an x-ray. But it’s still not ready to take the implant. He played a laser light on it. I have to go back after the holiday and have more laser treatment until he can finally insert the new tooth.

I had an implant done thirty years ago in England. At that age it all went very quickly.

Raul kindly said that I am looking well. I told him about Pilates. I think I look better too, but it may be subjective.

Afterwards Kate wanted to go to our new house. She spent an hour making notes of the changes she wants. The architects are coming in the afternoon. Before then we went to the Spanish restaurant. To go with my huevos rotos we shared a bottle of Pesquera wine, though I drank most of it. We returned to the new house at 4pm. Feeling sleepy I went to the only bed there and had a siesta. I awoke as the architects were leaving. So much for my contribution.

In fact I haven't achieved much at all today. I had not even got to the office. It left a feeling of dissatisfaction. The office puts some discipline in my life. I work from 7am to 4pm and don't drink at lunchtime. When on holiday drinking seems to start early and go on through the day. Kate aids and abets.

"A drink My Love?" "Yes, why not".

Tomorrow, 4th October, is my fiftieth wedding anniversary. Normally we would hold a big party to celebrate it. There would be jokes about surviving so long together, and wishes for many more years to come. But we certainly can't do that this year. I sent a text to Ceci. Would she like to have lunch with me at the Union Club?

I got a very sad reply.

"No thank you Darling, I would spend the lunch crying. I am thinking of all we have done together in the last fifty years. The family we have raised, the business we have built, the many holidays and wonderful times.

I will always love you."

She sent me our wedding photo.

That made me cry.

How difficult life can be.

We have many memories, but curiously few photos. Before the cellphone era we never carried cameras. We had what we called the Great Armstrong family holidays. We went together to Yellowstone Park in the USA. We went on safari to Kenya and Tanzania, where we stayed under canvas for two nights and listened to the lions in the camp. Then we had two more nights at the wonderful Ngorongoro Crater Lodge.

We went to India and the Taj Mahal and stayed at the Amarvilas Hotel. Finally, we went to New Zealand, Australia, Hong Kong and Beijing.

So many wonderful times.

I called the florist to deliver her a large bouquet of orchids. I have done that every year, and will continue to do it.

That left me feeling down. Christmas is coming. I will spend it with Kate and her family at our new house. So I won't be with my own family, for the first time ever.

Of course I will see them. Diana, Steve and their three boys, Oliver, Roco and Domenic, will come to Guayaquil as they always do. We will meet for meals. But not for Christmas dinner on the 24th December. I can't be in two places at the same time.

Though two years ago I was barely present at the dinner anyway.

It was the first time Kate brought her family to Guayaquil. They went to a hotel at the beach after Christmas. I had not met her father, grandmother or brother. We were to meet at the bar of the Hilton Hotel at 5pm on the 24th. I was nervous about meeting them. Kate had told me that her father is very severe. What's worse he doesn't know about us. She had never told him anything. Now he is going to meet her boyfriend who is considerably older than himself!

I must explain. Her parents have been divorced for years. But they are still friends. They have come together to visit her. Her mother knows me well, but Kate had asked her not to tell him about me.

I got to the bar early and had a couple of drinks. Kate arrived and joined me. The others were shopping. They will soon be here. By the time they came we had finished the first bottle of wine. In fact they were all very friendly. Her father and I got on well. We talked about the ranch, horses and cattle. A meeting of minds.

I looked at my watch. It was 8pm. I should have been home ages ago. I said goodbye and left them. I drove as fast as I could but the traffic was heavy with families gathering for the big event.

When I got home I was not well received. Where have you been? Look at the time. How could you let the family down.

I changed quickly into my dinner jacket and went to the sitting room with the family, all nine grandchildren too.

Dinner was delayed until ten thirty pm. By this time I had drunk a lot more.

We finally sat down, with me at the head of the table, Ceci beside me.

Then disaster. I fell asleep!

Ceci nudged me. I woke up and promptly knocked over the wine glass.

She ordered me to go to bed.

The grandchildren watched in horror as their drunken Grandfather sloped off to bed.

What a disgrace!

Today, Thursday 3rd October, Pilates was cancelled. The trainer had something else to do. But I was not let off. Kate called me at the office and told me to put on my kit, we are going to a gym at 4pm. Panic, I haven't been to one since school days.

I have seen photos of her gym where muscle-bound men lift huge weights. I am going to look a proper wimp there.

But no, it's not her gym we are going to, but the small private gym in the garden of our flat.

We had it to ourselves. She put the air conditioner on. There are five machines plus a selection of weights. I fancied the walking machine, but for some reason it didn't work, although it was plugged in. So she put me on the Eliptico where I walked and used arms and legs together. I managed this for ten minutes. Then she suggested weights. She gave me two kgs ones, and she took 5 kgs. We flexed arms and then raised and lowered arms out straight. Then we flexed our knees.

After that she stood on her head, while I hugged my knees to relax. We took photos to show to my sisters that I have indeed been to the gym. (I can't send photos of us together to Ceci or my children).

Finally school is out at 5pm.

It had been an experience, but I preferred Pilates. In the gym there are few things to do, and we spent too long on each. In Pilates each exercise is in multiples of ten flexes. Then we change to another, alternating between arms and legs. The hour passes quickly.

We went to the new house, taking Snoopy with us. We are learning not to leave him alone when Yaneth and Emilie go home. The last time we did, he got onto the dining table, there was a chair left out, and gnawed three marble chess pieces, two pawns and a castle.

Luckily for him he didn't damage the orchids, Kate's pride and joy. They have recently flowered again after many months of nothing. That is the beauty of orchids, they always return.

I don't think I have described Yaneth. She is a short, very round, lady. I guess about fifty years old with grown-up children. She has a lovely sense of humour, and enjoys a chat so much that if not terminated, she will get little work done. She cleans the flat and washes clothes. She used to leave cooked food for us. But we often left it, as we were out, or preferred something else. She has stopped doing it.

Her niece Emilie is twenty-five years old. She too is short, but slim and wears glasses. Despite coming from a poor background she is studying at university and will hopefully have a good career.

Cristina's carpenter has finally finished re-painting the last piece of furniture at Rodeo Grande. She sent it today, together with my saddle on its stand.

This piece is a mock antique cupboard painted red and gold with panels in the doors with pictures of angels. It's looking smart now, with new red and gold paint.

Ceci bought it forty years ago for Rodeo. There is a workshop in the Sierra which makes them. She has another green one in her (our) house in Guayaquil.

My saddle is looking the worse for wear. Since I last saw it it has cracked in two places. I guess it dried out, and has not been oiled as it isn't used. But it's still my saddle. The stand looks good and has a hook on the front for the bridle. I will put it in a corner of the house with my boots, hat and whip. A small shrine to my happy days at Rodeo Grande.

I thought for a moment about Leopoldo, my grey horse. I had ridden him for the last four years, since my previous horse was butchered by rustlers, who sold the meat.

It made us furious to think that they took a trusting noble animal and killed it for the little meat there is on a horse. They got Kate's horse too.

Leopoldo, named for the head waiter in the musical White Horse Inn, is a very comfortable ride. He was fast enough for me, but safe. He rarely tripped or reared up.

I guess the new owner of Rodeo Grande will ride him now.

Outside in the garden we looked once again at where the jacuzzi will go. We are getting together on this one. I have moved from my 2 x 2-metre pool to a slightly bigger size. She has given up the sunken seating area, and the surrounding water feature.

We have one more thing to work out. It's the aerial silk. When we first saw the house with its double-height sitting room we thought that she could hang it there. But once the furniture arrived that was not such a great idea. She will swing in it and so can't be near the huge glass chandelier, which we had bought with the house.

But if we move it over we are in contact with the sofa. We don't want to have to move the furniture each time. What is the solution?

We found it. We will build a tall, thin structure in the garden, about six metres high and three metres square. The architects did a mock-up of it. It fits in well.

So that is Kate sorted. Her pole can go in her dressing room upstairs, and the telas outside.

We sat and drank wine for a while. But sadly we can't yet sleep in the house, and we are conscious of the guards waiting to go home. They don't leave us until we are safely back in the flat.

We talked about Christmas. Her family will come for a few days and stay with us. We can spread them between the house and the flat to sleep.

Kate asked about New Year. That caused an argument. The tentative plan had been to go to Australia and see Catherine, and Emilie. But now they won't be there. They leave for Ireland in November. Anyway it's too far to go for a just a week, and I don't want to leave the company for longer at our busiest time of the year. I suggested we stay at home. It will be the first New Year we are together. Well the second.

In December 2016 I opted out of the family party at the beach house to stay in Guayaquil with my beagle, James, who had had an accident and was dying. He was uncomfortable in the car and cried all the time. I would stay to be with him. In the end he didn't die then. He lingered into January and we had to put him down, to avoid more suffering. I cried for my poor James. I swore that he would be the last of the line.

Seven beagles, all buried at the pet cemetery in the garden of Rodeo Grande.

He was my main reason to stay. But Kate and I were both in Guayaquil. She had returned from spending Christmas with her family in Ibague.

So we spent our one and only New Year together at the Hilton Hotel, where there was a party. As it was a masked ball we thought we would escape recognition. As far as I know we did, as it has never been mentioned.

Kate has set her heart on travelling this New Year. But it's a bad time to travel. Flights are overbooked and very expensive. She suggested we go to New York. She wants to mingle with the crowd in Times Square. I said no way. It's freezing at this time of the year.

To suggest somewhere I said perhaps Santiago, Chile, or Buenos Aires. It's summer there. We could do either in four days. She wasn't fascinated.

We left the subject and drove back to the flat.

"What would you like to eat?" she asked. I don't want takeaway again. I looked in the fridge. But there is very little there. I will make a bacon sandwich. She examined the bacon and declared that it was mouldy. She threw it out. That left only a piece of mousetrap cheese. I made my sandwich. She didn't want to eat.

My mind went back to living with Ceci. The fridge there was always well stocked. She enjoyed shopping at Supermaxi. Kate never has time, with her exercise program.

We call home delivery to buy the essentials. But even those are scarce today.

We are going on holiday in a week's time. So we run supplies down.

We watched the never-ending series The Game of Thrones.

Saturday.

We had my last Pilates class before the holiday. Adrian, the Cuban coach, insisted that I do it at least once a week in Madrid. Otherwise when I return it will be like starting all over again. I agree. I feel I am getting benefit. Today he commented that I managed two exercises that I couldn't do at all when I first started.

Kate wants to buy a camera. We went to the Mall del Sol and to the Sony shop.

Arturo, the very knowledgeable assistant, helped her to choose. The whole process took over two hours. There are five in our price range. It's not just the cameras but the multiple choice of lenses. I soon lost interest and wandered around the shop looking at the TV screens. To demonstrate them they showed scenes from movies. But annoyingly they repeated the same scene over and over again. One was the film Napoleon, which we had seen at the cinema. It's a good film, but to my mind they showed the same battle scene for each of the five battles in the film. They were all won by cannon fire eliminating the enemy cavalry or infantry. There is no discussion of tactics with his staff, nor do we see the enemy generals planning theirs.

We need a large TV screen for the new house. We are making a piece of furniture to encase it. The screens vary in size. We thought a 75-inch screen would be enough, 85-inch looked to be too big, or we would have to sit further back to watch it.

Finally she has her camera. I admired it and lamented that we have done ten safaris together, in various parts of the world, without so much as a camera. We simply take photos with our phones. Perhaps we will have to do another one?

Then we went to Su Casa store to look for a mattress. Ours is too soft. I can't lie straight without getting backache, so I have to curl up. We laid on three mattresses, being careful to not to get our shoes on them. One soft, one medium and one firm.

I opted for the firm one. Kate, to my surprise, agreed. We bought it today, as there is a sale on. They will deliver it in November when we move into the house. We still have builders to come and we don't want it covered in dust.

Before leaving the store we looked at dinner services. We liked one in white with a silver edge. Its ninety-two pieces and costs about three thousand dollars. That sounds a good price. Where is it made, Denmark?

No, Sri Lanka. Well, that explains the price.

We had a lovely holiday there in March 2021 when we stayed in a tea plantation called Dunkeld. The British colonial bungalow has beautiful gardens and a large swimming pool. It stands at the summit of a steep hill with magnificent views over the valley below. The tea bushes are planted in hedges along the contours of the hill.

It's much cooler than in the sweltering valleys below. Dunkeld is a large plantation so the manager would have been a senior man. In colonial days they served three years between holidays to Britain, so they made themselves comfortable. The plantations are now all owned by Sri Lankans but the names live on as Dunkeld, Castlereigh and Osbourne. The tea quality is associated with the name.

They charmingly serve afternoon tea in the garden complete with scones, cream and strawberry jam. There is bread, butter, a selection of honey, jam and even Marmite. Among the cakes we found Battenburg (church window cake). Kate loves it. We try to find it wherever we travel.

We went on safari and saw leopards hunting a deer (luckily it escaped). There was a male elephant on musk. It secreted a pungent liquid from glands behind the ears. The guide said that a female elephant can smell it even five miles away, and come to mate with him.

An animal version of Tinder!

We went whale watching too. While setting out from the harbour in a catamaran, we noticed small fishing boats, each with an outrigger. We asked the guide if they still dive for pearls in Sri Lanka. He replied no, today's pearls come from other countries. But it was once a big industry. There is an opera called The Pearl Fishers based on Ceylon (as it was then called). The music is by Georges Bizet and contains one of the loveliest of all male duets sung by a tenor and a baritone.

We had been desperate for a holiday that March after a year’s lockdown with Covid. We asked our friend Chinmay what's open? He replied Sri Lanka. So we went there, and put up with eight Covid tests on the way!

Olga's party is tonight. But I am nervous about going to it. It's in a high rise. We will not be able to take the guards into the building. We haven't seen Olga for over a year, and then all of a sudden she invites us to dinner. She made a strange remark to Kate, that after all her good luck she deserved a bad experience. She said she knew we would both be freed. An odd way to commiserate with your best friend.

We don't know what crowd she is mixing with now. I called Joseph, he said if you are not sure don't go.

Kate called her to plead a diplomatic illness on my part. Janina, hearing that we were not going cried off too.

Olga rang. She was furious. After a year's absence that is a bit rich.

We are still being very careful. We don't want a repeat performance of the kidnap. Next time we might not get out alive.

Celso, our new house boy, has passed his polygraph exam. One more piece in the security jigsaw.

Today, Sunday, I went to the office as normal, to catch up with work. Once that was done I turned to my book The Wide, Wide Sea. There were only thirty pages left, so I finished it.

It has a sad ending where Captain Cook was killed on the island of Hawaii. It seems that he was suffering from some mental problem on his third and last voyage. The kindly captain of before, who rarely flogged his crew, now became a tyrant.

The cause of his death was the theft of the ship's cutter, the largest of the ship's rowing boats, by some natives. Furious about it, he hatched a plan to kidnap the chief of the island, bring him aboard his ship HMS Resolution, and ransom him for the return of the cutter. This turned to violence both on the side of the Hawaiians and the British. A sad end to the good relationship enjoyed up until then.

I will start a new book on the plane to Madrid on Tuesday. My choice is The Lincoln Highway by Amor Towles.

At 1pm I went home for lunch with Kate. Strangely she wasn't in the flat, and neither was Snoopy. She hadn't said anything about going out. Anyway I had the guards with me, so she couldn't go far. Perhaps she was walking him.

I took a beer and went to the balcony. Looking down at the pool I did a double take. There is a naked woman lying face down on a sunchair. Her head is covered by a towel.

Then I recognised Kate. Looking carefully I saw that she was not entirely naked, I could make out the line of her thong. But she wasn't far off! Luckily there was no one else in the garden.

But where is Snoopy? Dogs are not allowed in the garden. I looked in all the rooms, then heard a plaintive barking coming from the laundry room. He must have gone in and the door closed with the wind. Poor chap, he went straight to his water bowl.

Kate came up soon afterwards to show me her very red back and bum. She had already burned her front half a few days ago, by falling asleep in the garden. Now she had lain for three hours to get the same effect on her back. She complained that it hurt.

Talk about self-inflicted wounds! She has not sunbathed like this for a long time, since we lived in the penthouse.

Departure day. Tuesday 8th October.

The flight is at 11am. We should be at the airport by 9am. We had packed the day before, all I have to do is to get Kate up and dressed.

Janina is flying with us. She will come over to the flat and leave her car here.

We have plenty of time for the flight.

But it wasn't that simple. Kate announced that we have to pass by the new house in order to fix something to do with the wifi. So my careful timing was out.

I feared the morning traffic. The house is in the opposite direction from the airport.

But we still got to the airport on time. There is a lull in the morning traffic about 9am. School children and those working have already got there. Wives have yet to emerge for shopping.

We checked in, bought two straw hats for the girls at duty free, and went to the VIP lounge for the customary gin and tonic. We took photos of the three of us and sent one to friends.

The holiday has begun.

The flight on Air Europa is comfortable and we managed to sleep part of the ten hours. On boarding, one passenger who I didn't know shook my hand and said he was so glad I got out of the kidnap. I thanked him. Just after the event there were many who did this, but I was surprised that people still remember.

There is a couple who I knew, we said hello. He is a neighbouring farmer.

Now, I don't mind meeting people on flights. It wasn't the case while we were still a secret couple. I was afraid that gossip would get back to Ceci. And it did, many times. Even one, so-called friend of ours, took the trouble to let Ceci know that she had seen me in Bogota Airport, with a girl!

It was the chief cause of friction between us, that I was openly travelling with Kate.

But we were not prepared to take separate flights.

We arrived at Barajas airport, Madrid, at 5am, ahead of schedule. Which airlines love to point out.

We luckily found a large taxi which could take the three of us and four suitcases. Not always the case.

We had slept a few hours on the plane. What to do now? Obviously, we opened a bottle of wine. By 9am we were sleepy and went to bed, and slept all day until 5pm.

Then after several more glasses of wine we got hungry. Kate reserved the Papua restaurant in Plaza Colon for 9.30pm.

It's not my kind of place, all atmosphere and slow service. But the girls enjoyed it, and drank innumerable cocktails.

After getting home, I went straight to bed. They watched TV. Some hours later I found them both asleep on the sofa. I turned off the TV, and nudged them to go to bed.

Janina has the spare bedroom, which means I lose my bathroom and have to share Kate's. That's not perfect, we like our own.

Thursday.

Kate's mother Margarita is due to arrive in Madrid at 10am, from Bogota. Her sister Luisa, will collect her from the airport and put her up in her flat, which is not far from ours.

They didn't come to see us until the afternoon. When they did they brought a friend of Luisa's, Julieta, with them.

After the greetings the inevitable bottle was opened. This time it was champagne.

I had been to the deli nearby and stocked up with champagne, red and white wine, as well as bread, cheese, cold meats and anchovies.

Just as well. Before they left after midnight we had drunk seven bottles, and eaten practically everything.

There was an interlude when we went out to have dinner at the Mexican restaurant Bakan, and then returned here. It had been a jolly party with a great deal of banter and laughter.

I fell asleep first, about midnight, and Kate ushered me to bed.

Earlier in the day we had received a lovely present from Tina of Tiffany. An orchid, a bottle of Dom Perignon and an expensive wine called Termanthia.

I saw today that Dom Perignon has been consumed. Luckily I still have the wine.

Tina has offered to take us to see a zarzuela show. Its a Spanish form of opera. That will be lovely. But once again she is putting us in a difficult position. As in Dubai in February, we are not able to buy anything from Tiffany this year. We still have to find and pay for the upgraded flat in Madrid, as well as making changes, and improving security, to the house in Guayaquil. Also Kate has her eye on a new baby grand piano for Guayaquil.

By the end of the holiday we still had not seen Tina. She is a good friend, but she comes with commitments.

Janina and Margarita shared the spare bedroom last night. We all emerged today a bit worse for wear.

I noticed that we have broken another of our Thai champagne glasses. There were originally 24 beautiful wine glasses that we bought in Chiang Rai in Thailand, when we went there and rode elephants in 2021. They have elephant motifs engraved on them. One after another they got broken. Now there are only ten left.

The event was described as bathing the elephants. We had visions of a hosepipe and brush. But it wasn't that at all. We rode one elephant each, sitting on the animal's head, together with ten other tourists. A mahout walked alongside giving the beast orders what to do.

When we got to a river the mahouts mounted on the elephants' backs. Half way across they gave an order and the elephants sank down in the water and it was us who got bathed. They got us even wetter by blowing water from their trunks.

All good fun. It was a hot day. We were dry again by the time we got back to the hotel.

We had upgraded from a tent to a spacious cabin with an attached private swimming pool, where we swam at night in lovely warm water.

Kate had her twenty-eighth birthday there. The hotel made a private dinner for us in a little pavilion with three musicians. Afterwards we went to the garden and released kites into the sky. They had a small flame under them and flew to a great height, carrying our wishes with them.

One thing we have to do while in Madrid is to revisit the eye clinic. Me for a post-operation checkup, and Kate as she is having trouble seeing at a distance. We got both appointments.

Having sorted that out, we went to the travel agency in Corte Ingles and planned a short trip to Croatia from the 18th to 22nd October.

We will spend two days in Dubrovnik and two in Split. The lady at the agency took details of what we want and will get back to us. She confirmed that is where part of Game of Thrones was filmed. We looked forward to seeing the castles.

I was surprised when Kate asked the lady if she was Nuria. She replied no, but she knew her. She used to work here. Kate told her that it was Nuria who had organized a trip to Italy for her in 2015.

I remember it well.

It was the first time we travelled to Madrid together. Kate was still a secret from my family.

I had invented some work reasons for going to Madrid. Then I would meet them in Yorkshire.

We stayed at the Hotel Principal on Gran Via. I took her to one of the few restaurants I knew at that time, Casa Lucio. As luck would have it, when one wants to keep something secret, I saw a member of the Phoenix Club there with his wife and family!

I put my finger to my lips, he smiled and nodded. Male solidarity.

Coming out of the restaurant we saw a strange character who we nicknamed the Midnight Cowboy. He is an old man with a drooping white moustache. He was dressed in a white shirt and white pants decorated with a red fringe and wore a white cowboy hat. All his clothes and hat had lights on them. He rode a tricycle with fairy lights and booming music. He charged people for a photo with himself. Of course we got one of Kate with him.

Then, as we walked back to the hotel he heard the sound of bagpipes. It was a folkloric group from Galicia, one of the few places apart from Scotland, that play the bagpipes. There were pipers and dancers dressed in colourful outfits, the women in long flowing dresses.

We enjoyed the sound so much we decided to follow them down the street. Then one street after another, like the Pied Piper. Finally, they got into a bus and went home. Only then did we realize that we were totally lost! There were no taxis. We set off to walk, until we recognised where we were, and eventually got back to the hotel.

To fill the time that I would be away in Yorkshire, Nuria had prepared Kate a tour of all of Italy by bus, taking fifteen days. It was exhausting. There were early morning starts and late-night arrivals at three-star hotels. But they covered a great deal of the country, and all the major tourist venues.

Her fellow passengers were mainly Mexican. The tour guide was a Spanish ex-Hells Angel. He was very kind to her, as she was the youngest person on the tour at twenty-one (bar families). He looked after her when some Italian wolf got too close. This happened quite a lot, including a policeman. In Capri a suave middle-aged man invited her to come on board his yacht. He was quickly told to get lost.

Today is the twelfth of October. It's known by several names as Columbus Day, Día de Hispanidad, or Dia de la Raza. It's either celebrated by those who conquered Latin America, or condemned by the Indians who were conquered.

In Madrid there is a procession which blocks the Castellano all day.

In Guayaquil it is marked by the Feria Ganadera, the Cattleman's Fair, where they hold rodeos. Teams from ranches compete to ride a bucking bronco or bull, to rope a running horse on foot, or a steer on horseback.

It begins with a parade of the twelve members of the team, on matched horses, led by their madrina, a pretty girl, wearing a dress which covers the horse's back.

For some years Rodeo Grande had a rodeo team. But recently we have not competed.

There are stalls at the fair selling agricultural and veterinary products, as well as saddles, boots and hats. Agripac is there as always, in our traditional place.

Cristina sent me a WhatsApp with videos of the rodeos. She said the Fair is not the same without us.

For many years it's been an outing for all the Rodeo Grande employees and their partners. I provided a bus for the thirty people to come to Guayaquil, then I took them for lunch at one of the open-air restaurants. After that they are free to do what they want. I gave each of them cash. Mostly it was used to buy beer.

This year it's only Cristina and her son Mati who went. The new owners of Rodeo Grande have not maintained the tradition. Anyway they are not cattlemen. They are busy planting bananas where the land is high enough to avoid the annual floods.

For many years I have been a member of the Cattlemen's Association, once I was even vice president. The Fair is where we meet once a year and drink together.

I am still a member, though today I don't own even one cow.

The 12th October 2013 is a day I won't forget.

I had met Kate on 28th August that year, during the casting for the Agripac 2014 calendar.

As she won the job she got to do the calendar photos and also several Agripac events during the year, where a model is required. These are expositions where the company takes a stand. Aquaexpo is for the shrimp sector, there are others for rice farmers, banana farmers and today's Cattleman's Fair.

She and another model were attending the Agripac stand, signing and handing out company calendars. They are dressed in skimpy cowgirl outfits,wearing calf-length boots, hot pants, a short blouse knotted to reveal the midriff and cowboy hats.

Up to this point our relationship had not even begun. We had chosen her for the calendar. I had been present at each photoshoot, giving the team the benefit of my preference.

I take credit for the very first shot we did. We went to Ceci's beach house as I had noticed that when the local fishermen drew in their nets to the beach there was a cloud of seagulls and frigate birds hovering overhead, and diving for the small throw-away fish that got caught in the nets. It was a Saturday (and incidentally my 68th birthday).

I had offered cash to the fishermen to make a show for us. They would not normally fish at the weekend.

They went out at dawn in boats to cast the nets with floats, and by ten am were on the beach hauling the nets in. We arranged for a small boat to be positioned on the beach close by. Kate, dressed in a bikini was lying in it. Pollo had his camera positioned nearby. The birds were the willing extras (no charge).

What a photo it is. I am looking at it now, eleven years on. The sky is full of screeching birds who fought for the fish. They swooped very close to Kate. She, brave girl, did not shrink away. Inevitably the fishermen came to oggle her, but that didn't phase her either.

Pollo took ages getting the right photos. In those days there was no attached laptop to check them, he kept passing me the camera to look at each photo.

We got two more shots at the beach, taken in a nearby tourist hotel with a background of a stuffed marlin, pictures of sailing ships, ancient anchors and memorabilia. She is wearing a captain's hat and a skimpy naval uniform.

The remaining three photos were taken at Rodeo Grande. We would go back there many times over the years using the flowering trees, cattle, buffalo and horses as props.

oak floors. Really all we wanted to see was the windows and views, the overall size and of course the price.

They asked us which of the ones that we had visited we liked most. I said the Velasquez one, Kate said the other one, because it has a garage. Even though the bedrooms have windows onto the patio. But the patio is in the centre of the block of flats. That is important. The residents association controls both sides, so the walls are well painted, there are no rusting air conditioners and no drying clothes. The garage has an option to connect it to the flat with a lift. This seemed a great idea. We would be able to drive into the garage, close the street door, then take the bags up the lift to our kitchen.

We discounted two other flats because from the back windows you looked out onto a courtyard where the neighbours indeed hung their washing out! In this day and age of driers. It seems primitive. Our present building has a bylaw prohibiting it. Why not others?

The flat that Kate likes had another plus. They are prepared to buy our flat in part exchange. This is great news. Otherwise what would we do? We need the money from the sale to complete the purchase of the new one. But if we sold too early we would have to store our furniture and rent an Air B and B. Also we thought that we would save the estate agent's commission of 4%. That idea doesn't fly. They want their commission both on buying and selling.

The two ladies came to look at our flat. Before they arrived Kate rushed around making it tidy. They are impressed with her dressing room with its rows of smart shoes and handbags. They saw the Agripac calendar on my desk, and asked if that is Kate. I said yes, and we told the story of how we met. They thought it very romantic.

From what we have seen from other similar sized flats we should be able to get our price. Unless the part exchange is at a discount?

After they had left we took a taxi back to the Corte Ingles. I had stupidly lost the airline booking. It had been printed and fell out of my pocket. The travel agent gave me a copy, and to be safe she emailed it too.

Kate had wandered off to look for a Dyson hair styler. When I finished at the travel agent I called her.

Then began a back and forth conversation that got increasingly bad tempered.

Where are you?

In the second Corte Ingles across the street. I will wait for you by the entrance.

But it's not so simple. The two buildings have several entrances onto different streets.

Where are you? Waiting by the entrance, as I told you.

Which entrance? Etc.

Eventually I found her. She is with her mother and sister.

But what she had found made up for the misunderstanding. She showed me a shop called FNAC. They sell opera Blu-Ray DVDs. I had looked everywhere for them without success, during the last few years. So today I bought six operas, and she chose two ballets.

Even better, there is a bookshop with a good English section. While I was starting along the shelves she brought me Never, by Ken Follett. That was clever. A new book by a favourite author. She also produced a Bernard Cornwell of his King Arthur saga. But I had already read it. I found an Ian Rankin too, A Heart Full of Headstones.

I have finished The Lincoln Highway, so I need a book urgently. I can't be without one.

Having got those and what she wanted, we walked down the street looking for somewhere to eat. It was 9pm.

We went into the first restaurant we saw, De Maria. It was an excellent choice. We had an enormous gin and tonic at the bar while we waited for our table. They brought us a courtesy glass of cava and then we polished off two bottles of wine. The ladies had meat or tuna from the grill and I had sweet breads, for only the second time in my life. This time I enjoyed them.

As we looked out of the window onto the street we can see a tramp sorting through a rubbish bin. He is an old man and looks so sad. Luisa gathered up what was left of her steak and went to give it to him. They talked for a while. She returned to say that he was grateful and would share it with his friends, but could he have some money too. I gave her five euros for him. Kate thought that was not enough so she went out and gave him ten more, for which she got a hug.

We all laughed. We had done our good deed for the day.

Wednesday.

We have an appointment with Dra Paloma Martinez to check my vision at 10am. The tests showed that both eyes are in good shape. She said that I should have a checkup next June to see if the lenses are dirty. They will need cleaning just once and then will last the rest of my life. We mentioned that Kate has an appointment on the 24th, as she can't see at a distance. Paloma described a few things that might be causing it. But asked us to wait for the tests.

On leaving the clinic on Velasquez Street we called in at an opticians shop and I bought a second pair of the same cheap glasses for reading in poor light. I still have the ones I bought in June, but I now have a second pair, just in case. They fold up very small and fit into a handy case.

We stopped at another shop close by, as Kate wants to buy a carry-on bag for her mother, who is going to Italy tomorrow with Luisa. While there I remembered that we are fast going through our glasses. I bought six champagne, six wine and six whisky ones in pink glass to match the set we have, and so not to use the Thai glasses.

They will be delivered tomorrow, so we don't have to carry them.

We went to a Pilates studio which she knew. Kate doesn't have an appointment. It it just for me. I got changed into my gym togs. My teacher is a young man, Gabriel from Extremadura.

He put me through my paces. Similar to Adrian in Guayaquil, but a bit harder. By the time the fifty minutes was up I was exhausted. Kate had not meant to do exercise today, but there was a cancellation, and she ended up doing it too, in her street clothes.

I came out without changing clothes. I thought we were walking back home. But she told me that she wanted to go to the Corte Ingles on Castellana to look for the hairstyler she had failed to find the other day.

I would never have gone into such a place dressed in gym kit. But today I did. We found what she wanted and then went to the bar at the foot of the elevators. We used to go there for champagne and caviar, but today we settled for beer and egg benedict.

I seemed to get by without curious stares.

Friday 18th October

We flew to Naples. I checked that I had everything I needed and we got a taxi to the airport. Only then did I realize that I had left my reading glasses at home. Before my eye operation I would have had to go back for them. But not now.

I bought the Economist at the airport and read it successfully. I have been using reading glasses since my operation, but I don't need them. It is just a habit.

In Naples we picked up the car from Avis. We put Amalfi on the GPS and set off, with Kate driving. It took ages to get out of Naples. Turn right, turn left, turn right again. We got onto a highway and passed a toll station. One euro twenty. Then turned left and right and we came back to the same toll, another one euro twenty, in the other direction.

Eventually we picked up the Naples to Salerno motorway. We went along this until we got to the wonderfully named Angri Sur. Here we left the motorway and turned down a narrow road heading towards Ravello. And then the climbing began. The road snaked up the mountain with hairpin bends. It is very narrow, some parts used traffic lights to make a one way system. It reminded me of the time I had gone with the family to the glorious Caruso Hotel. Son-in-law Steve was driving. Though today as we passed Ravello I couldn't see the hotel or even signs to it. There must be another winding road on the other side of the mountain.

We reached the watershed and then snaked down the other side, emerging on the coast road. We turned right to Amalfi and found the Hotel Miramalfi on the left side of the road. It's an upside down hotel. You park on the roof, the reception is one floor down and the rooms are on lower floors down the cliffside to the sea.

Ceci and I had stayed at a similar one in Positano, further along the coast.

We had booked a normal room, as it is non-refundable, just in case we changed our minds.

The hotel gave us an upgrade. It's the end of the season and it isn't full.

On 1st November the hotel closes down until April next year.

We got there at 5pm, changed and went to the bar, and then to the magnificent restaurant overlooking the sea with the lights of the small town of Amalfi to the left.

I had checked on Google in Madrid. The temperature was given as 22 to 27C.

But the first day it was cold and raining.

I got up for breakfast on Saturday morning, Kate slept on. It was in the same dining room. But with the daylight I got a much better impression of the town.

The staff were very solicitous. They asked which balcony table I would prefer, then tea or coffee, and handed me the a la carte breakfast menu.

I had put on a jacket and panama hat. I felt like the Gentleman from Peru, a novel by Andre Aciman, based on the Amalfi coast.

So much for the warm weather. There was loud thunder and pouring rain.

After breakfast I went back to the room and as Kate was still sleeping, I finished the Economist.

Fredy sent a video. He was opening the package with his passport, returned from the British embassy.

He made a drama of it. Did he or didn't he get the visa?

Yes he did. See you in London.

Of course he needed a flight to get him there. He had already contacted Janina. A few hours later she sent me a WhatsApp. She had booked KLM to Amsterdam and onwards to London. I apologized to Fredy that it was economy class. He replied that even if he rode in the baggage hold he would be happy.

We are now eight people in the UK, as Julieta is apparently coming too.

We got them an Air B and B to stay close to the Landmark Hotel. Friends may be friends, but the Landmark is expensive. Now I need to get Leo to book two more seats on the train from King's Cross to Darlington on Monday 28th. The logistics of it all!

Kate got up at midday. What shall we do today? The rain has stopped, but I had already discounted Pompeii. We will try it tomorrow.

Let's walk down the hill to the centre of Amalfi.

The road is very narrow. We hugged the low wall on the sea side of it. There is no pedestrian pavement. After a while we took a steep flight of steps from the road to the promenade.

There were a lot of people in the tiny town centre, buying souvenirs or eating pizza or gelato.

We walked through them, passed the douma, a spectacular large church set on the hillside. Its walls are clad in black and white tiles with yellow motives. We came to a small shop selling linen clothes. Kate loves linen. In we went. The diminutive old lady running it smiled at us and pointed to the clothes. But we couldn't communicate in Italian, nor she in English or Spanish.

Kate walked along the line of hangers and selected one after another which she handed to me. When my arms were full she took them and went to a dressing room.

I found the only stool available and moved it to where I had a sight line to the dressing room. She appeared in one outfit after another. They all looked good on her. I took a photo of each.

The lady owner warmed to us as good customers. We began to chat in our patois. She is a grandmother, a Nonna, so I admitted to being a Nonne. She has three grown-up children, one was married with a child, hence the Nonna.

We bought nine pieces. They weren't that expensive. Then we found a bar and had a couple of beers and shared a pizza, before walking back up the steps and the road to the hotel. It was much harder going up than it had been coming down. But from Pilates, I breathed deeply and that seemed to ease the pain in my knees.

We got back to the hotel about 8pm. Neither of us wanted dinner after the pizza. We filled the remarkably large tub in the bathroom with hot water to ease the pain in our legs.

That of course required a bottle of champagne. So we ordered a bottle of Ruinart Blanc de Blancs.

Kate washed my hair.

It must be seventy-five years since my mother did that, while I watched her in trepidation. She always had a cigarette in her mouth. The ash would be half an inch long, I knew that any moment it would fall and burn me.

Today I enjoyed being pampered.

One of my favourite operas is Tales of Hoffman by Offenbach. It has a beautiful aria sung by a soprano and mezzo soprano. It's called La Barcarolle. It describes a Night of Love.

Sunday.

Today the sun is shining. After my usual breakfast, Good Morning Mr Armstrong, I went to the reception and asked them to book us a guided tour of Pompeii.

It's at 2pm. We should plan to be there fifteen minutes early.

I discussed the route to Pompeii with the porter. I asked if it would be better to take the coast road to Salerno and pick up the motorway from there, rather than the narrow winding road through Ravello. He said no, the Ravello road has much less traffic, but if we wanted to drive along the coast we should allow more time.

We got going by 11:45am. I was driving.

Immediately we saw what he meant by traffic. We hadn't even got through Amalfi when it stopped. We knew we were in for a long wait when drivers got out of their cars and mooched about. Finally we got going again. The road is ridiculously narrow, with hairpin bends. There are buses that have to take the whole road just to get around the bends. We had seen from the hotel that part of the road is a viaduct on stone piers along the cliff face. They are the same tall narrow arches as the amphitheater in Pompeii. The builders have not improved much in the last two thousand years!

I drove thinking of all the easy improvements they could make to widen it by even half a metre, which would make all the difference as cars passed each other only inches apart. There is a solid stone wall on the sea side of the road. It is well-scratched by passing vehicles. It would be easy to remove the wall, which is half a metre thick, and put metal railings instead.

On some sections the road is right on the edge of the cliff to the sea, but on others there are gardens below it, which could be built over to widen the road.

Years ago I went to Sicily with Ceci and my family. There is a wonderful highway that circles the island. It tunnels through each mountain and crosses the valleys on viaducts. Why can't they do something similar here?

If I had known what to expect, I would have rented a Mini Cooper rather than the large Lynk and Co SUV.

I had never heard of the brand. But Google tells me that it's a Chinese/Swedish company allied to Volvo, owned by Geely.

Old man's chunter.

We got to Salerno in an hour and a half. There the GPS seemed to lose the plot. It took us through the town, down the hill to the promenade, through a car park, and back up the hill to where the motorway starts. Then I have to admit to my error. I got the wrong left turn. We went back down the hill, along the promenade (but avoided the car park), up the hill and so to the motorway.

After that it is easy driving towards Naples. The toll stations are a mystery, sometimes they are manned, sometimes not and there is a recorded voice in Italian. They don’t accept credit cards, just cash. There is a cup to put coins into.

We eventually saw the Pompeii sign and turned off into the town.

The GPS began to give directions. We followed them through the town and out of it, into an area of fields. Then we arrived at a dead end!

We backed out and followed the directions again. By now we had lost faith in the GPS.

There was a man standing by the side of the road. We asked him how to get to the ruins. In broken Spanish he explained we should follow the road to the church spire, and then turn left.

That wasn't too clear, so we again followed the GPS instructions. After ten minutes we passed the man again. This time he offered to show us the way. He got into his old and battered car and raced off. We followed him. He took us back to the centre of town and said the entrance to the ruins was up the street, which he pointed to. We thanked him and gave him twenty euros.

We found the car park and walked to the entrance. It is now 2.30pm.

We have missed the tour.

We showed our booking to the guard at the gate. He said we will have to pay again. So we did, and went in.

We have both been here before. Kate once on her Italian tour in 2015. I had been once just with Ceci and again with her and the family. Today we just saw a part of it. The city was destroyed in 79 AD when Vesuvius erupted. It was in the reign of my friend Marcus Aurelius. It happened so quickly that most of the residents failed to escape. There are mummified bodies in Naples Museum. The falling ash was relatively gentle so it buried the city without destroying it. In the eighteenth century it was rediscovered and since then the excavation has been ongoing. It's amazing what you can see. There are beautiful statues, walls painted with elegant designs and tiled floors. The houses are built with a small courtyard in the centre and rooms around them. The market square is huge with temples to Apollo and other gods. There is an amphitheater for gladiatorial contests and a theater for plays.

All this was built more than 2,000 years ago, when the British were living in squalid mud huts!

Today it is very hot and crowded. After two hours we left.

At the gate a lady artist is selling painted tiles. I bought the famous Cave Cane (beware of the dog). Though we didn't see the original today. We admired her painting of Priapus weighing his dick, but decided against buying it.

We bought souvenir books at the shop, one in Spanish and one in English.

And that was that for Pompeii.

Kate drove the return journey. We went via Ravello. It's true that the traffic is a lot less than on the coast road. We pulled over at a lookout point well up the mountainside. There is the most glorious view of the plain below us, full of houses, with the sea beyond and Vesuvius to the right. We took photos together and I took some of her sitting on the wall, looking pretty in her straw hat and shades.

Monday is our last day here.

It was a bright sunny morning. I got up early for my traditional breakfast. Today we have a pianist playing, how lovely.

There are a number of large ferries entering and leaving the port. They seem to be crowded. I asked the waiter if they are tourists. He replied no, most of them are local people travelling to Positano, Sorrento or Capri. It is quicker than taking a bus.

I can well believe it.

When Kate got up we decided to explore the rest of the hotel. We had seen the swimming pool far below the balcony of our room. We took the lift down to it. We were shown around by a girl who spoke good English. She said that the pool is seawater and not heated. I put a hand into it. It felt very cold.

We had a couple of beers at the bar. There were two other couples there. One couple went into the sea and played with rubber rings. They didn't seem to be frozen. Kate insisted we go in too.

I haven't been in the sea, even in Ecuador, for several years. I don't want to go in now.

But I have to.

We went back to our room and put on bathing togs. We returned to the pool bar. There are steps down to the sea. But the waves are strong and there is a large rock just to the right of the steps. I was sure we would be swept onto it and injured. Kate made light of it. She went in first, I had to follow. I threw in a rubber ring for her and one for me. Then came the moment of truth. We who are about to die salute you.

I dived in. It is very cold but not life-threatening. I swam fast to get warm. Then supported by the rings we played about.

After ten minutes I reckoned that duty had been done and went back to the steps. Kate came too. She went up first, giving me her hand to help me counteract the waves.

Time for another beer.

But she wants to go in again. Worse still, she wants to jump from the bar area, three metres above the steps. I said no. But she did it anyway, while I filmed her.

She splashed about and came out. Then she did it all over again.

This is getting like Snoopy with his ball!

We ate our last dinner at the hotel restaurant. She put on a white linen dress from her new collection. I donned my pink jacket. We gazed at the lights from the town. There is a full moon. It is very romantic.

There is a remarkable couple staying at the hotel. We have seen them several times. The girl is petite and very pretty with ash blond hair, her partner is tall, muscular and slightly dark skinned. We nicknamed her Daenerys and he Drakkari. They were very friendly, we smiled at each other, but we didn't talk. We guess they are on honeymoon, and don't want to meet people.

So the holiday ended.

We drove back to the airport in Naples. Once again we went over the mountains via Ravello. I drove, while she slept. I had time to think. Really the road wasn't that bad. It is our third time on it. I thought of driving in Ecuador from Guayaquil to Guaranda in the Sierra. The road is a bit wider than this one, but equally steep and winding. There we have to contend with huge trucks belching diesel fumes as they slogged up the hill. There is limited time to overtake them before the next corner. You need good acceleration, hence my BMW X5.

We have to contend with clouds too. You pass them about fifteen hundred meters above sea level. It's impossible to see even ten meters in front of the car. If you are behind a truck, there you stay until the cloud lifts.

We got home at 7pm. Gloria had been in while we were away. The place is spick and span. I found that I had another cold, which I blamed on the sea. But it's probably a virus.

We will soon go to England. Then when we come back to Madrid we have only one day before taking the flight to Guayaquil. I have to do whatever shopping today.

I need some skin creams for myself. Ceci has asked me to get her Imedeen. These are pills reputed to be excellent for the skin.

After three chemist shops I managed to find my creams. I bought three tubes of each to last me until we are in Madrid again next February. At each one I asked for Imedeen. They didn't have it.

I went with Kate and Margarita, in a taxi, to their Thai massage session in Calle Goya. They will be there for two hours. So I have time to search for Imedeen. I walked up and down Goya asking in five chemist shops. None stocked it.

One shop assistant suggested I try the Corte Ingles.

Bingo. I found it and bought a three-month supply.

I have Alex's belt which a friend of hers left here. So I am up to date with errands.

Kate has her eye appointment at the Martinez de Carneros clinic where I was operated. We go there on Thursday morning.

She does the same tests that I did. Then we got to see the principal doctor. This time it wasn't Dr Paloma Martinez, but her brother Ramon.

He explained that she has Myopia. It can be easily cured in an operation. It only takes five minutes surgery. But in some cases it can be painful for twenty-four hours. She hesitated.

But this time I took the lead. Yes she will do it.

We don't have time now, but we can do it when we return to Madrid next February.

Friday.

The gathering of the clan.

Fredy arrives in Amsterdam today, from Guayaquil, and will take an onward flight to London. We will meet him in the Landmark Hotel tomorrow at 7pm.

Janina is due to arrive on the Ave train from Barcelona at 4.30pm today. She will stay the night with us and we fly together to Heathrow tomorrow.

Julieta and Luisa will meet us at Barajas airport tomorrow.

Jorge Cepeda will arrive at Heathrow from Miami. He will meet us at King's Cross station on Monday at 12pm.

The clan gathers for the the all-important Kate's birthday party on Tuesday at Tupgill.

Leo has been constantly in touch with me to arrange details.

He called me today. He had gone to a great deal of trouble to get me an appointment with HM Passport office at Durham for Tuesday 29th October at 10am. I need to get a new passport urgently, I have only one page left in mine.

Today he called to say that due to flooding their office in Durham is closed until further notice.

Great!

But all is not lost. How much time do I have in London on Monday?

I have until 1pm when we get the train to Darlington.

The Passport Office will help out. They have me booked for an emergency appointment at 9am in their Docklands office.

At that time I should allow an hour and a half to get there from the Landmark by taxi, through the morning rush hour.

OK I can do that. But how long will I have to wait to collect my new passport?

In Durham they take four hours. But apparently they can do it in ten minutes in Docklands.

If so, whoopee. I can get my new passport and still be in time for the train to the North.

I went to Durham for my present passport on 17th July 2017. It is valid until 30th April 2028.

I had thought that it would be the last one. But no. I have travelled so much that it is now full.

Surely the new one valid for ten years to 2034 should see me out!

We went in two taxis to Barajas Airport in Madrid. We had booked economy tickets as I was paying for everyone, except Julieta. It is an easy two-hour flight so Business Class is hardly worth it. They have the same seats as economy, but leave the middle seat of three free.

Janina rearranged our seats at the check-in desk to the XL seats, which have a bit more legroom.

While waiting for the flight I noticed an extraordinarily beautiful blonde girl walk by. She is wearing a red leather pantsuit and red trainers. She looks to be a teenager.

When we got to the gate I saw her again. She is standing with an older man with a designer beard wearing shades. He is oddly dressed in a green shirt, yellow pants and trainers.

Kate saw me watching them. She told me that she knows the man.

He is a famous Iranian singer and disc jockey called Sasha. Kate had once been invited to his house for a party, along with her friend Paola, in a huge mansion in La Moraleja area of Madrid.

The party had been remarkable because in the early hours of the morning some rival had exploded a car bomb at the enclosure gate.

The police had come, and the guests were asked to leave.

The lovely girl at his side is Laura Niemas. She is an international model.

She had just turned eighteen and Sasha had given her a pink Rolls Royce for her birthday, which certainly got publicity.

On landing at Heathrow Terminal 5, we took two taxis to the Landmark Hotel and after checking in to our rooms, we went to the mezzanine bar.

We are a noisy group. I kept wondering when someone would complain. But no one did. We are together for the first time in weeks and have a lot to say, to recount and to laugh about. Fredy is the life and soul of the party, telling one joke after another.

When we got hungry we ordered from the bar menu.

Eventually it was bedtime.

Kate and I had stayed at the Landmark years ago. It had impressed us at the time with the lovely Palm Court in the centre. The Palm Court is still there of course. But now I get the impression that the hotel needs a makeover. The lifts are slow. Our bedroom furniture looks tired, and the waiter last night had been less than diligent with our orders.

Their computer keeps up a barrage of messages for me prior to arrival, mostly duplicates. For days after we left I got the same messages welcoming me.

On Sunday I got up for a very pleasant breakfast in the Palm Court.

I got the Sunday Times to read and went back to the room.

Eventually Kate got up.

We have a lunch appointment with Lien and his wife Rita at 2pm. Before then Kate decided that she would like a pair of shoes for her birthday present. That seemed reasonable. I had argued that the new house in Guayaquil is her present, but a lady likes something that she can unwrap (even if she sees it being wrapped first).

We got a taxi to Harrods.

To my simple mind, if you want to buy shoes you go to the shoe department. But she lingered a long time in Louis Vuitton, then Dior and Chanel, looking at handbags.

Eventually she said she would like a red Chanel handbag. It will go with her red shoes.

I asked her why she hadn't brought a handbag with her today.

It seems it was an oversight. But the Chanel bag one will fit the bill.

Having concluded our purchase for the day, we went to the Moet Chandon bar and had a couple of glasses of fizz, before heading to lunch at the Cambio de Tercio restaurant on the Old Brompton Road.

It is good to see our friends again. We caught up with our news. They are both coming to Guayaquil in November, we promised to show them our new house.

After lunch the ladies decided that they needed to return to Harrods. This time we did go to the shoe department, and Kate got a pair of knee-length black boots.

I was filling the time talking to Lien, when two men approached us and began a conversation. They said they were farmers. It seemed odd. Strangers rarely talk to you in London and their knowledge of farming was deficient.

Lien, who works in security, was suspicious and asked a Harrods security man to keep an eye on them.

Monday morning came. This is my passport day. I have an appointment at 9am. Being the nervous bloke that I am, I got up at 6am and was in the taxi just after 7am. Of course I got there an hour before the appointed time.

It's a bleak sort of place, an ex-warehouse in Docklands. There was one man waiting there already. He too was a Durham referral.

After standing in line for fifteen minutes, and being checked by several officials, we were told to go away and come back not more than 5 minutes before 9am, when the office would open.

It is a cold morning. Where to go? They said there is a cafe nearby.

I found it, and filled the time with a quite decent full English breakfast.

Promptly at five to nine I was back in the line, there were still just the two of us.

We were instructed to enter the building, where there is an airport-type strip search, coats and belts off etc.

We pressed the required machine and each received a numbered ticket.

I was called to stand before one of the twenty-four booths.

The man in charge looked at his computer, then got up to consult his manager. He returned to say that my application was on hold in Glasgow.

While I was doing a double take. He said, hold on. That is not yours at all. Now I can see your application on the screen. It's been processed. They will print a new passport.

Please take a seat.

I hoped I would have it by 9.30am and get back to the hotel to check out. I sat and waited. Meanwhile the office had filled up with other applicants. The monotonous recorded voice told each number which desk to go to.

Then I was called again. I expected to be handed my new passport. But no.

There is some delay, I can have it at 11 am. By now it is 10am.

It's tight timing, but I can still get back to the hotel before midday.

I was shooed out of the office a second time. Come back at 11am.

So I wandered the area. There seems to be a lot of hotels, including one which is a ship moored by the dock called the Sunborn Yacht Hotel.

But there aren't many people around, just a few dragging suitcases here and there. There is a large exhibition hall and other warehouses converted to offices.

I turned up my collar against the cold wind and walked quickly up and down the streets. I thought I might get a pint to pass the time. Sadly there is only Starbucks.

At exactly 11am I was back at the office. An official came to talk to me. He was apologetic, the printer had broken down. He hoped it would be fixed in the next half hour.

Now it is too late to get back to the hotel. I called Kate and asked her to pack the bags and check out, we will meet at King's Cross station. The train is for 1pm. I should be OK.

Finally I was summoned to the desk and given the passport. I was asked to check that the details are correct. They are.

I thanked them very much and took my new shiny passport. It's a blue one too.

Jorge had arrived from Miami that morning and was waiting with the others at King's Cross when I got there.

A few minutes later we saw that the Edinburgh train was leaving from platform three, calling at Darlington, among other stations.

We piled our luggage in and found our seats.

Then after the train pulled out of the station we ordered gin and tonics.

We have done it.

There were all eight of us on the train, and I had my new passport.

We were met at Darlington station by Nobby, whose taxi service does great work for family and guests at the Forbidden Corner. He had brought a van, but we couldn't all get in with the luggage.

Kate, Margarita and I went in a Mercedes owned by Ian. I sat in the front. He and I chatted about local people and places. I don't think we have met before, but we know about each other. Ian owns the Jervaulx Abbey ruins, and has a tearoom there.

And so we came to Tupgill.

Leo was waiting for us at the front door. We made the introductions and he helped us carry the bags to the lift.

His staff have decorated the house for Halloween. There is a scary talking butler figure in the hall, a spider's web over the stairs, with a giant spider in it, and plenty of pumpkin faces.

The first thing I did was to show my guests the bedrooms. They are all themed. They are the Mediaeval, the Chinese, the Arabian, the Indian and the Tudor rooms. I asked them to sort out where they wanted to sleep and then meet us downstairs for a glass of wine in the kitchen.

Leo pointed out my portrait hanging on the stairs. Now that I can see it clearly with my new eyes, I don't like it. My face has been overdone with wrinkles and the hands seem too large.

I have no doubt that when Ceci next comes to Tupgill it will be consigned to the store room, if not the bonfire.

I have a portrait hanging outside my office in Guayaquil. It was painted in nineteen ninety-six, just after I received the OBE. It's so much better than this one. But of course I was a lot younger then.

We sat around the kitchen table and drank wine. Several bottles later Leo escorted us to the White Goose pizza bar. This has only just opened. I had not seen it in its finished state.

I am suitably impressed.

It's named after Clarence, the famous goose who lived on the lake. He was with us fourteen years before dying this year. He has a grave with his name and dates by the lake.

He was given to us anonymously. We found him one December day with a label around his neck. The label said that his name was Clarence. He was given to us by a good lady to save his life, as her husband wanted to kill him for Christmas dinner. She attached five pounds for his upkeep.

That was very much a poisoned chalice. Over the years he has eaten hundreds of pounds worth of feed.

He was a funny old bird. He liked to be with people and would mingle with the crowd going into the Forbidden Corner.

But as he scared the children our employees had to keep returning him home to the lake, where he lived in peace with the dozens of mallard who inhabit it. They all feed from the tourists in the Summer.

Today, Tuesday, is Kate's birthday. She slept in until midday, which gave us time to get organized. Balloons were put outside the bedroom door, with a Happy Birthday sign.

We fetched a huge bunch of flowers from Leo's office and the birthday cake decorated with a parachute, made by one of our staff, Jessie.

We laid a rug on the lawn and put them there, together with more balloons, cakes, champagne and glasses.

Kate appeared at midday, looking very beautiful in a long lilac-coloured dress. She wore silver sandals and a tiara in her hair (albeit not the Tiffany one!)

We escorted her to the lawn. Then as she posed, first alone and then with each one of us, we took lots of photos. The champagne was opened after shaking the bottle and a lot of it sprayed over the lawn, in the best Le Mans style.

We went to dinner this evening in the nearby Blue Lion pub. I am trying not to repeat the venue in our five days here. The first night was the White Goose, today the Blue Lion, tomorrow we will eat in the Saddle Room restaurant. Thursday we will set the dining room table in Tupgill and eat in from the Saddle Room menu. Friday is the last night. Let's see what we do.

I am trying to organize a pheasant for that night. I am very fond of it, but I suspect the others have never tried it.

I woke today with the daylight. Now that the clocks have gone back, it's light at 6.45am.

Of course you can't have it both ways, it's dark by 5pm.

I looked out of the bedroom window at the trees in the park. My aunt Doris planted a few copper beech in her time. Forty years ago I supplemented them with a selection of fir and deciduous trees. Today they have caught up the much older copper beech to form a homogeneous mass.

Over the top of the trees I can see the lovely mountain Flamston Pin. It's the backdrop to Tupgill.

The Forbidden Corner hosts fifty weddings a year. Inevitably the happy couple want their portrait photos done on Tupgill House lawn with the mountain in the background.

When my kids were young, we used to climb Flamston Pin and have a picnic at the top. But I haven't done it in years. It's quite steep and hard on the knees.

Surprisingly when you get to the top it doesn't fall away on the other side.There are moors stretching many miles. On the Glorious Twelfth of August parties of guns drive up there to shoot grouse.

We have been lucky with the weather, it's been sunny and pleasant so far, and according to the Times it will remain that way until we leave on Saturday.

I saw my sister Jane yesterday. She walked up to Tupgill from her cottage. We chatted in my study with Kate and then went to the Forbidden Corner cafe for lunch together. I didn't introduce her to the rest of the group, as we have the language barrier.

Today she came again to see me. We talked about her son Peter. He had a very violent life in South Africa, and died young. It's the first time that Jane has talked to me about him. She suffered a great deal because of who he became and what he has done.

I was very pleased that at last she could talk about it.

I only really got to know Peter in the last year of his life.

This time we walked on Middleham Moor with the whole group, me acting as interpreter. On the way to the moor we looked at the building programme we are doing at Ashgill. The old Ashgill House has been demolished and is being replaced with three rental cottages. We started two years ago, but stopped while we built the White Goose. Now we are restarting it.

The moor is a lovely place to walk. It's always windy, but today was not too cold.

On our way back to Tupgill, as we passed the lake, we saw a group of four guineafowl. I had never seen them here before. Leo told me that he had bought six, but that they had flown away. As we got closer to them they ran off complaining loudly. How nice to see them.

Jane lives in a cottage at the bottom of Tupgill Park. I walked with her down the park. It was five o'clock, cars were coming out of the Forbidden Corner. As they passed us one stopped and drew into the side of the road. The driver asked me if I am the owner of the Forbidden Corner. I replied yes. Then he said he was very glad I had survived the kidnap. He had followed it on the news. I thanked him, and he drove on.

It's been ten months now since the incident, and people kindly still offer me support.

I hope he will come to my book launch next year. Then he will be able to read the whole story.

Jorge travels extensively for his business in South America.

Over a beer he told me that he was recently in Bolivia. He had been to see his distributor Agripac Boliviana. Today it's the leading supplier of agricultural chemicals in Bolivia.

Is there any connection with Agripac in Ecuador? Oh yes, there certainly once was.

Back in 1977 I founded the company with a Bolivian partner, Winston Suarez.

We had been to Harper Adams Agricultural College together and were great friends.

I had decided to branch out to Bolivia, and got in touch with him.

We set up Agripac Boliviana. It was not my most successful venture.

Winston was not cut out for commerce. I would set him on the right track and return to Ecuador. A month or so later he would call me, there was a crisis. There was always a crisis.

Over the ten years that we shared the business, I must have spent a total of two years in Bolivia.

We never made any money.

Then, when I had had enough of it, we decided to wind up Agripac Boliviana.

But unknown to me he found an investor to buy it.

He never shared the price he got for it.

The end of our friendship.

Years later I met Bertrand de Lassus, the French owner of the business. I joked with him that if he ever wanted to sell it I would buy it back from him.

But I don't want it back. It has bad vibes for me.

We are currently building Agripac Peru. This time with our own people.

Jorge told me today that Winston has died. RIP. But I shan't mourn him.

Which brings me to my conclusion.

The best number of partners in any business is ONE.

Last night was Halloween. We had a Ghost Trail. We had obtained special permission from the Yorkshire Dales National Parks to open the Forbidden Corner at night for Halloween.

We were told to be in the car park at 6pm, as each group was spaced out, to make the scary bits work better.

I thought that it would be cold, so I didn't put on my fancy dress, the others did, though they wore a coat over it.

In fact I was too warm in my famous Mammut jacket (the one I recovered from David).

The evening was quite mild. But more than that, we ran a lot of the time.

We had hardly got into the Forbidden Corner garden when an ogre sprang at us with a piercing cry. That started the panic. We walked on to be met by a werewolf with red fangs and claws who was hidden among the trees. There was the minimum of lighting to show the path to follow, but quite enough shadows to hide our tormentors. We went over the stepping stones (luckily the water jets had been turned off) and entered the underworld. Here there was even more scope for creatures to spring out at us. They not only sprang but shouted at us, tried to split the group into several parts, closing doors between us. It caused confusion. Do we go on, or go back for the unfortunates who have been taken? It was scary for me who knows it well. Imagine those who saw it for the first time!

We went down a passage which has niches in the wall for statues. I have done it so many times before. Today I thought there was one more statue here than there should be.

But if it was part of the show it didn't move. Perhaps it was waiting for a later, more vulnerable, group of guests.

As we emerged from the underworld there was a scream from a lady in the group in front of us. We heard the sound of a chainsaw. We slunk back inside. Who would go out first?

Kate, the bravest, did. She screamed too, but we had to follow her, the following group of guests were on our heels. The mad chainsaw man with a hideous face tried to push us back in. He said he hadn't had time to cut up the first lady. We had to wait our turn.

That did it, we pushed past him and ran for our lives down the walkway overlooking the field. Finally, laughing at our stupidity, we stopped to catch our breath. We walked slowly on. Then we were accosted again, by a creature behind the hedge.

This was getting to be quite enough for one night. But we still had the mausoleum to come. There, apart from the normal electronic screams and rattling chains, we met a clown (literally) who emerged from a coffin and chased us with a hammer.

But then it was all over.

Giggling, we walked back to the cafe, with other survivors, and had beers to calm us down.

We got back to the house at 8pm. I went upstairs to put on my Hugh Hefner outfit of a red silk dressing gown over my trousers, yachting cap and a pipe in my mouth.

Everyone had risen to the occasion. Kate went as the genie from the bottle (as in the Elizabeth Montgomery show, Bewitched). Fredy's was the best outfit. He went as Darkpool, currently showing in the movies.

Luisa was Audry Hepburn in Breakfast at Tiffany's, Margarita was a witch, Julieta a cowgirl and Janina a street walker. Only Jorge had not had time to get an outfit.

There is no fancy dress party to go to this year. Last year I won first prize at the hotel in Montego Bay. The previous year we had been in Punta Cana.

Tonight it was just the eight of us.

We decided to eat in the Tupgill dining room, rather than go to the Saddle Room restaurant, to avoid the stares.

We chose from the restaurant menu and they brought it over. It's only twenty yards away.

It was a fun dinner, interrupted by loads of photos, both in the hall and on the winding staircase.

Friday 1st November

Jorge left at 5am this morning to take a train to London and catch his flight from Heathrow to Miami. The car got a flat tyre on the A1 motorway. He was in a panic. If he missed his train he would miss his flight as well. The timing was very tight. Another taxi was called. He still missed the train, but got the next one and his flight. He called us to say that he was the last passenger to board. But he had made it.

Now we are seven.

Tomorrow we will do the same and return to Madrid. The Tupgill holiday is over. We have enjoyed it. The weather has been great, and I have seen Jane again. She is going to be eighty-four in January. Each time we meet we are aware that it may be the last one.

There was one more thing we all wanted to do. We drove to Leyburn and went to Campbell's grocery store.

The girls went from shelf to shelf happily picking things that they wanted to take home.

I was content with three boxes of Taylors Yorkshire Tea, a pack of four tins of Heinz baked beans and three Wensleydale cheeses.

But they filled the trolley between them.

I was amazed at the checkout to see what they were taking back. Even detergents, because they liked the smell!

We tried to pack all these items in our cases. But of course it wouldn't all go in. There was a lot to carry by hand too. When we got to security at Heathrow the tins of baked beans were about to be confiscated. We let out a collective "No".

The lady official relented, and we were allowed to take them. Applause.

We left Tupgill on Saturday to take the train from Darlington to London. We were in two cars. The first lot got there on time for the 9am reserved train. Kate, Janina and I missed it as Kate had left her handbag in Tupgill with her passport inside. We had got as far as Bellerby, six miles from home, and had to go back to the house.

We caught the 9.20 am train. Of course we didn't have reserved seats. We looked at the reservation tickets on the seats. Those still empty from Darlington were clearly no shows. The train stopped at York, after that it was straight to London. In York the carriage did fill up, but we still found seats.

The ticket inspector came around. I showed ours from the last train. She said there was nothing extra to pay.

We all met up at King's Cross and took two taxis to Heathrow.

Then we split up. We fly from Terminal Five to Madrid. Fredy flies from Terminal Four to Amsterdam today, and tomorrow to Guayaquil.

Once again, at Terminal Five,we ate fish and chips in the Harry Ramsden. Then, as we walked towards the gate, we passed a WH Smith shop. I can never pass one.

Begging indulgence from the others, I dived in.

I was looking for the Economist, but saw on the shelf the very latest Robert Harris novel called Precipice. Happiness indeed. I have read all his previous books. He must rank as my very favourite author.

The Iberia flight is delayed. The lady captain announced that to do with weight, some passengers will be asked to change seats and come forward. She said that not all the baggage can be loaded. But not to worry it will come in the following flight.

We arrived at Madrid an hour late.

As we waited in the queue for Immigration I remembered Kate's story of one time she entered Spain on her own. She was nervous that the immigration official might have counted the number of times she had entered this year and questioned her as to why so many. She approached the desk nervously. He greeted her in Spanish.

"Hola Kate, nice to see you again, are you going to Ocaña tomorrow?"

She did a double take. The official is a fellow sky diver. They chatted happily and he stamped her passport.

Today there was no problem, and my brand new blue passport got its first stamp.

We went to the carousel to collect our bags. We waited half an hour, but no bags appeared, not ours nor anyone else's. We went to the Iberia desk and were told that the bags will arrive on the next flight at 11:30pm. But that meant waiting two hours more. We were tired and wanted to get home. They will send the luggage to our place tomorrow.

Finally home, we opened a bottle of wine. We are all tired. We had started the journey at 8am and it is now after 10pm.

Sunday.

It's now midday. No sign of the luggage. Each time the intercom rings, our hopes rise, only to be dashed. I am beginning to regret not waiting at the airport last night.

I found a toothbrush here but no razor. I was going to buy one but Kate offered me her lady shaver. I have had the closest shave I have ever had, smooth as a baby's bottom, (so that's how they do it?). But I nicked my chin in the process.

Fall back position, if the bags don't appear on time we have other empty suitcases here. I have plenty of clothes but there are things I wanted to take to Guayaquil, not the least of which are my new books, tea, Wensleydale cheese and Heinz baked beans!

I called Iberia, giving the references for the four bags. Yes, they all arrived in Madrid last night, and should be delivered today to your address. They will text you the time.

I explained that we were flying to Guayaquil tonight.

Plan B would be for Iberia to send our bags to AirEuropa for the Guayaquil flight, and to Iberia for Margarita's flight to Bogota.

But the voice on the phone didn't want to know. He said they were already on the way to us.

Just before we left for the airport two of the missing bags arrived. They were Kate's and Margarita's.

And the others? Apparently they are in another place.

We left for Barajas at 10pm, in good time for the 1.45am flight. We went first to terminal four where Iberia has its lost luggage department. We explained the problem all over again and showed them our reference numbers. They said it is impossible to put the bags on our Air Europa flight tonight. They will send them via Iberia to Guayaquil tomorrow.

And so we arrived home in Guayaquil.

Josef met us at the airport with the security detail. It is 9:30 am Monday morning.

We went back to our rented flat. Fredy arrived with a local speciality breakfast of bolon, mashed plantain with cheese and pork scratchings.

We ate it and drank a glass of wine.

Snoopy is excited to see us. We were pleasantly surprised. We had expected to be ignored, in best beagle fashion.

We were told by Emily that she had taken him for a walk every day at 5pm, where they met all his doggy friends (and I suspect she made friends too).

To make him a happy dog, we took him out today at 5pm, and indeed all the other dog walkers knew his name. We let him off his lead on a large stretch of unbuilt on land, where he raced about. There was a young lady with a Highland Terrier bitch. She said that she (that is the dog) had been on heat, but now it is over. Snoopy seemed to think himself shortchanged.

Today seemed to drag a bit. I didn't go to the office as I was feeling sleepy. That will wait for tomorrow. We ordered supplies for the kitchen and sushi to eat tonight. Then we took our wine to the TV and once again watched Game of Thrones.

Will it never end?

Tuesday 5th November. Guy Fawkes Day.

But of course it means nothing outside of Britain.

I got up early and was in the office by 7am. After being away for four weeks there are a host of things to do. I worked manically to get up to date and reduce my computer intray to manageable proportions.

I had been away from Ecuador, and hence my barber Carlos, for four weeks. I called him for an appointment. He would see me at 4pm.

Both of us enjoy opera. He was waiting for me watching the Three Tenors, Luciano Pavarotti, Placido Domingo and Jose

Carreras. It was conducted by James Levine. It was an old version. Both Pavarotti and Levine have since died.

I asked Carlos if all his customers liked opera, he said that sadly only a few do. So he enjoys my visits.

Rather appropriately, before I left there was a video of The Barber of Seville, with the song Figaro.

We are going to the new house tonight to see how the architects have got on. From reports I hear they haven't done much. Now it's getting urgent. We want to be living there by Christmas.

We went, met them and lo and behold they had done almost nothing. I was annoyed.

Sadly, I gave vent to my disappointment, sarcastically admiring all the improvements which weren't there. They stood in silence while I listed everything.

They explained that the furniture for the TV, and the corresponding piece of the other wall, have been ordered. But they won't be delivered until December.

What date in December? They didn't know.

And the jacuzzi? They didn't yet have the municipal approval.

What about the bathroom fittings? Surely that could have been changed.

They were waiting for Kate to come back to decide which brand.

Is there no such thing as email?

There was a representative from a company that makes kitchen furniture, with them. He had samples of the surfaces to show us.

I thought we were long past this stage. We had walked the house with them several times. They had made computer renders, they had quoted for the work, and I had paid 50%.

All of this before we went on holiday, four weeks ago.

Now we get back and we are still deciding on the colour of the kitchen and looking at yet more computer images!

I demanded to know if we could be in the house by Christmas. They looked vague, i.e. no!

At this point Kate took over. She shepherded me to the kitchen, poured me a glass of wine, and sat me down in the pergola to count the stars.

Then she went back to the three men and carried on the decision process.

Two hours, and four glasses of wine later we left. In the car I thanked her for not getting annoyed with me. I had been very rude. She said that was OK, I was stressed. We were both disappointed.

But we have to think again about Christmas.

The house won't be ready for her family's visit.

To cheer me up, I got a reprieve from Game of Thrones. We watched an opera, The Daughter of the Regiment, by Donizetti. It starred Patricia Ciofi and Juan Diego Flores.

This is one of his most famous roles where he sings 'Mes Amis', with nine high Cs.

It's very challenging for any tenor. He sings it beautifully.

He had once come to Guayaquil and gave a concert in the Sanchez Aguilar theatre. We of course went to see him. He sang several operatic arias, but couldn't sing Mes Amis, which I shouted out from the front row. He explained that he was recovering from a throat infection. While there are techniques to get around this, the high C is not an option.

Thursday.

Finally my suitcase arrived. Janina collected it from the airport and brought it to our flat. I unpacked it quickly to see if the Wensleydale cheeses had contaminated everything. No, all is well. I had put them in a plastic bag and on opening it there was a greasy mess, but the cheeses looked fine, if a bit squashed.

We celebrated by eating one of them with a glass of wine.

Snoopy got a few pieces too. He enjoyed them but was not a happy hound as just before Janina arrived he had clearly expected to go for his walk.

He went to the door continuously and whined. We would have taken him earlier, but Kate wanted to wait until the sun had gone down.

Of course by the time that Janina left it was too late for a walk, and anyway we were ready for bed.

Both the tea and the four cans of baked beans are fine.

I put them in the kitchen.

This morning one can of baked beans is missing. Well not missing, there is the empty can in the garbage bin. Kate had enjoyed her midnight feast.

I ate half of a can with bacon and eggs. Delicious. I hope there will be some left for tomorrow.

Strangely Heinz baked beans are not available in Ecuador. I am sure there is a good market for them. All our group loved them at Tupgill.

We talked about Christmas and what our options are. Kate thinks there is no chance of moving into the new house. I disagreed, we should put pressure on the architects. We could do the interior work and leave the jacuzzi for later.

But if it is not available how do we accommodate her family?

Perhaps we can rent a house at the beach for the four days they are here?

But that doesn’t suit me. It's our busy season at Agripac, the rains begin in December and then the annual planting starts. Traditionally I would be at my desk until late Christmas Eve and back there from the 26th. The beach is two hours away.

Let's see what happens.

My daughter Diana and grandson Dominic, aged 10, have arrived in Guayaquil. Tonight we have a dinner for the family, to which I am kindly invited.

Tomorrow Alex's daughter Sienna, also aged 10, has her first communion.

They came for lunch today at Bandurria with Ceci. After lunch Diana said that Dom has a present for me. He led me to the piano, sat down and played a complicated piece without music. We all applauded, including the staff who were having lunch.

The dinner went very well. It was held in Ceci's (once our) house. My three children came over. She showed me some new paintings she had bought. Really her taste has never been mine, but now she doesn't have to ask me if I like them.

Magda made her wonderful roast chicken with mash, Yorkshire pudding and gravy.

As always, I ate too much.

Saturday. We went to a chapel close to home at 2pm.

Sienna was dressed in a pretty white dress with a green bow at the back. Both Alex and Diana looked very beautiful in their dresses. Ceci had on a pretty red dress. I had a suit, white shirt and tie for the occasion. Nick, who rarely moves out of the casual, wore a sports jacket and fawn trousers, loafers and no socks (a very Spanish habit).

It took an hour, with the Catholic priest talking to Sienna about the responsibilities of her relationship with God. There were about twenty people there.

I didn't follow the service too closely with the various readings and the singing of a lady with a guitar. We were continually asked to stand, then to be seated, then to kneel.

My mind drifted to the purpose of religion.

The Christian Church has done remarkably well since its days of persecution in Roman times. On the whole I accept that it has been a force for good, providing comfort for those who believe in it. It was the sole entity which maintained the flicker of Roman civilization throughout the Dark Ages of barbarism. The church provided literate priests who transcribed Roman documents and so preserved our knowledge of a lost civilization.

On the other hand it was responsible for immense human suffering in religious wars and the Inquisition.

Today it is in decline. We are in a post-religious era. Fewer and fewer people attend church. The Vatican, which once was the source of tremendous wealth, is appealing for funds to avoid bankruptcy.

When the service was over we grouped for photos of Sienna with her parents, then with grandparents, then with Nick's wife, Almu, who is her godmother. Then lots of photos with friends, rather like a wedding.

Afterwards we got back to our cars and drove to Alex and Javi's house for a buffet reception.

A lot more friends turned up, those who had ducked out of the chapel part.

Many of them I hadn't seen since Ceci and I split up last January. Her lady friends were polite, but a bit frosty. We began sitting together but after a while they all moved elsewhere.

But there were my children's friends Edward and Trevor Harding, whom I had known since they were born. They had no hang-ups and chatted to me.

Later an old friend of ours, Abel arrived. He is from Manabi province. He was telling me about something in Rocafuerte. I said I had bad memories of Rocafuerte, where I was held by the kidnappers.

Yes, he replied on Fito's ranch.

What? Is it known that I was on the ranch of a notorious narco?

Jose Adolfo Macias "alias Fito", the head of the Choneros gang. He is described as the Capo of Ecuadorian drugs.

He escaped from prison in January last and is still on the run.

Was it "Fito" I talked to on the phone? He was in prison then, but at that time the gangs ran the prisons. He is described in the press as living like a king in prison with all amenities.

A phone would be the least of them.

Did the police know about the ranch? Were they warned about interfering with it? At the time of the kidnap I had had day dreams of the sound of shots, police sirens, shouting men. Of being told to lie on the floor to avoid stray bullets, until the good guys could safely release me.

But of course that never happened. I was delivered to the police by the bandits, when they had got what they wanted.

In Colombia narcos have a thing about ranches. They pose as cattlemen, controlling vast areas of land. The advantage is that the police or army can't get to them without due warning, so allowing them time to escape.

The most famous narco of all, Pablo Escobar, had enormous ranches. He even had a zoo on one of them. Today, thirty years after his death, the Colombian government is trying to find a home for the herd of hippopotamus. They offered them to Ecuador, but it was not accepted.

Nick tells me that when he was in England in November he received a summons as a witness in the ongoing trial of the kidnappers (it's been going on since February!).

Like ourselves he did it by Zoom. He too found it disconcerting that he could see the prisoners, and they could see him. Though now there are only four. One more has died in prison and two have been released from lack of evidence. He related his telephone conversations with the head of the group, mainly at night, and the agreement to pay a ransom to secure my release.

The party was going well, and would go on until late that night, but I left at 6pm.

Kate had sent a message that she missed me. She is very good about me seeing my family, but I didn't want to leave her alone on Saturday evening.

As I was leaving Diana asked me if I would come to lunch at home tomorrow. She, Dominic and Ceci are flying on Monday morning to Los Angeles.

I drove unsteadily home, escorted by my security. I had drunk a fair amount of wine.

On arriving I suggested to Kate that we have a siesta. She thought it an excellent idea.

But before that she had a new outfit to show me.

Once again the lovely music comes to mind, La barcarolle.

I had eaten more than enough at the buffet, but she wanted dinner. After which we repaired to the TV. Surely the Game of Thrones can't go on much longer?

The whole chapter was a huge battle scene between the forces of good and the White Walkers.

It is nighttime. The Drakkari, their sickle-like swords aflame, charge in their mass formations towards the White Walkers. They are watched from the castle top of Winterfell. The mass of flame is slowly extinguished until none is left. Like the charge of the Light Brigade, at the battle of Balaclava in 1854, it is glorious, and a complete failure.

During the battle several main characters died, but at the end it seems that good has triumphed. Once the king of the White Walkers is killed, the skeletons of his army crumble to dust.

So on we go towards the end.

On Sunday I went to the office as normal until just before midday. As I drove home there was a police motorbike blocking an intersection.

I stopped and waited. Two motorbikes roared past followed by a police car, then four suvs with flashing lights, then more police cars and motorbikes and finally a pickup filled with soldiers in full gear with guns. I guess that President Noboa is in town.

In my consular days I once had the fun of driving like this. I drove our Ambassador to see the President of the day at the Governor's palace of Guayaquil.

I had picked him up at the airport and was surprised to see that I had an escort. The police captain in charge said that the President was pushed for time, so he wanted to see the Ambassador as soon as possible.

Well, that was a hairy drive. I crossed Guayaquil at a hundred kilometres an hour. The motorbikes skidded to a stop at each intersection, narrowly missing causing an accident, while I sailed through. It's great to be important.

Kate said that she is going to the gym today with Janina and her little daughter Kaila, who is seven years old. Kate loves children and always takes time to play with her.

I hope one day she will have a child of her own. I sometimes think that poor Snoopy is a surrogate child. She continually dresses him up in funny clothes, which he hates.

They left at 12.15 pm. I have to wait until our escort returns to take me to Ceci's house.

I called her to say that I can't leave Snoopy alone, he will destroy the house.

A case of love me, love my dog.

She relented and said I could bring him with me.

This is a big plus. Neither she nor my family have ever wanted to meet Snoopy.

The first problem is that he is Kate's dog, and secondly he is called Snoopy, which offends family history. When Ceci and I got married our very first beagle was called Snoopy. There can't be a second one.

I explained that she named him for the cartoon character, but no, she doesn't agree.

Now for the first time they will meet him.

And of course they like him.

When I arrived it was just Ceci and I. I let Snoopy off his lead and he explored the premises, he liked the garden most of all, and baptized it liberally. Then Diana came downstairs with Dominic. He ran around with Snoopy, over exciting him. We got a show of an electric beagle tearing around the room, leaping on and off sofas, to our amusement and Ceci's alarm that he would break something.

one. But I suspect that they have put off the moment of having to put hand to pocket.

The last three nights the generator has stopped for three hours a night, from 12am to 3am.

Last night it didn't come back on.

The mains electricity returned at 6am. I had woken thirty minutes before then, taken a partial cold shower (just the necessary bits) and was wondering if I could shave in the light of the telephone, when the light came on.

I have never seen a situation like this in Ecuador. Over the years there has been the odd crisis with the lights going out. Now it is a constant. We have power cuts of 14 hours a day in Guayaquil. The feed mill cannot produce enough to fill the orders, neither can the competition of course. No one has a generator big enough to run all of their machinery.

The government in their wisdom suggested that all factories take a week off. Until the Chamber of Industries explained to them the consequences of doing so.

It all goes back to an overreliance on hydroelectricity on the east side of the Andes which runs down to the rainforest of the Amazon.

A rain forest without rain? Oddly, every time I have been over there it rained.

The newspapers don't really explain much. The headlines run from 'Drought, empty rivers and hydroelectric dams' to 'Heavy rain causing flooding'.

What is the true picture?

Luckily I have the means to find out. Every one of Agripac's two hundred shops, spread around the country, has a rain gauge. We normally begin to use these in December to measure the coastal rainfall.

I asked that we begin today with the Sierra and Oriente (Amazon side) shops. This will give us an idea of when the electricity cuts can improve.

This afternoon I had my fifteenth Pilates class. Adrian was pleased to see us again, after our month away. He asked if I had done Pilates in Madrid. I admitted that I had only been once. But it was better than nothing. I haven't fallen behind. He applied a little more pressure today, but continually praised my ability to do the exercises, compared to when I started with him.

I am rather proud of myself that I have kept it up so long. The first time in my life that I have done so, barring school, when it was compulsory.

Kate on the other hand is an exercise addict. Today she told me that after her piano class at 8am, she has done an hour of pole dancing, two hours of gym and then an hour of Pilates with me.

After dinner Kate was occupied with her Instagram, so I watched another opera, or more strictly an operetta. The difference is that it contains spoken parts, an opera is all sung.

Today it was The Merry Widow by Franz Lehar. It is a beautifully made movie, filmed in the New York Met, starring Rene Flemming.

It's set in the French embassy of some imaginary east European country. The country is bankrupt. The only person who can save it is Hanna, the young Widow of the country's richest banker, who was left a huge fortune. All the men are courting her. It's their duty to the Fatherland, as well as a spot of personal interest. If she marries outside the country the wealth will go elsewhere.

The man she loves, and who eventually admits to loving her, is Count Danilo Danilowitsch. They had once had a romance, but at the time he refused to marry her.

Now he dedicates his life to the Paris nightclub Maxim.

The music is wonderful and the Maxim dancers finish with a cancan.

Marvellous.

Today, Tuesday, the same thing happened with the lights. But I am a fast learner. I took my toiletries and padded to Kate's pole dancing room, where she has her bathroom. The water is heated by gas here, unlike my bathroom where I changed it to electric.

Two days without a shower is unthinkable.

No breakfast for Snoopy today. He has once again forgotten his manners. Actually it looked as though he had eaten something that didn't agree with him. I admit to sharing a Wensleydale cheese with him last night. Or maybe it was whatever he found in the garbage bin, which was tipped over. Rubbish is strewn over the kitchen floor. Normally I put the bin in the laundry room, but last night I forgot to do it. He knew of course that no breakfast was forthcoming, he didn't even leave the bed, just opened an eye as I went to kiss Kate goodbye.

Today's Expreso reported that fifteen people were killed in the Guayaquil Penitentiary yesterday.

According to the article they are all members of the Freddy Krueger gang, who are enemies of the Choneros, led by Alias Fito. Once again the gang wars have flared up.

This is the first time during the presidency of Daniel Noboa that this has happened. Talk of having regained control of the prisons now looks hollow.

The article went on to say that the prison authorities have not released names of those killed. Outside the prison scores of parents of the prisoners are waiting to see if their son is among the dead.

I am still getting over my disappointment that Donald Trump will return to the White House next January.

I had hoped that we had seen the last of him.

What happens now in Ukraine? Will he still do a deal with his pal Putin, even though there are now North Korean troops fighting alongside the Russians?

Will US public opinion allow him to make a present of Ukraine to Russia and make Kim Jong Un a hero to the Russians, and even more of a menace to the West?

Will he destroy Nato, just as it needs strengthening against Russia or China?

God Forbid!

Then of course there is his crazy idea to ship millions of illegal residents of the USA home, wherever that may be. The majority of both Republicans and Democrats in Congress have a thing about not legalizing these immigrants, even though they have been residents for many years and have children and grandchildren who are US citizens.

It's not as though the USA is crammed full of people. The birthrate is falling and the population is only maintained by immigrants.

I feel strongly about this. I too am an immigrant to Ecuador. Though in my case a privileged one. I have maintained British nationality, especially because I was Consul for thirty-five years, but I could have acquired Ecuadorian nationality at any time.

I feel that I have contributed a great deal to the country, as have the US immigrants, legal or illegal.

Thursday.

Yesterday I went to the dentist at 4pm. It is a routine visit for him to check the growth of the bone where the implant will go. This has been ongoing since the tooth was extracted in March.

Kate is at a spa, so I went alone.

Once again it appears that the screw inserted in the jawbone, to take the implant, is still not firm enough.

Raul decided that the screw is the problem and he will replace it.

OMG this is going to hurt and I don't have Kate to hold my hand, wimp as I am.

“Come on Colin, this won’t hurt and it will only take me five minutes“ said Raul.

OK, if it is that quick I wont call Kate. Though she told me that she has finished in the spa and is enjoying a cocktail.

But nothing gets done in five minutes. He injected an anaesthetic into the gum, ouch!

Then he began to extract the screw. But it was still painful. So another anaesthetic was injected.

After that he brooked no further delay and set to work.

A dentist needs strong arms. Raul certainly has them. It's impressive the amount of pressure needed to extract teeth and fit implants.

The screw is removed and another put in. Then I am free to go. It took half an hour.

I was instructed to return once a week for five weeks to have a laser aimed at it.

It will be another three months before the implant can be put in. Which will make it a year since the tooth was removed.

I collected Kate and we drove home. By now the anaesthetic is wearing off and my jaw ached. On getting home I went straight to the bar and poured myself a large glass of wine. Kate protested that I shouldn't drink while taking anaesthetics. But no way. I need a drink. After two glasses of wine I thought whisky might give more relief. I don't normally drink it.

Today I have a headache to replace the jaw ache of yesterday!

I should have taken paracetamol, instead of trying to drown the pain.

Before bed I watched half an hour of Wagner’s opera Parsifal. I was in that sort of mood.

I have my Wagner moments, and can run through two or three of them one after another.

Parsifal, the perfect knight.

Amfortas, the king of the Knights of the Holy Grail has been wounded by the magician Klingsor. It's a wound that will never heal, until his own spear, that caused it, is returned to him.

According to legend no one can kill Klingsor, until he meets an innocent fool, who knows no fear.

That man is Parsifal. Raised in the forests by animals, he is a simple fool.

The opera is long on dialogues. I only began to enjoy it after seeing it three times. Most of the voices are bass.

But there is a happy moment when Parsifal arrives at Klingsor's garden which grows pretty girls (but hardly bothers about clothing). They try to seduce him, but without success.

He can't be that innocent!

Tonight we have our Opera Club at Bandurria. We never do Wagner. Our audience wouldn't appreciate it. Anyway Parsifal has only one soprano role, Kundry, and it's not a big one.

We choose operas where Viviana can star.

Tonight it's Rigoletto. I will do the introduction and a brief resume of the plot. The Duke of Mantua is a notorious womanizer. He sings the well-known aria La Donne e Mobile (women are fickle). Rigoletto is his hunchbacked court jester. He helps the Duke seduce the wives and daughters of the courtiers, who he despises. One of them, on his way to the scaffold, curses him.

Other courtiers take their revenge on him by kidnapping his beautiful daughter Gilda and delivering her to the Duke's bed.

Rigoletto is shattered, she is the only person in the world whom he loves. He contracts an assassin to murder the Duke. But Gilda has fallen in love with the Duke, and sacrifices herself to save him.

Thinking that he has the corpse of the Duke to throw into the river, Rigoletto discovers that it is Gilda's corpse.

He cries out in anguish "The Curse".

We have done some work on the stage since the last opera. All that is left to do is fit the curtains, and position the projector for the subtitles, which are promised for this morning.

Friday.

What a night! I am late to the office today. It was close to midnight when we left the opera group.

For the first time Kate came with me. It had always been difficult before as Ceci normally comes with a group of friends. But she is in Los Angeles. Kate knows Vivi of course, she got her to sing at both my birthday parties. By coincidence she met a great friend of hers among the audience, Cecilia Niemes, an attractive woman in her fifties. She was once Miss Ecuador. She owns a model agency, and was the first person to give Kate a chance to model in Ecuador, when she was only sixteen.

I joked that she was amiss not to have sent her to Agripac back then.

I had to wait three more years to meet her.

Vivi insisted that we begin right at 6pm tonight.

Because of the traffic, and Kate having to wash her hair, we arrived five minutes late. I greeted a few of the guests before being called on to open the proceedings.

I had put on a grey-striped suit for the occasion. This one fits better than the blue one I had on for the first communion, which seemed a bit big. They are all bespoke, but go back many years. In 2010 when I bought this one I was more akin to today's figure.

Henry Poole makes each suit to measure. They have a weighing chair in the shop. This is to avoid customers saying that the suit is too tight, when it is they who have put on weight.

Fashion may come and go but they never made drainpipes or bell bottoms. The trousers are comparatively wide, all have turnups. Looking at mine today I noticed the white stitches inside the legs of the trousers. They are put in by the cutter, and strangely never removed, though they can't be seen from the outside. The jackets are a couple of inches longer than a normal blazer.

I walked out from behind the curtain and gave a short synopsis of Rigoletto. Then I returned to Kate at the principal table.

Yes indeed a table. The audience, of about a hundred people, sits on chairs to the front, slightly lower than our platform, and to the sides. I need a table as we are served wine during the performance. And that is the problem. The waiters are attentive and continually fill my glass. But opera and wine go well together.

Vivi is a talented producer and actress, as well as having a magnificent voice.

We performed Rigoletto with only the six principal voices and no chorus. But she added six dancers from a ballet school. It worked beautifully. The dancers made the opening scene in the Duke's court realistic. Normally there is a crowd of people, we did it with only seven.

Vivi sings the part of Gilda, her brother Alex is an imposing Rigoletto and Andres is the Duke.

There is a scene in the assassin, Sparafucil's, house where the Duke is trying to seduce his sister Maddalena, while Gilda and her father Rigoletto watch from outside. All four voices sing at the same time, but not together. They are distinct, a baritone, a tenor, a soprano and a mezzo soprano. It can only be done in opera, it wouldn't work as theater.

The opera itself took an hour and a half. Then the buffet supper was served and the others got to the wine (I was way ahead of them).

Afterwards, as is our tradition, it becomes a group of friends who enjoy singing.

Though we didn't have a chorus today, some of them came to watch it. They all aspire to be principal voices. Now is their chance. One after another they went to the stage and sang operatic pieces.

Vivi's husband Carlos found the backing music for each of them.

Which opera will we do next in January? Vivi suggested the Merry Widow. Andres opted for Pagliacci (the clowns). To convince us that he can do it he sang the main aria for us, and did it with great aplomb.

Our homemade theater, Bandurria, is our company dining room, which we have altered to make a stage. What we didn't have to alter is the acoustics. I don't know why, but they are perfect. Perhaps because of the central atrium, which was once an open-air garden, until we roofed it with glass.

So we don't need microphones or speakers, the space is quite small and the voices easily fill it.

I had a guest for lunch today in Bandurria. Alex and Javi brought Sienna with them.

"Hi granddad". She was cuddling a small stuffed toy.

"What is that My Love?"

She told me it is a Capybara. They are herbivores of the rodent family, and can grow to be more than a metre long. They live in the Amazon rivers. They are said to be the least aggressive of all animals, in fact they are friendly to humans.

There is a song about them, which she played for me.

After I had admired it she demanded to know when I would bring Snoopy to see her again.

I laughed at that. "Anytime you like. I can leave him with you when I go away." I saw Alex and Javi exchange worried looks. They had refused to have him when I went to Madrid.

Now I have a fifth column. Mummy, can't we have him to stay, pretty please?

And while talking about Snoopy, today is his second birthday. 17th November. But of course we didn't get him until he was weaned in January 2023.

Kate talked of having a party and inviting other dogs he knows. But I said no. They would end up fighting, or mating!

She went to the mall and came back with a Happy Birthday 2 sign, doggy balloons, six marrow-filled bones, a conical hat and a birthday bib for him. She put them on the sofa and grabbed him to sit among them with his hat on.

She made a cake out of dog food paste and put two candles on it.

Then we took turns to hold him there and take photos.

He got rid of the hat, we grabbed the candles, and the cake was soon gone. He took all of half a minute to eat it all. The marrow bones are a great success. He is still on the first one several days later.

He picks it up and drops it noisily on the floor, while all the time we hear him gnawing it. He has hidden it several times under the pillow on the bed, and behind cushions on the sofa.

Happy Birthday Snoopy.

As I drove home from the office today I noticed that the trees in the street were in flower.

The office is in downtown Guayaquil, not the prettiest of cities.

But there has been a regeneration programme in some streets. Ours has benefited. The municipality have removed the spaghetti of electricity and telephone cables from poles, and put them underground. They planted trees for shade, and in this season, just before the annual rains, they flower. We have the glorious yellow of the Tabebuia, and blue Jacarandas.

I drove in a melancholic mood. It reminds me of Rodeo Grande.

How we loved this time of year. We would ride and point out to each other the pink flowering Robles, the orange to white Fernan Sanchez, the blue Pechiches, the pink Cañafistula and the yellow Buttercup trees. The mango trees are in fruit. We would ride up to them and a cowboy with a long stick would knock the fruit down. The trick is to catch it before it hits ground and squelches. How delicious they are on a hot day's ride.

Then hopefully the rain will advance south to Ecuador too, and solve the problem.

I looked at my rain reports today. There have been sporadic rains both on the Coast and in the Sierra. We are nearly there. Jaime sent me a photo of Cotopaxi, the mountain is visible from Quito. It had been bare. Once again there is snow on the summit, a good sign.

But as someone remarked to me, the supermarket shelves are still stocked, there are no food shortages. So the food industry is getting by, just.

We left Snoopy with Celso and went to a nearby restaurant for lunch. Then, with nothing else to do, we collected Snoopy and went back to our flat. The security men can now go home until tomorrow morning.

I filled the afternoon by finishing my book Precipice. It is the true story of an extraordinary love affair between the prime minister HH Asquith, aged sixty-two, and a young aristocratic woman Venetia Stanley, twenty-five. During the First World War he writes to her several times a day, sometimes even sending her secret government telegrams. The police discover it. It would cause tremendous harm to Britain should those messages fall into the hands of enemy agents.

The author explains at the end of the book that all the Prime Minister's letters to Venetia Stanley have been preserved and are now in a library. The ones from her to him have been destroyed. HH Asquith burned them on his last day as Prime Minister.

Another wonderful Robert Harris book.

By seven pm I was tired of reading, and Kate had finished watching her gruesome documentaries about famous murder cases.

What shall we do? We returned to Game of Thrones.

Surely that must be the very last chapter. Daenerys and Jon Snow attack Kings Landing.

Jon and most of the leaders want to do just enough to get the townspeople to surrender, and not to have a massacre. They send a messenger to tell them that if they want to surrender they must ring the church bells and open the city gates. That appears to be working and the bells are ringing. But Daenerys, riding her last remaining dragon, goes berserk.

She flies back and forth over the city burning and destroying the buildings until all that is left is flaming ruins and mummified bodies, as in Pompeii.

Most of the few remaining characters are killed.

Rather like Wagner's Ring Cycle, it is Gotterdammerung. The twilight of the gods.

Everything is destroyed.

Tomorrow we are again dining with Lien and Rita. They have been chatting to Kate this week about swapping KLM porcelain houses. They are collectors. They want to swap any duplicates they have for ones they don't have. We have never been serious collectors. Each time we fly KLM in business class they offer a selection, we get one each. But we can never remember the ones we already have. There again, half of ours are in Madrid, the other half here.

But we are happy to help them out.

Lien suggested Kate and I watch the film Proof of Life, starring Russell Crowe and Meg Ryan. I had heard of it but never seen it. The film is about the kidnap of an oil executive by the FARC in Colombia. It was actually filmed in Ecuador. At the time, the year 2000, Colombia was considered dangerous and Ecuador safe!

Last night we watched it.

The kidnap lasts for four months, while the poor chap is moved from place to place on the Amazon side of Ecuador, by drugged and trigger-happy members of a narco gang.

Russell Crowe is an ex-member of an elite British SAS regiment. Now he is employed by a security company which specializes in kidnap and extortion cases.

Unlike my kidnap, which lasted only four days until I was released, Crowe and a few fellow tough guys storm into the enemy camp, guns blazing, and rescue the hostage who is then taken out by helicopter.

There are lovely scenes of Quito and the beautiful church La Compania with its vast amount of gold filigree. Also of the Ecuadorian jungle. All of which I know well.

Amazon is a wonderful place to buy books. They have everything. But the problem with Ecuador is that parcels sent from abroad get held up by customs. Malcolm Tempest once kindly sent me a Christmas hamper from Fortnum and Mason in London. It arrived mid-December, but took me until February to get it released. Fatuous questions were asked as to what it contained. The customs had it down as chemicals, when in fact it was jam, biscuits, preserves, crackers and a Christmas pudding.

To avoid that I asked my daughter Diana to buy me two books and send them back with Cecilia in December.

The first book is titled The Donkeys by Alan Clark, the same man who wrote the Alan Clark Diaries. I met him once when he was Minister of State for Defence. He stopped in Guayaquil on his way to the 1992 Santiago Air Show in Chile. The Ambassador and I entertained him. He describes me in his diary as being tall, distinguished with a military moustache, who he understood to be doing rather well in business.

The Diaries are notorious for their description of the many affairs he had while a Member of Parliament and Minister.

But he has also written two acclaimed history books. I have already read Barbarossa, the definitive account of Hitler's attack on Russia. The Donkeys is a disparaging account of the Generals who led the British Army in the First World War. Both Field Marshals Sir John French and Sir Douglas Hague come in for criticism for sacrificing so many lives in their constant futile attacks on the German trenches.

HH Asquith was Prime minister. Field Marshal Kitchener was minister for war, and Winston Churchill was First Lord of the Admiralty, so it ties in with Precipice.

The second book is one I have seen reviewed in the Economist recently.

It's Kingmaker by Sonia Purnell.

It's the story of Pamela Churchill, Winston's daughter-in-law.

Her marriage to his son Randolf was short-lived.

In 1941 Winston asked the help of this beautiful, fascinating twenty-year-old woman to change the mind of the US isolationist envoy Harry Hopkins. He is opposed to the USA giving any help to Britain in its war with Germany. She seduced and convinced him. He in turn convinced President Franklin Roosevelt. The rest is history. The USA began the Lend-lease programme to supply arms to Britain in her hour of need.

She went on to have liaisons with a number of important men during the war, all to Britain's advantage.

She later married Averell Harriman in 1971 and became a Washington hostess, who had tremendous influence with the Democrats. Pamela Harriman finished her career very successfully as US Ambassador in Paris.

Yesterday when we got home from Pilates at 5pm Yaneth was still there.

She said that she was worried about the house in front of our building. It had been for sale. Now it was either sold or rented. She had watched it for the last couple of days. Burley men came and went by motorbike. There were no women. The blinds were drawn all day in every room.

We went to the kitchen window with her and looked at it. There is a smart blue and silver motorbike by the front door.

I sent a text to Josef telling him about it. He said that he would check up who it is tomorrow. Now it's too late the administration of our compound has closed.

Kate and I became nervous about it.

What if they had rented the house to watch our movements? Could this be a second attempt at kidnap? Motorbikes had played a part in that.

I asked Josef if we should have security tonight, two men either to sit in the car outside, or within the flat?

He replied no. That would only draw attention to ourselves.

He told us to lock the doors and balcony windows, and not to go to the car in the basement car park until our guards arrive tomorrow.

We went to bed and locked the bedroom door. I awoke at midnight, Snoopy was sniffing at the door. I feared someone might be in the flat. I didn't get up to look. I had the phone by the bed. If I hear anything I will call Josef. He had said to call him anytime.

But Snoopy returned to bed. I went back to sleep.

I dreamt that the same men who took us in December had returned.

"You made a promise to us. You haven't kept your promise. We will take you again. This time we won't be so nice to you."

I woke in a sweat. All was quiet. It was 2am. It was the same time as we were taken in December.

I put out my hand and took Kate's hand. She is asleep. No she isn't either, she squeezed my hand. We didn't talk. Just lay there taking comfort from each other's presence.

My thoughts continued. If they took us in the night they would just have to cross the road to their house. They could keep us sedated there until say a builder's truck came in the morning which they could use to smuggle us out. The river is the other side. But there is an electrified fencing along the edge, and a police launch patrols all night.

I must have slept. I saw it was 5am.

Time to get up. The danger has passed. It will be daylight in half an hour. There is already movement in the street. The newspapers are being delivered, the rubbish collection van with flashing orange lights is moving slowly down the street. The first joggers and dog walkers are already about.

Perhaps there never was a danger, it was all in our minds.

There have been a series of robberies in one of the urbanizations near to us. It caused a furore. The mayor has demanded that the police increase their presence.

That would be nothing compared to a kidnap from one of the most heavily guarded compounds. Then no one would feel safe in their beds.

Our escort turned up earlier today, Friday, at 6am and I went for my car. At this time of day the traffic on the highway outside the compound is thin. I accelerated to ninety kph. Today will be a quick run to the office. Near our flat there is a new shopping centre which has just opened as well as a Toyota showroom. There are others in the building stage.

They are finally building more pedestrian bridges over the road. I have seen people trying to cross it, dodging the traffic. It's something a driver has to be very aware of. People misjudge the speed of the traffic, they dart out and then find they can't reach the other side, so are stuck in the middle with cars racing by each side of them.

Downtown, at Puerto Santa Ana the 'Yoo Guayaquil', the tallest building in Ecuador at forty-six floors, is well under construction.

This all makes me happy. This is my town. We won't give way to the mafia. We will continue to build, and work and live here. One day they will be beaten.

Looking at the traffic I think of all these people going about their business.

There are school buses, commuters by metrobus, motorbike or by car. The everyday rush to school, the office, the factory.

We are the silent majority. We will overcome.

I get to the office and have my presidential moment as the guards stop the traffic, with flapping arms, to let me race into the office car park.

Always supposing that one of the five office cats is not sleeping there.

Later in the morning Josef sent me a message. He had talked to the administration of our compound. He was told that the house in front of us is empty. A man with a motorbike goes to clean it once a week.

I wrote back that I didn't believe it. Our maid had seen several men coming and going. Also there were lights on last night.

He replied OK, he was still checking. He will get back to me.

In the afternoon I got another message. Now he knows the facts. The man living there wanted to keep a low profile, he has body guards. He is no threat to us. There have been complaints about his bodyguards from neighbours.

I asked his name. He replied that it was better I didn't know. But he repeated there is no threat to us. I thanked him. Stand down the guard.

A mystery man. But if he is living there alone the complaints probably arose from his partying. Yaneth had seen no women. But that was not to say that they did not come at night.

Anyway it is a relief that we are not under siege.

Fredy and Omar have a small farm where they have, among other things, a lot of free-range hens. Kate and I once overnighted there when we had an Agripac event nearby. It was a memorable night as we couldn't sleep for the blasted cockerels. They had clearly got out of sync. Instead of greeting the dawn at 5am, these wretched birds began crowing at midnight and kept it up until dawn.

At 7pm today Omar sent us a message that he is in Guayaquil with Fredy and would like to visit us and deliver a basket of eggs. I gladly accepted. It's thought that eggs from hens that roam with the cocks are better for you. Huevos de gallo in Spanish.

I told Kate. I expected she would be happy to see them.

She gave me a quizzical look and said,

"You invited them, so be warned I may not be fit to go to Pilates with you tomorrow".

"Nonsense, Pilates is at 11am. They are only coming to deliver the eggs. We will have a glass or two of wine and they will leave."

Fredy had said that he would be coming in his uniform. What was that all about?

Halloween has come and gone.

They arrived at 8pm. Fredy, his mother and Omar. Then I understood. Today is his graduation from Espol University. He has been awarded his master's degree.

He is dressed in white shirt and tie, grey suit and wore academic robes and cap.

We congratulated him. It has been a year's course. In fact he was lucky to have survived it.

The course had a module of two weeks in Israel. He flew to Tel Aviv in the first days of October last year, and spent ten days in bomb shelters during the Palestinian offensive.

We tried to get him out earlier, but the airport was closed and no airline wanted to fly there anyway. Eventually he returned via Istanbul and Amsterdam.

Tonight we laughed about it, over the first glass of wine.

Kate wanted a photo of us together. I was dispatched to put on a jacket and tie.

Then we chatted and told jokes. From time to time I opened another bottle of wine.

I must have fallen asleep in the chair about 11pm. Kate sent me off to bed.

Waking at two am I heard raucous singing. I went back to sleep.

I woke up again at 4am. Kate wasn't in bed besides me. I padded into the living room, the lights were all on but there was no one there.

I found both her and Snoopy on the sofa in the TV room. They were both asleep. I turned the TV off.

I couldn't wake Kate, but Snoopy followed me back to bed.

The next day I went to Pilates on my own!

I had made breakfast of bacon and the new eggs. They are smaller than normal ones, rather like bantam eggs, and the shells are coloured white to light blue, rather than the normal brown ones. The taste is the same, but I am sure they are better for me.

Sitting in my office I have a fine view of the River Guayas. There are flat-bottomed river boats moving up and downstream. They are the ferries for the shrimp farms. They go downstream carrying trucks loaded with shrimp food from the factories in Duran to the shrimp farms located on islands or the river banks.

They return with large plastic tanks filled with ice and harvested shrimps. They take them back to Duran where packing plants are situated.

There the shrimp are packed for export, either headless or head-on. Some are shelled completely and packed directly for sale in the supermarkets of the world.

Today Ecuador is the biggest shrimp exporter in the world.

I have just seen figures. In 2009 Ecuador exported 300 million pounds of shrimp, in 2023 it was 2,700 million pounds (Americans like to work in pounds).

There are a few white to grey clouds over the river. They are not yet the black rain-bearing clouds. Those will come in December. But the very presence of clouds is encouraging. The annual rains are on their way. Winter is coming.

Fredy reported that he went through a shower on his way to Manabi yesterday.

The temperature is rising too.

During the dry summer months from May to September, the temperature in Guayaquil is from 23 to 29 degrees centigrade.

The thermometer in my car now shows 26 degrees in the morning and 33 when I return from work.

We sat out on the balcony of our flat last night and had our glass of wine. It's still pleasantly warm, after the sun has gone down.

For the last few days my chest has been itching. The temptation is to scratch it. If I do so then little bits of skin slough off. Kate told me to apply hydrating cream, not just once a day but several times. I do and that helps.

But we both know that I am in denial. Sooner or later we have to return to see Dr Jose Maria. It's been three months since he gave me the all clear in August. Shaking his hand in gratitude I asked when I should return to see him.

He replied whenever you are worried.

Today I called him and got an appointment with his secretary for 4.30pm.

There were several people in his waiting room, but we were called in immediately.

"Hello Colin and Kate, what can I do for you?"

Kate took over. She unbuttoned my shirt and showed him the red blotches, and an angry-looking spot.

He asked me to remove the shirt and lie on the operating table. He pointed the reading lamp at my chest, and put in his eyeglass.

"Well the cancer has returned. There must have been some roots left beneath the skin. But it's not as bad as last time. Let's say 30%. The spot is not dangerous. It's a small infection, you must have scratched it.

So once again you have three options. All three are painful, you have to choose."

On the grounds of the devil you know, we opted for Imiquimoid.

He agreed with us. It will take up to sixty days to treat. We still have six small tubes of it from last time. I asked him to prescribe Diprogenta, which gives relief when the pain is too much, as well as something for the spot.

Then Kate asked him to look at the other cancer spot on my head. He did, and said that it looked much better. This he can treat today with liquid nitrogen.

Well OK. Let's get it over with. Kate held my hand as the freezing blast was applied twice.

I am well stocked with paracetamol. Here we go again.

I suppose I have to admit that the whole cancer thing began in Rodeo Grande. For many years, before it manifested itself, I rode with an open-neck shirt. Two hours in direct sunlight every week. So if it kills me. I will have died for love of my ranch.

After that we went home. At least I have faced up to it. Last time he said sixty days, but we went back to him in forty-five and the job was done, or so we thought at the time.

I had an odd idea that by doing Pilates I would somehow improve my resistance to skin cancer. All the wonderful endorphins of adrenaline, dopamine, testosterone and oxytocin would ride to my rescue. I have done twenty hours of Pilates so far, but it doesn't appear to have helped. I live in hope.

While at the doctor's Kate had pointed out my swollen ankles. It happens at the end of the working day. It is clearly not his field of medicine, but he recommended that I get my blood pressure checked, and depending on the results I might need to wear support stockings. He pulled up his trouser leg to show that he uses them.

Otherwise I should walk about in the office, or put my feet up on the desk.

That would look a trifle laid back to my troops!

He suggested that I see a cardiologist to check out my heart.

He warned against eating salt. Well Kate is already on to that. So sadly no salt on my chips. But I am allowed chili peppers. I got addicted to them when I lived in Mexico. Bandurria makes a really hot chili hot sauce and I ask them for a jar from time to time to eat at home.

So yet another doctor's appointment is lined up.

We got in touch with the cardiologist Dr Alex Rossi. We knew him as he had done our checkups prior to going to Antarctica.

He kindly came to the flat. After taking my blood pressure several times (with oddly differing results) he made a list of the blood and urine tests I should have, also a pelvic doppler scan and an electrocardiogram. He said that the swelling might involve just my lower legs, or there could be a problem with my heart or kidneys.

Hang on there, I thought it was just a case of support stockings!

As we say in Yorkshire, old age is a bugger, but the alternative is worse.

A week has gone by. Kate applies the acid cream to my chest every night. So far so good, there is still no pain. I wear the elastic, knee-length support stockings. They have made a big difference. My shoes go on so much easier than before.

I have not yet done the tests. Putting off the evil moment.

Last night we were invited to the Christmas Nutcracker ballet by the owners of one of the large supermarket groups. The invitation came for Mr and Mrs Armstrong.

Kate enjoys ballet so we went. I have been to this sort of event many times before. It normally involves the good and the great, the Consular Corp and upmarket personalities.

I put on a suit and tie and Kate a long, light blue dress. I wondered if friends of my wife would acknowledge Kate.

But it wasn't at all as I expected. I was the only one in a tie. The theatre holds a thousand people, and while not full, there was a reasonable crowd. There were only half a dozen people who I knew, and they all came to say hello.

The ballet itself was wonderful and perfectly performed. The cast is composed of guest professional dancers, the Arts University and En Avant, the Guayaquil ballet school. There are some wonderful children who are just beginning lessons. One tiny girl of about five, fell over. There was a collective Ooh! from the audience.

There was enthusiastic applause, I suspect in good part it was from the proud mums and dads there.

We went to our new house on Friday evening to meet with the architects. Now, at last, we can see progress. The ripping out of units has finished and the new ones are ready to be put in. The back-up generator is installed. It runs off gas, and we are told won't be too noisy.

We await municipal permission to build the jacuzzi, but it's expected next week.

They said that they hope to have the house 90% finished by the end of December. But that came with a rider, as long as they have the funds in time. The estimated price, as always happens, is now twice what the original one was. Well we can't stop now. So I will put hand to pocket next week.

Once we finished at the house, I invited Juan Gabriel and Sebastian to have dinner with us at our favourite Spanish restaurant nearby. We have been friends for years. I felt that I was out of order to criticize them when we got back from Madrid, and wanted to make it up. We laughed a lot and enjoyed dinner.

By coincidence I saw Gustavo, the Agripac managing director, walking outside with his wife Paola, she is their sister. I signalled them to come in.

It was not only them but my personal lawyer Alfredo and his wife Rocio, the parents of Juan Gabriel and Sebastian. We said hello, but they couldn't stay, they were going elsewhere. All the family was here bar one. He is Alfredo Jr, who is an Agripac director and legal counsel.

A real family business.

I have only had five managing directors in the fifty-three years of Agripac, apart from Ceci who from time to time was the second legal representative with me. But with our young family she couldn't work full time.

Mario was my partner at the beginning. Then came Elena, Chris, Nick M and finally Gustavo, the best of them all.

As he is in his fifties he will be the link from one generation of Armstrong to the next.

Chris retired and now lives in London. His youngest daughter Marna works with us in Alex's area of the business. Today she came in tears to tell Alex that her father had had a serious operation. We pray for his recovery. And we hear two weeks later that all is well.

There are several people working in the company who are descended from my group of friends at the time I arrived in Ecuador. Martin is the son of Stanley Wright, my best friend for many years, until his death. Jorge Hidalgo is the grandson of my good friend Godfrey Berry and James is the son of George McCracken. Then of course there is Jordy Molina, Simon de Montfort's godson.

They are all English speaking (as well as Spanish obviously). The lingua franca of the company board is English.

Jorge Cepeda once worked for the French chemical company Rhone Poulenc. He said that the directors had to speak English in meetings. That must have offended French sensibilities.

This week we are repeating the meeting of our two hundred shop managers. The same as we did last June. But now it's pre-season. Nick has made a promotion in which we raffle three pickup trucks and twenty-six motorbikes. We want to explain this to the managers in person and get their feedback.

Once again I have asked Geronimo Alcivar, the shops supremo, to tell the lads not to overdo the handshakes. They seem to think the firmer the handshake the better the friendship. My poor hands suffer. There is no problem with the lady managers, just a kiss on the cheek.

We have three days of meetings here in the head office and then we fly to Quito and Cuenca to cover the Sierra and Oriente shops.

We need an excellent December to recover from a very slack year.

But we rely on St Peter, who is thought here to be the rain bringer. It always rains at this time of year. If it starts in December then it's an excellent end to the year. If in January that's another year.

After the meeting we had a group photo with one of the motorbikes. I had to be the clown who straddled it, pretending to ride it, while one after the other our lady managers got up behind me. It took all my new found leg muscles to keep the wretched bike from toppling over.

Yesterday Kate got her new Colombian passport. In her case it was a simple trip to the consulate in Guayaquil. That used to be the way the British did it too, when I was first Consul. Now some bright spark has ruled that it can only be done in the UK (though I believe online too). Issuing of passports has been taken away from the Foreign and Commonwealth Office and given to the Home Office. Which by definition doesn't have much overseas coverage.

We went once again to Pilates. Every time the coach asks me if there are any after effects. Today I tell him yes, my backside aches. He replies that is from the liga. It's an elastic band around both thighs. You stretch it and release, so working your bum. Well I hope to improve it!

We did a lot of stretching of the spine. He told me that I will be taller for doing it.

Intrigued by this, I bought a tape measure and measured myself on the office wall.

It came out as six foot one and a half inches. I might yet get back to the original 6 foot two.

Jorge Cepeda is back in town. We are going to have dinner with him. We went home to change. But today there is no electricity until the mains come on at 8pm. Finally the heroic old generator has given up the ghost. The administration is buying a new one. Each flat owner will have to pay $2,000 towards it. Luckily, that's for our landlady to pay. Though we have been billed each month for the diesel for running it.

With no electricity, Kate can't finish ironing her hair. Let's go to the new house. We have heard that our generator is now installed and functioning. Anyway it's closer to where we are meeting Jorge for dinner.

As we get near to the new house we see dozens of iguanas on the communal lawns. They are lovely to see. We used to have a lot of them in Rodeo Grande. The young ones are green and the bigger, older chaps are yellow to brown. They can measure up to three feet long. If threatened by people or dogs they leap into the water. They can swim remarkably well.

Yes, indeed the generator is working. We can hear it as we park the car outside the house. We happily go around switching on lights. We can't try the air conditioning units as they are all disconnected. There is nowhere to sit. All our furniture is covered in plastic and dust. Kate had to stand to finish her hair. We didn't stay long. It's almost 7 pm when we are due to meet Jorge in an Italian restaurant.

Normally our escort sits at an outside table of the restaurant, and we send the menu out to them. So they eat what they choose (at my expense). But today we have Snoopy with us. Dogs are not allowed in the area where the restaurant is. So the guards have to take turns. One walks him in the car park and the other eats. It's on my conscience that we have eaten out Saturday, Sunday and Monday. These are long days for them, and they miss their weekends. But when we leave the country they can use these extra holiday entitlements.

Kate is back in touch with her friend Olga. There had been a cooling in the friendship since we ducked out of her party. Today they talked on the phone for two hours. Poor Olga has a dilemma. Her mother is ill, possibly she is dying. Olga wants to go back to Ukraine to see her. But it's not easy. Because of the Russians bombing Kiev, the airport is closed. If she goes she will have to fly to Warsaw and take a train, all of twenty hours to Kiev. Then take a bus six more hours to where her family live. Bombs are falling all over, it would not be a safe journey.

Kate and she are going to meet on Thursday, when I am in Quito. Kate tells me that this will be the first night we have not slept together since we became a couple last January.

Before that of course we were apart more nights than we were together.

Fredy has driven past Rodeo Grande. He sent us a sad photo of uprooted trees. But for the moment they have had to stop knocking them down. There is an investigation by the Environmental Ministry. Last year my daughter Alex was working with them to establish Rodeo Grande as a carbon sink to offset Agripac's footprint.

I guess that it's because of this that they have made an inspection and found a great number of the trees have been felled.

I don't suppose the order will stop them for long.

After the meeting today with the shop managers Nick took me aside to tell me that he had heard from our lawyer that three of the remaining six men in prison for our kidnap (two have been murdered, one died of natural causes) have been sentenced to seventeen years in prison. The other three have been released, as there is insufficient evidence against them. That is the good news. The bad news is that the state prosecutor has had a death threat from the Tigerones, and has left the country for a while.

Our family has been warned to take even more precautions.

It's been almost a year now, will it never stop?

The big season is about to come for Agripac. But it hasn't yet started raining. Rather as in the last World War, the first weeks are the phony war, nothing happens.

To fill the time I am consuming books.

The latest is called The Six, by Laura Thompson.

It's the story of the six extraordinary Mitford sisters. They were born between 1904 (Nancy) and 1920 (Deborah), the daughters of David, second Baron Redesdale and his wife Sydney Bowles. Their father was against formal education for girls, so they had governesses at home. Despite this they were remarkably well read.

Nancy became a well-known author. Pamela became the wife of a country squire. Diana married the leader of the British Fascist party Sir Oswald Mosley. They were both imprisoned during the World War as Nazi sympathizers. Unity became a friend and confidant of Hitler. She tried to commit suicide when war broke out.

Jessica married a communist and emigrated to America. The youngest, Deborah, married the heir to the Duke of Devonshire. She was the least keen on education.

Even when grown up she was teased by her intellectual sisters as having a mental age of nine.

But she achieved a great deal in her lifetime, and outlived them all, dying at the age of ninety-four in 2014.

Her achievement is Chatsworth House and estate, in Derbyshire.

When her husband Andrew inherited the title of Duke of Devonshire in 1955, post-war death duties were in force. They were draconian. Eighty per cent of the estate had to be sold to pay them.

Their stately home, Chatsworth House, with its one hundred and seventy rooms, had been a boarding school during the war, and was in very poor shape.

Deborah set herself the task of bringing the house back to life, as near to its glory days as she could. Then she opened it again to the public.

She achieved her dream. I have been there. It's a wonderful place.

A Noel Coward song comes to mind:

The Stately Homes of England,
How beautifully they stand,
To prove the upper classes have still the upper hand;
Though the fact that they have to be rebuilt
And frequently mortgaged to the hilt
Is inclined to take the gilt
Off the gingerbread.

Saturday 7th December

I am back from Quito and Cuenca. It's been an excellent trip. We met ninety more shop managers and made our presentation.

I have to say that I am really proud of Nick. He has taken the lead all the way through this programme. It was originally my idea to do a promotion, raffling five cars. I handed it to him in October. Then heard little more. I was rather anxious that it would not be well put together.

But I stand corrected. The prizes were changed to three cars and twenty-six motorbikes, so that we can raffle two bikes each week, thereby generating more interest.

He contacted our main suppliers as sponsors, who covered a large part of the cost.

I made my contribution at the end of each session adding to the promotion extra credit for those who invoice in December, rather than January.

It's been well received. The troops are enthusiastic. I may add that my reputation as the rain bringer is intact. It rained both in Quito and Cuenca while we were there. I got an applause for that.

It's been a feature of my travels to visit the shops pre-season every year. But as we do it in December and January, the rains normally start anyway!

After finishing in Quito and taking the obligatory group photo, Jaime, the Quito area manager, drove us to the airport. We were in plenty of time for the flight to Cuenca so we went to a bar and shared two bottles of an Argentinian Malbec wine, called Enemigo.

Cuenca stands at 2,500 meters above sea level. It's an attractive city built of red brick with red pantile roofs. It has a mild climate and is home to many thousand Americans who retire here, looking for a cheaper place to live. It has five rivers which all drain to the east. On these rivers stand two of Ecuador's most important hydroelectric dams, Paute and Mazar. So rain in Cuenca is of great importance to the electricity supply for Ecuador.

Hopefully the power cuts will now be less.

My relationship with Nick sadly had been one of rivalry since he joined the company. We spent ten years scoring points off each other.

But I have to admit it he has now become the stronger of the two.

The old silverback gorilla is about to be supplanted in the troop!

Alex too works in Agripac. Her domain of Corporate Responsibility, brings us less into conflict, if only because I don't understand it as well as I do sales.

My two inlaws, Almu and Javi, handling personnel and production are fine.

It's only with my children that I competed.

After our meeting in Cuenca yesterday I went with Nick and Geronimo to visit a factory which makes meat products. They have a large herd of pigs and produce hams, sausages and cuts of cold meats.

We recently made a contract with them to supply dog food.

Like Agripac it's a family company. We met the founder and his wife, both sons and their wives who all work together, in apparent harmony.

We toured the factory to see how the products are made.

I was nervous about this after being lectured by their head of health and safety, who said that to visit the factory we would have to change our clothes, shower and put on overalls to prevent contamination. I have done this before when visiting a food factory, and it's a slow process.

I looked at my watch, we only have an hour before we have to be at the airport for our flight to Guayaquil.

But it wasn't so bad. We were only required to put on a white coat over our clothes, and a plastic cover on our heads. The walkway was above the factory floor and we looked down through windows.

That also shielded us from the smells.

I have a weak stomach for organic smells. I have visited slaughter houses for cattle, pigs and chickens. On each occasion it was all I could do to avoid vomiting.

On the other hand I have no problem with chemical smells in our Laquinsa factory, where others have difficulties.

While waiting for the flight from Cuenca to Guayaquil, we had a beer at the airport.

We heard the first Christmas carol of the season. I always enjoy the first one, and then rapidly get tired of them.

It reminded me of the first one I heard two years ago. It was the year before the kidnap.

At that time I could still travel to visit the shops. Albeit with protection.

I didn't want to have an escort. I thought it unnecessary. But the family insisted. Kate and I drove to Manabi in my BMW, and two armed men followed us in a pickup. To me it was a joke and we played the game of trying to lose them by driving fast in restricted areas.

In fact we got pulled over by the traffic police while doing so. Then we saw the advantage of the guards. They told us to keep driving. They sorted it out with the police.

We were going to Plan Maize.

It was an annual event at Colon, before the planting season in Manabi. Agripac put up marquees, and invited a thousand small farmers and their wives. We gave them beer and lunch while we displayed our wares for the season. We showed them the latest maize hybrids which we recommend for their area, and explained how we can give them credit until harvest, which is the only way some of them can plant, as there are few government bank loans for farmers today.

Then there was a show with live music and dancing. Kate, as our calendar girl and hostess, held a fashion show for the ladies present and handed prizes to the winners.

Next to our shop and warehouse in Colon stands Proman, owned by my great friend Simon de Montfort. We have been in partnership for many years. Proman is dedicated to multiplying maize and rice seed for Agripac.

After the event we stayed with Simon. He has a lovely house and indoor swimming pool.

Simon is an Englishman whose roots go back to Ireland and before then to France. His forbears were Huguenots who left France after religious persecution in the sixteenth century.

He came to Ecuador as a forestry expert with British Overseas Aid after taking degrees at both London and Oxford. Then, like me, he stayed and set up his own business.

He never married but has helped his three godsons with their education. One of them Jordy, who graduated from London University, works in Agripac.

We enjoyed dinner together, that was where we heard the first carol of the season. We recounted old times and for Kate's benefit he told stories about Sri Lanka. He had grown up there as his father was a government official.

I haven't seen Simon since then. He is nervous about coming to Guayaquil and I am prohibited from going to Manabi. Hopefully one day that will change. We correspond regularly and I forward him the Economist each week after I have read it. We both prefer the paper edition as opposed to online.

The flight from Cuenca was on time and we arrived in Guayaquil. My escort was waiting and I drove home to the flat at 7.30pm.

Kate had a lot to tell me. Despite being heartbroken that I had left her, she had filled the time happily. She had lunch with Olga and Janina, she had sent photos of the three of them together. Last night she had gone to a disco, Ventos, with Karen, her pole dancing teacher, her husband Frank and brother Orlando. She had got home at 4am today and slept until midday.

She said that she had really enjoyed Ventos. She used to go there a lot, but I am not a disco man, and was rather jealous of the men she met there, so banned it. She told me she had seen a lot of friends.

I protested that she had kept our security detail with her until 4am. She said yes, but she hadn't needed them at all today, until they collected me from the airport.

She was watching Two and a Half Men on TV. I can't watch shows that have canned laughter after each line. She kindly asked what I wanted to see. I was sleepy but suggested we watch part of the Wagner opera Lowengrin. I told her that the famous wedding march comes from it.

I had forgotten that it's in the second half of the opera. So even though I fast-forwarded to show her it, she was asleep on the sofa before I got there.

In fact it's not the wedding march so much as the bedding march. It takes place after the wedding of Lohengrin and Elsa. The court escorts them to their bridal chamber and then the ladies help them to remove their outer clothing, before leaving them to get on with it.

The DVD was recorded at the Bayreuther Festpiele in 1982.

Lohengrin is sung by Peter Hofmann and Elsa by Karan Armstrong (I have never heard of her before. A long lost relative ?).

Today, Saturday, I am in the office catching up on work after two days out of the office.

Alex called me to come to Bandurria to say hello to the Juconi children at their Christmas party. Juconi is a charity run by Rocio Torres MBE, my sister-in-law and British Vice Consul of many years, both with myself and now with Nick. Her two daughters work with Agripac, Maria del Mar here and Daniela in Peru.

Juconi was founded by a British lady, Sarah Benitez and her Mexican husband Thomas, in 1995. Today Rocio is the director. The aim of the charity is to save children from broken homes from working in the streets and not going to school. The charity helps the family on condition that the parents allow their children to attend school. Over the years they have many success stories. There are Juconi kids with university degrees who tell the new ones what they can achieve, if only they study.

We traditionally invited 250 children and their volunteer helpers to Rodeo Grande each December.

There they could ride horses, play football, dance, paint pictures and have games. We gave them lunch and provided them with a takeaway for their families. We had seen that they ate little and saved food to take home. So now they can both eat and have something for their parents.

I was surprised how many of these town kids knew how to ride a horse. But, of course, they are not long removed from the countryside. They are products of the mass migration from the countryside to the towns which has gone on since before I got to Ecuador and continues today. In 1972 Guayaquil had only half a million inhabitants, today it has three and a half million. Back then 70% of Ecuador's population was rural, today it's 30%.

By contrast only 1% of Britain's population are farmers.

But of course Rodeo Grande has gone. I didn't go to Bandurria and join in today. There is no way to do it quickly. I would have to give a few minutes speech. The kids would want photos with me. The Juconi people would want to thank me.

I was rushed with work and I had to go to Pilates, so I missed it for the first time in many years.

I saw the photo today of the 250 kids sitting on the floor of Bandurria looking up as the group photo was taken from above. There are tables and chairs in the car park for lunch. They won't all fit into Bandurria.

I asked Maria Dolores later how it had gone. She said it went well, but the kids missed Rodeo Grande with its riding and football. Yet more collateral damage.

In Colombia the 7th December is called the Night of Candles. It's a festival to celebrate the patron saint Maria del Carmen. Families light candles and put them in front of their houses. They take all the chairs they have and put them outside. Neighbours visit each other and hospitality is given. Each person can ask seven wishes from the saint.

Kate decided that we should celebrate it. We went to Supermaxi and bought Christmas hats and pyjamas with the picture of the Grinch on them. For those not in the know, Grinch is a cartoon character who hates Christmas. We have watched the film several times. He does his best to ruin Christmas for children. We nicknamed Snoopy Grinch last year, as three times when we left him alone he pulled over the Christmas tree and damaged the ornaments.

Today he was made to wear his Grinch outfit too.

A typical Colombian treat that day is buñuelos. They are a type of sweet pancake. I followed Kate up and down the shelves of flour, looking for the right one. There was wheat flour, maize flour, bean flour and more. She wasn't sure which one to use. So I called Margarita and passed her the phone. After some time she rang off and told me that the recipe was too complicated. We will get takeaway buñuelos from a Colombian restaurant.

We bought lots of candles and cardboard plates to stand them on, and two bottles of Aguardiente, Colombian firewater. Finally we bought a speaker for her cellphone so that Kate can amplify her Colombian music.

Tonight we are noisy neighbours!

On getting back to the flat we lit thirty candles and stood them on the balcony. We dressed ourselves and Snoopy in pyjamas. Kate had bought pixey slippers with turned-up toes from which hung a woolly bobble. She had to fight off Snoopy who took to trying to remove the bobble.

Then Janina and Joanna arrived. I opened a bottle of Aguardiente. Viva la Fiesta.

Sunday. I awoke still dressed as Grinch at 7am. My escort was already waiting in the car outside the flat. I am normally on time for them, but today no way. I sent a WhatsApp to say I needed a few minutes, but it was an hour before I finally made it to my car. I could have slept on of course. But Sundays I like to go to the office and continue this book.

What I shall do on Sundays once it's finished, I don't know.

On the office floor I saw what I thought was a cockroach. Looking closer, before stepping on it, I saw it was a grillo. They are crickets.

So they have arrived. They come in swarms every year. The eggs were laid in the last wet season in the earth of the countryside. With the first new rains they hatch. As soon as they can fly they make for the city lights.

You can see them in the streets, black masses around street lights. They used to be much worse and cars would skid on them. Today the streets are fumigated before they can massify.

We went to the new house on Saturday. There is some progress with the builders, but not enough.

We decided that we needed a deadline.

I texted Juan Gabriel to say that we want to hold a Christmas party for Kate's family and friends in the house, on the 23rd December. For that we need the sitting room, kitchen and at least one toilet to be finished.

He replied at once that he will do his best. We will meet next Friday and see what that surprise announcement has achieved.

I got home at 2pm. Kate was watching TV. Neither of us felt like eating or being sociable. We were still nursing hangovers. I had to collect and throw out the cardboard trays on which the candles had stood on the balcony. Snoopy had already gnawed three of them.

I sat on the balcony with a beer (hair of the dog) and finished my book The Beekeeper of Aleppo by Christy Lefteri. She had worked in Athens as a volunteer among the refugees from Syria during the civil war there, which raged between 2011 to 2023. From her experiences at that time she has written this moving account of a refugee couple trying to reach Britain.

The Syrian president, Bashar al-Assad, cruelly destroyed his own cities and people to ensure his survival, with help from Russia.

Today's newspaper tells me that the insurgents have suddenly regrouped and in just twelve days they have taken Damascus. Bashar al-Assad has fled to Russia. It's the end of a fifty-year dictatorship of the al-Assad family.

This is a great loss of prestige to Vladimir Putin, after having backed al-Assad for many years.

The US President, Joe Biden, said that with so much loss of men and armaments in Ukraine, Russia can no longer afford to get involved in Syria.

Ceci is now back from Los Angeles, where she stayed with Diana, Steve and family. She has been away for a month. She has travelled a lot this year, I suspect that I am the cause of it.

We met for lunch yesterday at Bandurria. It was lovely to see her. She was pleased to see the changes we have made to the stage. It lets in much more light, and the new area serves for extra tables in the restaurant, when there is no opera.

She kindly asked about my new house. I told her that we are not living there yet. We still have the builders in. She asked why there was so much work to do, as it is a comparatively new house. I replied that Kate wants things changed, rather than using the previous owners' items.

She enquired about the Rodeo Grande furniture, and said that it won't look right in a modern house. I explained that we are using more wood fittings and painting the doors brown to change it from modern to more rustic.

She asked if I had the Rodeo dinner service. I replied no. I have given it to Cristina. She exclaimed that it was an expensive set, why didn't I keep it.

But the fact is at the time I was overwhelmed by selling the ranch. I wasn't even going to keep the furniture. So when Christina asked for it I gave it to her without a second thought.

Diana has bought me three books on Amazon. Ceci carried them here. I now have twenty up front to read. That should take me through until we leave the country again next March.

I have done nothing about all the tests required by Dr Alex. It's been two weeks since he asked for them. Last week I was occupied with the shops. This week I can't think of an excuse.

Yesterday Kate insisted that we get them done. We went to a clinic at 7am, when it was just opening so as to be the first in the queue. The receptionist added up the tests to be done and we paid for them. There was one they couldn't do, it is the Echocardiogram. Their machine is not operative. We will have to go elsewhere for that.

We were led to a small room where a nurse took blood samples. There were a lot of tests so he had to fill four syringes with blood. He got three and then the vein seemed to empty. So I had to stand a second jab in another vein. Kate held my hand.

The urine sample is easier.

That was all for now. The Doppler scan can't be done until 11am.

So we went to the office. Kate left me there to go to her gym. She returned before eleven and we drove back to the clinic. The Doppler machinery requires near zero temperature. The doctor was accustomed to working in it, I was not. I lay on the operating table shivering. It took more than half an hour to do it. But the results seem to be OK.

That's all for today. We asked Dr Alex to book another clinic so we can complete the heart scan.

Kate and I had words the other day. Among other complaints was that of all the photos in my office there was not one of us together. There are photos of Ceci and I, and of myself outside the palace of Holyrood House in Edinburgh, when I received my CMG. There are photos of the children and grandchildren, but none of Kate and I. I guess I didn't want to cause more trouble by putting our photos there, especially when the relationship was still a secret.

Now it doesn't matter.

I suggested we go back through the thousands of holiday photos we have and enlarge the best one. But that doesn't work. Photos taken with a cell phone can't be enlarged without distortion, something to do with pixels.

So we need professional photos. We have some of these. There was a photographer aboard the Queen Mary II. We have a pen drive of them. I took my laptop home and we looked at them. But we didn't find what we are looking for. Although there is my favourite photo of myself. Not sure how he did it. I have a sort of Noel Coward look. Slightly supercilious.

We had bought a new Sony camera before going to Italy. She found a memory chip from her previous camera when it stopped working. Now she plugged it in to the new one. Lo and behold we have hundreds of photos which we can enlarge. We spent a long time looking at them. There are so many memories. We forgot about choosing one and just looked at them all. Today we will choose the best.

She will give it to me for Christmas in a silver frame.

I don't often meet my customers face to face. I leave that to Nick to do. I always found that it is better to keep a distance, as I am the ultimate authority on credit. Nick can always say that he is sorry but Colin has decreed that the debt must be paid before extending more credit. Face to face I can’t appeal to anyone.

But yesterday I had a meeting with a big customer from Manabi province. He is offended that we sent his name to the credit buro as a defaulter. True he was six months late in paying us. But of course he has a dozen reasons why.

Jacinto, the area manager, asked me to invite him to lunch at the Union Club to kiss and make up.

I did, and it was successful. He will buy from us this coming season, after vowing never to buy again.

But, after a lot of wine, I was feeling sleepy when we went to meet Juan Gabriel and Sebastian at the new house. Today we begin to see progress. The large piece of furniture to hold the TV in the sitting room is there, but not yet assembled. Most of the doors are painted brown, the new loos and basins are fitted in the bathrooms, and the hole for the jacuzzi has been dug in the patio.

They promise to have the sitting room ready for the family party on the 23rd.

I have bought a real pine Christmas tree from a market garden in Quito. I asked Jaime to truck it to Guayaquil this week. It's been a long time since I enjoyed the smell of a real tree. Today they are mostly artificial. Of course they don't last long, but I wanted it for the 23rd. Our first Christmas together.

So home for supper. Then Cristina called me. She has lost her job in what used to be Rodeo Grande. I suspected she wouldn't last long after the cattle were sold. She was brave about it, but after Christmas will have to interview for a new job. We chatted to her and to Mati and made jokes to cheer them up. I half offered her a job in Agripac. But she said no. She is not cut out for sales.

She said that Ciprano and the cowboys will soon be out too. They can't adapt to being banana workers.

So my relief at their being taken on by the new owner was short-lived. I became emotional, and broke a wine glass, yet another one gone.

Reading today's newspaper I see that six members of the Lobos mafia have been sentenced to seventeen years in prison. One more victory for law and order.

I also saw that Ramon Barranco is retiring after thirteen years as director of the Sanchez Aguilar theatre in Guayaquil. He has produced over thirty shows in that time, including the Nutcracker ballet. His last production will be Snow, a Christmas fantasy.

He used to come to my operas. I joked that the director of Ecuador's largest theatre, with a thousand seats, condescends to visit the smallest with only a hundred.

But perhaps one day we will grow. The magnificent Glyndebourne opera house, near Lewes in England, began as a stage in a private house in 1920, with a hundred seats. Today it stands by itself, a purpose-built opera house.

I have been there three times with Ceci over the years. The program begins at 5pm, which allows a break of an hour for a full dinner in their Wallop restaurant. Guests arrive early and picnic on the lawn before it starts.

We took the early afternoon train from London, dressed in evening clothes. Which got a few strange looks, until once on the train we saw we were far from the only ones dressed up.

It's the Glyndebourne train.

Sunday 15th December. As usual I come into the office in the morning. On a Sunday, transit police put cones down one side of the road to provide a safe passage for the cyclists and joggers. There are a lot out this morning either singly, in twos or in groups.

Every time Kate is with me in the car she puts on her own music. When alone I switch back to opera. I have eight operas on a pen drive, providing twenty hours of music. They are played at random. I try to guess which opera it is before looking at the title on the screen.

They are La Traviata, Lakme, La Forza del Destino, Tales of Hoffman, Ernani, La Gioconda, Andre Chenin and Romeo y Julieta.

Today Monday 16th December, it's a year since the kidnap. I have been allowed one more year of life.

The last time that I met my uncle Stuart he was living in Evelyn Gardens, Chelsea.

He had sold Manor Farm, Rockbourne. I was recently married, so it must have been about 1975, I took Ceci to meet him. He prepared us lunch at home wearing his striped butcher's apron. He declared "If I am spared, I will be eighty-two years old come Michaelmas". Sadly he wasn't spared, he died that year.

To the family's great surprise he left a widow. He had been a bachelor until his last years, then had secretly married the widow of his best friend.

In my case, "If I am spared I will be eighty years old come Michaelmas".

Fredy sent us a WhatsApp yesterday with photos of the last supper in Rodeo on the 15th December last year. How happy we all looked. It was the end of the age of innocence. One year later I have no ranch. Many of my beloved trees have been knocked down. The cattle and horses have gone and Cristina has lost her job.

The electricity continues to come and go. I wondered what would happen if I was in the office lift at the moment that the mains electricity goes off and the generators come on. There is a gap of several minutes. Today I found out. I arrived at 7am, got in the lift and then there was a blackout. I was suspended between floors. Resisting an impulse to call someone, I waited, the light returned. I stepped out at the fifth floor.

It happens several times a day, which is annoying if I am in the middle of doing something on the laptop. After the light returns there is a further delay until the internet is restored.

The President has stated that there will be no power cuts at Christmas. Remember there are elections in February. We mustn't spoil Christmas for the voters.

The rider to that is that industry will be cut off totally for fifteen days. Once again there is panic and lobbying by the Chamber of Industries. Today I see the government has partially backed down. They have sacrificed the biggest electricity users, the cement factory, mines and steel furnaces will close for two weeks.

Christmas is getting near. Our Pilates coach will be away from next week until the first week of January. We have one last session today, it is my twenty-ninth. We have become good friends with him. He confided that his wife is four months pregnant. We congratulated him. It's their first one. It will be the first grandchild for both their parents and will make his grandparents great grandparents. He will find out in January if it's a boy or girl.

(He has just told us, it's a boy).

Kate looked dreamy. I know she would like to have a baby one day.

Today we had a new exercise called jumping. It's done horizontally. A board is placed at the end of the former. Then you push against it and the springs to jump with both legs, and then with one leg at a time holding the other in the air. While not difficult it's like cardio, it leaves you breathless.

When we finish at 4pm there is always the same man who has the following class. He is in his sixties. He told us that he comes to Pilates following a serious operation. He has to lose weight.

We always say hello to him. Today he told us that he collects stickers and showed me one of myself, with me wearing my cowboy hat.

I asked Kate how on earth he could get that. She replied that there are thousands available. She showed me another one of myself which came out last January. It has my photo and the caption 'Colin is free.'

I have been back to see Dr Jose Maria. Kate was busy, so I went alone. He looked at my chest and was satisfied that we are on the right course. I told him that it doesn't hurt at all, despite a month's application of the cream. He reasoned that it is such a small area to treat and that the skin now is thicker than it was before. All to the good.

He asked me a strange question "What did you do in World War Two?"

"Very little, I was only born in 1945!"

Had I been in the armed forces I would be approaching a hundred by now.

Do I look a hundred?

Then he said that he had just seen the Churchill film The Darkest Hour. We talked about it and the fight Churchill had in cabinet to avoid a government motion to approach Hitler and offer terms. It was touch and go, half the cabinet, many upper class people, including most of the Mitford family, were in favour of it. If that had happened, today we would be a small part of the German Reich.

'Ich bin ein Engländer. '

Kate has the results of my blood and urine tests. She knows a lot more about this than I do.

She says that my cholesterol level is too high. I need to cut out fried breakfasts. I will wait for the doctor to confirm it. I have the heart scan this afternoon and then we can meet Dr Alex again. Or maybe leave it until after Christmas, if I am facing a restricted diet!

Kate has already banned my standby, Alka Seltzer, as it contains aspirin. Now I have to take Andrews Liver Salts, which apparently don't.

A sign of the approaching New Year in Ecuador is that you see the Años Viejos in the street. There are now two outside the office block. They are papier mache figures of a person or animal. They are burnt on New Year's Eve, supposedly to get rid of the bad things of last year. The real purpose is to beg for funds to celebrate the New Year with a party. I always donate to the office ones, it's expected. The guards got me at the entrance to our flat tonight. I gave them a sub. They have looked after us for nine months.

There is another custom too, called las Viudas, the widows. This is a man in drag with exaggerated boobs and backside. They approach people in the street crying that they are the widows of the old year, left destitute and asking for donations.

All good fun.

I have a dilemma. With whom to celebrate Christmas? Kate's family is arriving on Monday from Colombia. The idea is to go to a rented house by the beach on the 24th.

If I go with them it will be our first Christmas together. But what about my own family?

Nick, Almu and their kids have already left for Madrid to spend Christmas with her mother.

Diana, Steve and the boys are coming here from Los Angeles. She, Alex and Ceci made it clear that I should be with them and my grandchildren for Christmas dinner, in Ceci's house. I can't be in both places at the same time, they are two hours apart.

I asked Kate. She generously conceded that I could be with my own family, rather than hers, for Christmas. Then drive to the beach on Christmas day.

So that is decided.

Thursday 19th December. Her sister Luisa arrived from Madrid last night. We met her with Janina at the airport.

There is a handy stall there which sells 'Welcome Home' balloons as well as flowers. Kate bought a purple balloon. Luisa was soon out with her luggage. She loved her balloon. We drove back to our flat. Tomorrow she and Janina will head for Montañita for three days. It's a beach resort noted for discos and wild parties. The smell of marihuana hangs over it.

Reputedly it's one of the only two places in Ecuador recommended for young travellers in Lonely Planet, the other being Baños. I don't suppose there will be many foreigners there this year, with Ecuador's bad publicity.

But tonight we will drink together. The party went well, or I think it did. There are five empty wine bottles in the kitchen this morning.

I stayed until the food arrived. We had ordered bandeja paisa, a famous Colombian mixed grill with pork crackling, arepas and beans.

After eating, the talk was between the three girls. I was out of it.

I crept away to the TV room and finished the evening watching a bit more of the opera Turandot which I had started a week ago. Princess Turandot has lost the contest of the riddles to Kalaf. But she has not yet demanded that all Pekin must not sleep until she discovers his identity, which leads to his famous aria Nessun Dorma.

Before she could do that, I fell asleep and was sent to bed.

Waking at 4am this morning, they are still talking.

Snoopy and I went back to sleep.

Friday. Laura, the lady artist who painted my portrait, called me. Can she come and see me? She has four more paintings which she has framed.

I had forgotten about these paintings. She arrived and Jorge helped her carry them to my office. The first she showed me is a painting of my favourite 'Noel Coward' photo, taken on the QM II. I love it. It's so much more flattering than the one I took to Tupgill. It measures two feet by two feet six inches in its frame. It's much smaller than the Tupgill one, but it will replace it.

There is one of Kate sitting on my knee. It's more of a caricature.

The third is a painting of Marilyn Monroe, painted from a photo. I like this one too.

The fourth is a present to us. It's a picture of a white horse rearing up on a dark blue background. She painted it years ago. I have seen it in her catalogue.

She said that she is returning to Argentina. Ecuador hasn't been a success for her.

She would like us to have it.

I thanked her for all the work that she has done for us. We have eight of her paintings.

I kissed her goodbye and wished her a Happy New Year.

Saturday 21st. Following her meeting with Cecilia Niemes of her former modelling agency, Kate has been asked to judge in a junior beauty contest for teenage models tonight.

She has been to the hairdresser and done her makeup. Which dress would I prefer, the maroon or the white one? They were held up on hangers. I chose the white one, luckily as that was her choice too. She put it on and asked me to zip it up. I looked at the tiny dress and said that it wont zip up. She said that it will. And indeed it did. But the result left her barely covered. You can't go in that!

Nonsense the event will be on TV, I have to wear something exciting.

With that she left at 4pm.

I am reading Never by Ken Follett and really getting into the several plots. It's the story of how the third World War might begin. Starting in a very small way, it escalates and escalates until war between China and the USA looks to be inevitable.

Kate got back at 8pm. She was thrilled with the event and her part in it. She is on a high. Please take me to dinner.

I suggested that she change out of this risky dress. But she said no. She is perfectly comfortable in it. We drove to the Riviera restaurant. We had to take Snoopy. He can't come inside but there are outside tables where our guards, Pedro and Jose can dine and hold on to him.

The restaurant was full, but as she predicted she wasn't stared at.

When Janina and Luisa returned from Montanita we demanded they tell all. Had it been as good as ever? Sadly it had not. There were power cuts a lot of the time. Most venues were closed and there were very few people there. A damp squib.

Monday 23rd. The buildup to Christmas. Diana, Steve and the boys have arrived from Los Angeles. They will stay with Ceci.

Kate's parents Margarita, Gildardo and her grandmother Leonor, arrived at 6pm from Colombia.

Kate is busy at the house, so I am delegated to pick them up from the airport. They will stay the night at a hotel before they go to the beach tomorrow. My instructions are to take them to the hotel to book in and freshen up. Then bring them to our new house. We are having a pre-Christmas party there.

I worried about the traffic. It would take ages to drive to the hotel and then back to the house in the other direction. But I was in luck. They are not tired.

Let's go straight to the house.

I was in my car with my escort, Pedro. He suggested that he drive so I can chat to the guests. He had told me about a course he had taken in Colombia on defensive driving. Now I saw what he meant. It was a fast and hairy ride. He drove aggressively pushing in on lanes of traffic. My conversation was soon cut off as I gripped the door handle.

We had asked the architects to prepare the living room for the party. They had done it. It is clean and the furniture is set out. The tree is decorated, and the air conditioner works fine. We are set for the party.

When we arrived Kate welcomed them in. Luisa, Janina and Fredy were already there. The music blared from her new speaker. I had asked Celso to stay and help serve the drinks. So we were quickly provided with glasses of wine.

Tuesday 24th December

I went to the office early. We work today until 4:30pm, so almost a full day. The sales are beginning to pick up at last. I spend the day approving credits.

Kate called to say that she is on the way to the beach with her family, two security guards, and Snoopy. I will go there tomorrow with another two guards.

Josef was adamant that we needed four men to guard the house there. It's not isolated, but the houses are scattered along the beach front. It could be vulnerable to attack.

I went home to the empty flat at 5pm. It was only then that I realised how Kate fills it with her presence. She will only be away one night. But it seems desolate.

I was expected at Ceci's house at 7pm. I put on a suit and tie and drove there. I was a few minutes early. The family was still getting ready upstairs. Alcides handed me a glass of wine and I walked into the garden.

The melancholy mood from the flat is still with me. We built this house twenty-six years ago. At that time Ceci and I were still good together. It's a lovely house. We enjoyed watching it being built over a two-year period, and the details that we included. It's large with five big bedrooms. At the time we built it there was a bedroom each for Nick, Diana and Alex, one for us and one for guests.

Now of course they have all flown the nest. But when Di comes to visit she fills the rooms with her family.

I walked around the garden. It had been my house too, and now it's not. I am a guest.

The new house I have bought with Kate is about half the size of this one. But then there are just the two of us.

Dominic, the youngest at ten, was the first to see me and he came to give me a hug. Then Rocco, thirteen, gave me one and finally Ollie, sixteen. He has inherited the Lamplough height. We stood back to back and he is taller than me.

Diana and Steve came downstairs and then Ceci. I moved inside and we talked happily as a family.

Alex, Javi and their little ones, Sienna and the twins Christian and Olivia, aged seven, arrived.

Olivia, in the way of children, asked me "Granddad, why don't you live with Grandma?"

"Well My Love, that is difficult to explain".

Matt Haynes and Lilly arrived with their two little ones.

We went to the table at 9pm, earlier than normal. I think Ceci remembered the last Christmas here when we didn't eat until almost 11pm, and I fell asleep at the table. Tonight she was taking no chances. But I am on my best behaviour, taking tiny sips from my wine glass.

Magda is here and has cooked a wonderful lobster thermidor. I don't much enjoy turkey.

We pulled crackers and put on paper hats. It was a lovely dinner.

Afterwards I thought I had better leave early. No way could I get to midnight without falling asleep.

I told Ceci. She begged me to wait a bit longer. The children want to open one present each. That is the house rule. The others are for tomorrow.

Dom played the piano. I made a video of it. He played beautifully. Not to be outdone Rocco played and then Ollie. Di did a duet with Dom, then it was Steve's turn. Finally Sienna played for us.

How lovely. Music soothes the soul.

My mother was a wonderful pianist. She graduated from the Royal Academy of Music (LRAM). I only remember her playing when I was very young. After she got arthritis in her hands she stopped altogether. Something of her has come out in her great grandchildren.

Before I left I was given my presents. Then finally I said my goodbyes.

I am still sober

The flat is so empty.

Christmas Day

I had told Fredy that we will leave for the beach at 8am. He arrived at that time, left his car in my parking space and we set off for the beach. Well not quite. Kate had asked that we take some special Colombian pudding with us. We looked in the fridge of the flat. It's not there. It must be in the other house. We drove there. It's not there either. Finally we found it in the freezer of the flat.

Only then can we leave.

Fredy had found and rented the beach house for us at Punta Blanca. He had gone there yesterday and settled everyone in. Then he returned to Guayaquil to spend last night with his family.

Now we are going together. He will cook for us.

We got there at 11am to find the party was ongoing. They had got up for breakfast and were already well into the beers. Two more friends had arrived, Orlando and Nichol. The only one still in bed is Kate.

I was shown which room she has and gave her a kiss. She turned over and mumbled that she wanted to sleep on.

I joined the group on the terrace.

It's an odd house on several levels. It stands on a hill overlooking the sea. There are other houses below it, closer to the beach. It has five bedrooms, and sleeps eleven people. But the bedrooms are tiny and there are two-tier litter beds. The top ones look positively dangerous, as they are high and have no railings.

Our bedroom has a double bed, but the bathroom is miniature, and there is no hot water.

This is not at all like Ceci's palatial beach house. But on the other hand it was not expensive to rent for two nights.

After two hours and four beers, I was feeling sleepy and went to join Kate in bed. But she is now getting up, so I have the bed to myself. She told me that they were about to have lunch, but I'm not hungry.

When I woke up the strange melancholy mood returned. I wanted to be on my own. I took a book and avoided the noisy group in the dining room. I found a secluded space on a lower deck to read.

After a while Kate found me there.

Why was I antisocial? Come and join the party. But no. I tried to explain that it is to do with my having left my family last night to come here. It's the first time that I have done so. They would be eating pork sandwiches. We always did that on Christmas day.

That didn't sit well with her. I had spent Christmas Eve with my family. The least I could do was to be friendly with hers today.

OK. I put down my book and we joined the others.

She wanted to go into the sea with Nichol and Orlando. They changed into bathing suits. I certainly wasn't going to show my blotched chest to everyone so I took Snoopy and walked with them to the beach, accompanied by three guards. The house has a path that snakes down to the beach between other houses.

The sea was apparently quite warm. They went in and played with an inflatable duck and shark. But the wind was cool. There is a difference between Guayaquil and the beach of about five degrees celsius.

Margarita and Leonor joined them in the sea. I sat on a deck chair and talked to Gildardo.

Snoopy was off his lead. He raced about the beach and even went into the sea when Kate called him.

By 7pm it was getting dark. We all returned to the house.

Having had a break from alcohol I could now enjoy a glass of wine. Fredy made a barbeque, but most of them had eaten too much lunch and didn't want more food. I was hungry and enjoyed it.

Thursday 26th.

We have to leave the house by ten o'clock this morning. I had breakfast at 8am with one or two early risers. Then began the process of rousing and chivying them all to get ready to leave. Where is my hat? Have you got the presents? Where is my phone?

I joked to the guards that it is like herding cats.

We left just before 11am. There is not much traffic. In fact there are not many people at the beach. The majority, like Ceci and my family, come here for New Year when you can see fireworks all around the bay as far as Salinas.

There was a lot of beer left over. It was divided among the four cars. Kate and her parents, plus Snoopy rode with me. They enjoyed the beer. One can after another, with the odd sip for myself, the driver. Of course we didn't reach Guayaquil before we needed a loo stop.

Once back at the flat, I quickly changed and left for the office. I wanted to see the sales and have plenty I can do there. But I also wanted to escape the party that will go on all day. By the time I return at 6pm they will be well on, and I will be ready for my first wine.

I had reserved a hotel for them tonight, as they leave tomorrow morning. But Kate has cancelled the reservation. They prefer to sleep in the flat.

What? How can they all sleep here? There are only two double beds. Kate and I have one, how can the four of them share the other? But she had thought it out. Her father can sleep in the maid's room, Luisa on a sofa, and Margarita and Leonor in the bed.

Friday 27th December

I went to the office at 6:30am. The party is over. I can gratefully get back to work.

Kate's family leave today for Colombia at 10am, and Luisa to Madrid at 8pm.

Then we are back to normal. Ceci has gone with Di, Alex and crew to Peru. They sent me a photo today of the hotel where they are staying for three nights in The Sacred Valley, by Machu Picchu.

I have been there with Ceci many years ago. They will be back in time for the New Year.

That is the next event.

What are Kate and I going to do about it? I don't know. We haven't planned anything.

We are happy to be together. Neither of us wants another party.

So we come to the year 2025.

What will it bring?

About the Author

Colin Armstrong, born and educated in the UK, has spent the last fifty-three years of his life in Ecuador.

He founded Agripac SA, which has grown to become one of Ecuador's principal companies. From 1981 to 2016 he was the Honorary British Consul in Guayaquil, Ecuador's largest city. He was awarded both the OBE and CMG for services to the British community in Ecuador.

He continues to live between Ecuador, Madrid and Tupgill, his home in the Yorkshire Dales.